I have a confession to make, my opinion about this book is heavily biased!

Dr. Georgia Miliopoulou, Zozeta for me, is a friend - Many, many years ago when I was a junior strategist (we were called planners back then), she was a mighty Creative Director who demanded my briefs to be brief and bright. And that taught me a lot.

Equally, her book is going to teach you a lot regardless your experience. It will reveal secrets for creative advertising's form and function, and it will position for you Advertising in its rightful place, at the intersection of culture and commerce. Refreshingly the book avoids falling in the trap of the many pseudo-dichotomies that torture creative advertising today (i.e., equity vs. performance, traditional vs digital, long term vs short term, mass vs personalized) and sticks to timeless principles and how they can be applied in today's environment effectively. In that sense it doesn't simply rally for a return "back to the basics" of advertising creation but arms the reader with the ability to move forward with basics.

Highly recommended to anybody who considers himself a student of advertising.

– *Antonis Kocheilas, Global CEO, Ogilvy Advertising*

Creative Advertising Concept and Copy

Considering perspectives on creative advertising through a unique media and communications lens, this book encompasses both the theory and practical tools needed to approach and understand creativity in advertising with an original eye.

Drawing from diverse subject areas including Social Anthropology, Narrative Theory, Consumer Psychology, Semiotics and Cultural Studies, *Creative Advertising* provides a solid grounding in advertising education away from the traditional business and marketing literature. Notwithstanding the need for independent inspiration and originality, the author guides readers through the entire process of campaign planning, moving from strategy to creative idea to finished piece whilst employing concepts and principles relevant to 'design thinking'. Taking into account ethics and regulations, the use of text and images, and storytelling across radio, TV and video platforms, readers will come to a holistic understanding of what advertising can (and cannot) do, and how to achieve the best results.

Written for students involved in creative advertising as an area of academic research and professional practice, this book will also be of interest to early-career advertising professionals seeking a fresh perspective on their work.

Georgia-Zozeta Miliopoulou is Associate Professor in the Department of Communication at Deree, The American College of Greece. She has over 25 years of experience in creative advertising and holds a Ph.D. in brand communication. She has been teaching creative advertising and new media since 2003 and still offers workshops for communication professionals. Her research interests include creativity, strategic content & storytelling, and the managerial aspects of creative agency work.

Creative Advertising Concept and Copy

A Practical, Multidisciplinary Approach

Georgia-Zozeta Miliopoulou

Routledge
Taylor & Francis Group

LONDON AND NEW YORK

Designed cover image: THEPALMER / E+ via Getty Images

First published 2024
by Routledge
4 Park Square, Milton Park, Abingdon, Oxon OX14 4RN

and by Routledge
605 Third Avenue, New York, NY 10158

Routledge is an imprint of the Taylor & Francis Group, an informa business

British Library Cataloguing-in-Publication Data
A catalogue record for this book is available from the British Library

Library of Congress Cataloging-in-Publication Data
A catalog record has been requested for this book

ISBN: 978-1-032-35795-9 (hbk)
ISBN: 978-1-032-36204-5 (pbk)
ISBN: 978-1-003-33072-1 (ebk)

DOI: 10.4324/9781003330721

Typeset in Galliard
by Taylor & Francis Books

To my children who raised me to an adult,
teaching me boundless love and boundaries.

Contents

Illustrations

Tables

Boxes

About the Author

Zozeta has worked as a copywriter and creative director in global advertising agencies in Greece for over 25 years, including Lintas, FCB, Leo Burnett, Saatchi & Saatchi, and Publicis, before serving as a Founder and Head of Creative & Content Services at Tenfour Agency, Athens. Her work has been awarded in Greece, while she has offered creative consulting services to major advertisers.

Holding a bachelor's degree in philosophy and psychology, she pursued graduate studies in cultural management years later, and earned her Ph.D. with Honors, studying brand communication.

For over 20 years she has offered courses in advertising, creative communication, and new media, while she also conducts tailored workshops for professionals.

Her research interests include creativity, creative literacy, strategic content & storytelling, and the socio-cultural & organizational factors affecting brand communication. She has published papers in the European Journal of Marketing, Gender, Work, and Organization, the Journal of Research in Interactive Marketing and more, having presented her research in the European Academy of Management and other distinguished conferences.

Since January 2015 she has worked at Deree, The American College of Greece, School of Liberal Arts & Sciences, Department of Communication, currently serving as Associate Professor, and Head in the Department of Communication.

Preface

This is a book about creative advertising concept and copy, approached through a social sciences & humanities lens, providing not only a theoretic background for students to understand creative advertising, but also specific tools that help students develop their creative skills.

The book presents an academic background that relies less on marketing management tools and more on constructs and theories from the cultural or media studies, providing tools not just for the analysis but also for the making of creative advertising.

The aim is to contribute to advertising education by focusing on advertising creativity as a distinctive skillset, supported by a multidisciplinary theoretic perspective and combining tools that help ideation and idea development. The scope and tools presented can also support professionals in creative advertising to develop, enrich, diversify, and reflect on their ideas.

The book adopts a European perspective especially when it comes to the discussion of regulations or other topics of non-globalised theory and practice, but attempts to provide global best practice and understanding where applicable.

Acknowledgement

Dr. Anastasia Logotheti, a mentor and friend, returned a sample chapter with over 3.000 comments. The last one, half-way, read: "I can't go on beyond this point". I survived the hit. If it wasn't for her scrutiny, and her input that made me re-write half the book, this effort would have been much worse. Dr. Antigoni Kyrousi and Dr. Athina Zotou provided precious, meticulous insight and I am grateful for the time they dedicated to reading sample chapters; and for their friendship, most of all. Dr. Stamatina Katsiveli offered valuable comments that allowed me to continue at a time when I felt exhausted, hopeless, and burnt out. Dr. Ioanna Tsivakou has shaped my thinking and being, as a Professor in 2003 and a dear friend ever since. Themis Petropoulos contributed largely with his love for storytelling and his acute professional perspective.

I am grateful to Lizzie Cox who pulled this book out of me remaining a steady, reliable voice throughout this process, and to Hannah McKeating who was always there to address my concerns and offer help, spot-on.

I am also especially grateful to the three reviewers that examined the first proposal providing fruitful yet encouraging comments. Dr. Anastasiou, Dr. Copley, Dr. Dugmore, thank you. I hope the outcome does not fall too far below your expectations.

Because no woman is an island, and gratitude is contagious, I also ought to thank the people who have supported my late transition to academia, starting with Dean Helena Maragou who knows how to bring out the best in people, even when it's hard to find; and moving on to my colleagues in the Department of Communication. I hope we can all keep working together, making each other better day by day.

Special thanks to the people who keep popping up in my life unexpectedly, proving the power of love and friendship.

And heartfelt thanks to my good friends, you know who you are, for sharing all of life's joys and hardships for over 40 years now. Our lifelong commitment has kept me going. I don't know where I would be without you, but I do know that I have been locked up writing for too long and you all deserve good treats and big hugs. No worries, you don't have to read the book!

Thank you.

1 Advertising: Bridging the economic and social sphere

1 Advertising studies

In most UK and US programs, advertising is taught through two different lenses: the lens of business and marketing, and the lens of social sciences and humanities, through communication or media or cultural studies programs. These two lenses affect the understanding of advertising that students acquire.

In the former case, students focus on understanding much deeper the planning and distribution of advertising; hence on its strategic and financial aspects, while its creative aspect is often approached through a managerial perspective and a techniques-based approach (indicatively: Drewniany & Jewler, 2014, pp. 97–140 & 170–200). Such programs draw on theories from business studies and try to foster practical skills, mostly around advertising research, strategy and media planning. There are books which try to provide a holistic understanding of advertising and the thinking processes that lead to successful, appropriate advertising (indicatively: Altstiel et al., 2023; Fill et al., 2013; Drewniany & Jewler, 2014) or of integrated marketing communications campaigns (indicatively: Belch & Belch, 2003; Egan, 2015) which are most helpful but there is room for more insight into the tools that enable creative work. Successful creative professionals also publish books which reflect their view on creativity, frequently presenting case studies which enable an intuitive understanding of techniques used in the creative process. A lot of these books follow what could be characterised as a "reverse engineering" approach. They present a campaign and then explain how it came to life and the challenges along the way. However, when it comes to forward thinking and designing from scratch, it is not easy to find instructions or steps which support ideation and development.

In the context of media, culture, and communication studies, students focus on understanding much deeper the content and the implications of advertising as a cultural artefact or sum of artefacts. These studies have contributed to a greater understanding of advertising, its sociocultural role, and its significant influences both on the individual and on the social and cultural level. Significant contributions have been made by combining advertising studies with social psychology, social anthropology, linguistics, semiotics, narrative theory, political economy, media studies, cultural studies, gender studies, and more. Through this lens,

DOI: 10.4324/9781003330721-1

students develop stronger analytical skills and critical skills. However, there seems to be less focus on practical skills that would enable ideation and idea development. The business and professional aspects of advertising in the everyday life of the agency are sometimes underplayed.

This book attempts to support advertising students with different backgrounds, in a multidisciplinary way. Not all theories addressed are introduced in detail, but basic constructs are outlined, and sources are provided for further readings. The book draws from the marketing literature especially in Chapter 2 which discusses objective setting and measurements in alignment with business requirements; in Chapter 3 presenting some established tools for audience segmentation; and in Chapters 7 & 8 where the media side is presented, combined with the need to prove results within a business context. Beyond that, the attempt is to bridge creative advertising with disciplines from the social sciences and the humanities, by following a practical approach; that is, by offering not just knowledge but also tools which can help copywriters and creatives conceptualise and develop their ideas.

The book aims at a multi-disciplinary understanding, in one of the many ways such an understanding can be achieved. The social sciences paint a vivid picture of advertising audiences. Cultural and communication studies demonstrate the appropriation and use of advertising messages in everyday life. Creative studies offer a better understanding of the individual and team processes that occur in the everyday life of the agency and, particularly, of creative advertising professionals. Semiotics, linguistics, and narrative theory provide interesting, relevant, and efficient tools for creative ads and campaigns, addressing both students and professionals. Thus, this book aims at combining critical skills for the understanding of the implications of advertising with creative skills for the making of advertising, taking a stance towards ethical, sustainable, socially responsible advertising practice. This is one of the ways to bridge the gap between the business sphere and the social sphere; between marketing and communication; between traditional and transformative (Gurrieri et al., 2022) advertising research.

2 Advertising: definition and scope

> Advertising is the placement of announcements and messages in time or space by business firms, nonprofit organizations, government agencies, and individuals who seek to inform and/or persuade members of a particular target market or audience regarding their products, services, organizations or ideas[1].

Advertising has been defined in many ways which affect the scope of our understanding. Most definitions highlight the persuasive aspects and the appeal to mass audiences. In this book, we follow the above definition which is somewhat narrow and classic. Below, the basic aspects of this definition are discussed in relation to the scope of this book and to the contemporary advertising landscape.

Advertising is paid placement of messages: this is what differentiates the practice of advertising as opposed to other communication activities. Public Relations seek to attract attention by addressing professional stakeholders or press representatives without usually paying to have their messages placed. Product placement is about paying to insert a product within information or entertainment related content but does not involve the making of any messages. Content marketing places messages on social media but these are not paid. Well, when we talk about "organic content" we refer to content that is posted by a brand and, hopefully, shared or acted upon by the users (which could relate more likely to Public Relations). Paid content is content promoted via paid campaigns on the web and social media, in which case this feels more like traditional advertising.

Advertising messages are placed in media time or space. This may include the traditional mass media; digital, social, and mobile media; as well as cinema advertising and outdoor advertising. Communication activities like sales promotion also disseminate all types of materials and messages including but not limited to free samples or pamphlets; but sales promotion does not use media. Flash mobs or pop-up stores that may also be organised for advertising purposes might not be considered "advertising" under this definition. However, because such activations often involve some sort of media coverage and content dissemination, they are often organised in the context of an advertising campaign and thus frequently constitute part of advertising planning.

> "Advertising is the nonpersonal communication of information usually paid for and usually persuasive in nature about products, services or ideas by identified sponsors through the various media."
>
> (Bovee & Arens, 1992, p. 7).

"Usually" is the operative word in the above definition, leaving some room for exceptions like the ones addressed above. However, there are more aspects to discuss here, which are reflected in the rest of the book:

First, advertising is mostly persuasive in nature – a common statement between the two definitions. Indeed, information has never been the sole (or even the main) objective of advertising. Information is means to an end, not an end in itself. This is a default position and unless the recipient lacks media literacy skills, they know, and they are expected to process advertising content accordingly. Being persuasive in nature, advertising always relies on some sort of emotional appeal. Advertising is more about persuasion and emotion than about information and reasoning, though both are required for a successful campaign and should not be seen as contradictory. This is a central premise of the book, for strategic and ethical purposes.

Second, even though advertising is always audience-oriented, it is mostly nonpersonal. Advertising messages reach their audiences by estimating which media these audiences consume and when. This differentiates advertising from direct (aka personal) marketing activities which involve personalised contacts with consumers. Email campaigns are such an example: messages sent to lists of recipients through automated platforms that support such listing as well as design, dissemination, and measurements. Email campaigns can be regular and periodic, or emails can be sent ad hoc, for multiple reasons like, for example, to announce news or offers. In some parts of the world, this means that email can be used to reach out to new audiences. In the European Union though this is less likely the case. The General

Data Protection Regulation (GDPR)[2] requires consumers' consent to receiving such emails. This means that consumers opted to give their email to stay in contact with a brand, thus email campaigns are more likely used for customer retention, upselling and cross-selling, i.e. offering new products to existing customers.

A challenge here is microtargeting (Danaher, 2023). Is it personal or non-personal? Microtargeting occurs in the digital environment and, much more likely on social media, where an advertiser can use multiple filters to include a handful of consumers who present specific characteristics. The brand does not "know" the consumer, but such advertising often feels painfully intrusive. Furthermore, microtargeting allows brands to deliver different messages to different consumer clusters and one consumer will never know what the other consumer saw. This means that two next-door neighbours could get an offer for the same pair of shoes, but with a different price, which is not legal in some countries; or that a political party might address specific consumer clusters (Baviera et al., 2023) with statements or promises that were never made in public, or fostering polarisation (Prummer, 2020).

Third, according to Bovee & Arens (1992), advertising must come from "identified sponsors". Why is this important? Because advertising should not conceal its intention to persuade and promote; and should not mislead consumers into thinking that its content is solely informative or entertaining. They should know who tries to convince them. By signing an ad, the brand takes responsibility for the content of the ad. In the new media environment, such lack of transparency poses challenges.

One challenge is native advertising. Native advertising is paid advertising where the ad matches the form, feel and function of the publication's editorial content[3]. Native advertising used to be regulated by law in many countries before the new media. The practice transcended to the unregulated online environment where consumers often access a lifestyle website content not knowing that this content is meant to persuade them to buy. Generally, a good rule of thumb is that if a brand pays for native content but discloses so and signs this content, then native advertising is acceptable, especially if it combines education and entertainment. If, however, users do not know that a brand has paid for the content they access, this could mean they are misled to believe that the product is recommended rather than promoted, which is not ethical.

Another challenge is influencer marketing defined as a collaboration between a brand and an influencer, to promote products or services. An influencer is a social media account with a significant number of followers and, sometimes, some sort of expertise in an area. Celebrities can be influencers but also, for example, architects or well-being experts. Again, if the influencer discloses that their post which includes a brand is paid for; discloses the sponsor, then the practice is more likely to be considered ethical and fair. If influencers appear to promote branded goods as if this were a personal recommendation, however, then their practice is misleading.

So, you see, we are not in the nineties anymore when the above definitions emerged. The changes in the advertising landscape go way further than seeking a new definition, especially since all brand activities on social media are now monetized one way or another. New ways to communicate blur the boundaries between previously separate forms of communication. New or re-emerging challenges become even more complex because countries and states cannot easily tackle these with legislation and policy making. The web is global, transcending boundaries, with websites often found in server-heaven places where poor practice is not regulated.

Advertising changes fast, always has, always will because, to be effective, advertising needs to adjust to ever-changing consumers and contexts. Distinctions that were once important appear to have become obsolete. But have they? Even if the landscape changes by the hour, or because it does, we need to go back to the basics, establish a fundamental understanding, frame key terms and notions, and take it from there. By following a narrow and traditional understanding of advertising, we manage to outline its activities precisely and to pinpoint areas of concern. We also manage to combine the past with the future, without shaking the foundations of advertising as a concrete and established area of studies. Perhaps we do not need new definitions; we need more alignment between past practice and new challenges.

3 The product and the brand; marketing and advertising

Whereas the AMA definition provides a list of possible advertised entities, the Bovee & Arens definition refers to products, services, or ideas by identified sponsors. Before delving into the "how's" and the "why's" of advertising, we should dedicate a few words to "what" and "who" is advertised.

Brands are advertised. Brands sign and declare their presence at the end of each video advert, at the bottom of each poster, on the left of each social media post. Brands may talk about their products, but this is not necessarily the case. Brands may also talk about their social responsibility; or their corporate assets; or about social issues they choose to address, like in the case of "#likeagirl", the campaign by Always that aims at the empowerment of girls entering puberty.

Brands may represent products or services or retail stores or corporations or non-governmental organisations or political parties and politicians. Broadly defined, brand management also addresses celebrities or even individuals pursuing a competitive career. The question "what is a brand" might take many different answers. For the purposes of this book, we start by acknowledging that:

- A brand is any sign on symbol that signs an ad.
- This symbol indicates who approved and financed the message of this ad, not who created the ad.
- This symbol may be linked to anything or anyone who has the resources to advertise and can benefit from advertising.

We draw the line between branded and non-branded products which cannot sign an advertising campaign. We also acknowledge that a brand may use advertising to promote much more than its products, including values, beliefs, financial performance, collaborations, or joint ventures, and more. So, in this book we discuss brands, not products. Where the word "product" is used, it is in synecdoche, to refer to anything branded.

This is not a new distinction, albeit it is often neglected. The seminal paper by Gardner & Levy (1955) brought it to light decades ago. The importance of setting the two apart goes far beyond acknowledging that brands may also signify much more than products. The distinction between the product and the brand should underline our understanding of the entire advertising process.

The "product" or offering can be purchased and used. The brand can be appropriated and exchanged in interaction. The product might have verifiable benefits, tangible to some extent. The brand possesses symbolic value that can only be verified in communication. Even when promoting a product, advertising builds brands. Products may be tangible; the brand never is. We tend to have opinions about certain brands. These opinions might stem from actual product or service experience or might be the result of discussions, connotations, associations, habits, emotional connections that go back to childhood; and, of course, advertising.

There is nothing tangible about the brand. To each of us, every brand is a jar we fill with meaning deriving from personal experience and advertising or other forms of communication. Our jars look alike but are never identical. *My* jar of, let's say, Nike contains not only the ads *I* have seen which may not be the same with the ones *you* have, but also *my* personal experience and the way Nike aligns (or not) with *my* beliefs and values. Brands try to communicate consistently and cumulatively but our brand jars are bound to differ. Marketing or advertising only constitute part of what our jars contain.

The more a brand invests in advertising, the more each consumer's jar contains and the richer our view of this brand. The more money a consumer intends to spend on a brand, the more they need to fill its jar before purchasing, by seeking information and referrals. The more money consumers have put in their brand jar, the more likely to stay loyal to this brand. And so forth. Thus, is explained the cumulative effect of all branding and advertising efforts. There are jars that are half full even if we are not the target group for their products. Just consider how many detergent brands you could recognise long before you moved out of your parents' house. This is one way to explain brand equity in relation to advertising and to argue that sometimes returns on advertising investment occur long after a campaign has ended.

This approach also helps distinguish between marketing and advertising. Marketing is about creating, pricing, distributing, and promoting offers, in the broad sense of the term: products, services, corporations etc. Advertising is about creating, distributing, and promoting meanings, ideas, values, connotations, all intangible offerings that help us make consumption-related choices – and a lot more as will be discussed in the following chapters. Respectively, marketing is part of the business world, the economic sphere, as Bell would argue (Bell, 1978) while advertising has one foot in the cultural sphere, being close to the cultural and creative industries (Hesmondhalgh, 2007).

This book approaches each ad as an artefact, commissioned by a brand, signed by a brand, created by an advertising agency. The brand uses this artefact to encapsulate and carry meaning beyond the marketplace, in our social and cultural contexts. To delve in the making of creative advertising, therefore, one must understand how audiences perceive, appropriate, and exchange such meanings.

It is quite popular to argue that advertising existed in the ancient or even in pre-historic times. It is also quite risky to assess one era using criteria established in another era. Ancient sword makers and olive oil producers would mark their products to distinguish from these of competitors or would likely place posters on walls and mark their workshops. Back then, though, paying to place a message was not an established practice. Based on the definitions above, it is quite a stretch to consider ancient signage as a form of advertising. Even more so, the brand could not easily be separated from the product and had no reason to exist without it. What changed with the mass media and with advertising, is that brands can exist, travel, be exchanged, and used without the product being anywhere near. It's the separation of the product and the brand that makes a difference between antiquity and the present, which elevates the importance of the brand in today's global, cluttered markets and cultural landscapes. Many people have bought the idea of a BMW without ever having bought a BMW. The brand not as mere descriptor but as symbolic means of exchange emerges in the mass media era and, so far, there is no similar historic precedent (For a more thorough discussion: Beard, 2017; Conejo et al., 2015; Moore & Reid, 2008).

This book builds on two metaphors. The first is the metaphor of the jar which describes brands as meaning-carrying entities residing in consumers' minds and hearts, as discussed above. The second metaphor that is now introduced is the metaphor of the bridge.

We approach each ad as a bridge between a consumer and a branded product. One pillar of the bridge is cemented in the business or organisational sector; the other pillar is grounded in the world of consumers and their everyday culture and lifestyle. The creative strategy is the bridge skeleton, its backbone, ensuring that the two points are appropriately and solidly connected. The creative idea is the bridge design, that makes it fun to walk or drive through, memorable, a landmark if possible. For an ad to be successful, the two ends of the bridge must meet halfway. The business pillar requires that objectives are met and returns on investment are achieved. This is defined as appropriateness. The people pillar requires an original, authentic experience. Appropriateness and originality are, roughly put, two key ingredients that define creativity as will be discussed in Chapter 4. In various parts of the book these two metaphors will be revisited as we delve in the creative process.

4 The practice of advertising in steps

There are many different types of advertising agencies, offering creative services, each fostering and promoting their own unique way of delivering good work. Despite all differences and points of uniqueness, however, there are notable similarities in the way agencies work. In this section, we highlight these similarities rather than focus on the differences. We start by describing some key functions and then proceed by describing specific steps usually required from the moment a request appears until the moment when an ad airs. Knowing these functions and steps may work as a beacon for younger professionals and help students acquire a better sense of the profession of advertising.

A creative agency needs at least two organisational units, or departments, to function: a) one that offers service to clients, coordinating all parties involved in the making and airing of an ad, and ensuring that creative work responds to client requirements and b) one that conceives and materialises creative ideas. Imagine this is the kernel, though. Beyond that, the more an agency grows, the more departments, activities, and processes are added, thus allowing the agency to offer more and more holistic services to larger clients. For example, many agencies separate client services (aka account management) from advertising strategy (aka account planning); they also include separate departments that oversee production of creative materials like photo shootings, radio commercial recordings, etc. Furthermore, larger conglomerates have separate business units that may offer allied services in the area of public relations or advanced digital applications and so forth. And, of course, media planning which is often offered by specialised media shops – at least in most of the EU countries – is in full alignment with creative work. These are the primary functions. For an agency to operate, we also need supporting functions: departments for finances and accounting, human resource management, and so forth. Some graduates know what they want from a very early stage, while others might need to explore the agency before finding their preferred area of work.

Advertising agencies run like businesses, but advertising also belongs in the cultural industries which have distinctive processes and procedures. The term "creative industries" or "cultural industries" describes those companies or organisations whose primary function is the production of cultural texts and social meaning. "Texts" is a term used here as a synecdoche to refer to all kinds of cultural products including but not limited to art, culture, and the media (Hesmondhalgh, 2007, pp. 11–17). Advertising produces such texts whose main purpose is to be perceived, remembered, or even appreciated, appropriated, and exchanged by the intended audiences, and hopefully used for consumption related decisions, based on their individual criteria which comprise rational, emotional, and social factors.

An interesting aspect within the cultural or creative industries is the need to combine creative freedom and openness with viability and revenue. So, although one might imagine that people in an advertising agency sit in a meeting room brainstorming and generating ideas, this is only part of a set of complex, concrete processes that professionals follow on their everyday professional life.

Advertising begins when there is a problem to solve or an opportunity to grasp. Clients assess their marketing challenges and pick up the phone delivering a request; or they calculate the following fiscal year's needs and plan for the type of advertising support they will need throughout, to reach their marketing objectives. Agencies might think of a way to offer added services to clients or even do proactive work for their client. Nobody ever wakes up in the morning thinking: "let's run an advertising campaign". Advertising is the answer to marketing problems or opportunities, as will be discussed in the next chapter, but not always the right answer. So, let us start from the moment a client picks up the phone, and examine what usually happens.

Step 1: identify the client's issue. As a series of communications begins, the client services team or person must gather all available information relevant to the client's needs. Such information covers two broad sources of interest: first, the markets and second, the people. So, first, the team must understand exactly what the market situation is: what is the problem or the opportunity? Is it measurable? What evidence is there, from the market and from competitors? Is there any past practice worth considering or eliminating? Many agencies have a semi-structured list or questionnaire for this initial client-agency interaction but as collaboration evolves, this flow of information is often simplified. Simplification often appears more intimate and time efficient but might prove to be detrimental as important things are often taken for granted and omitted, thus leading to inappropriate work or waves of time-consuming changes.

The second source of interest is, of course, consumers: what do we know about them? What do we need to know? What do they know about the brand and product? How do they feel about it? This is not just for big campaigns and significant projects. Even for trivial everyday work, affirming our understanding of consumer behaviours, thoughts, ideas, and reservations is important, even if only for team alignment purposes. Knowing the consumer is essential to define appropriate objectives and appropriate target groups.

Step 2: define the strategy. Processing available data and approaching client needs from different angles, the team of advertising strategists, also called account planners, must make a set of decisions considering four distinctive elements: i) objectives, ii) targeting, iii) message, and iv) media. These decisions will constitute the backbone of each ad and will be used to assess ideas and to support these ideas when presenting to the client. Creative strategy is presented internally to the creative team, using a templated document called the creative brief.

Step 3: ideate, create & verify. Once the creative team studies and assimilates the brief, they must respond with their ideas. This is one of the most exciting aspects of advertising and yet one of the toughest as well. Ideas are floating in the air, mouth to ear, mouth to pencil and back, doubted, twisted, killed, amended, or not. Approvals and rejections can make or break one's day, and pressing deadlines keep everyone on edge. However, what is important is that in advertising creative work usually begins once some sort of strategic framing has taken place. There are plenty of examples of creatives coming up with a unique idea and then tailoring the strategy around it. However, this is not the rule. Strategy frames right from wrong which means that strategy ensures work can be not just original but also appropriate and therefore successful in achieving objectives.

Roughly speaking, strategy specifies what an ad must say and do; and creativity specifies how best to say it and do it. However, strategy and creativity go in tandem, and one blends with the other in many instances throughout each step of campaign generation.

Step 4: present. The moment of a presentation is important. The entire advertising team is represented, and all members must have ensured that their work is tied together, has a great flow, solid grounds, and significant potential, hence read-throughs and rehearsals often take place before an agency presents important work for larger campaigns. Some smaller tasks might go back and forth via email, though personal contact with the client is essential even in such cases. During the presentation the client's representatives might approve or reject on the spot, while more often than not, they will provide some initial feedback and return with comments and changes. Though an approval is the holy grail, sometimes rejection is better than amendment, as some changes are hard to implement or fit within the proposed ideas.

Step 5: execute. Once an idea is approved as amended, final artwork is completed and approved, including any video production or digital material. The media plan is finalised to its merest detail, and the campaign can go on air.

For a large campaign, these steps might take months. Smaller tasks may be completed in just a few days. Accordingly, the process of implementation and finalisation of an approved campaign, might last anywhere from a couple of days to several weeks, depending on production demands and on the number of creative materials that need to be ready before airing.

In some cases, these processes might appear linear and serial, as if mounting car parts on an assembly line and indeed some agencies operate in such linear ways. However, many agencies follow the above steps with variations. There are two significant areas of variation. First, many agencies tend to blend the transitions from one step to the next: alignment meetings, involvement of one department to the activities of the other, and so forth, so that their efforts do not feel like a relay race but a combination of different areas of expertise, that are well blended and aligned. Second, many agencies involve the client or even the consumer in various stages of their work. Clients may provide feedback on the creative strategy and on raw ideas, while consumers may participate in focus groups for copy testing purposes (indicatively: Turnbull & Wheeler, 2017). Furthermore, new media have imposed changes in both the structure and the processes described above: new skillsets, new procedures for new media artefacts, as well as new ways to collaborate have emerged yet are not standardised across the sector (Stuhlfaut & Windels, 2019). There is room for more research on the different ways agencies work and on the impact of their internal procedures on quality and on client long term satisfaction.

Agencies must be flexible and agile to meet client demands, especially when competition is tough, and the market has ups and downs. However, they must also ensure high quality work with high production values and prove the client's budget was used well. Striving to achieve time efficiency and value for money is not an easy task. In many offices, the old quote still hangs on the wall: time, quality, price: pick any two!

5 The creative brief and the outline of the book – a parallel structure

We are now delving in the second step described above. Combining brand and market data with consumer data, account planners must make decisions about how advertising can help, and what advertising should try to do. All these decisions are written and explained in the "Creative Brief". The creative brief is not the client's brief. The creative brief brings together both client's and strategists' input; incorporates the agency research and know-how; is tailored to the needs of the specific task; is meant to be helpful to the creative team. The creative brief is the creative strategy on paper (Altstiel et al., 2023; Henry, 2011), taking a synoptic form but containing elaborate information where applicable, to support the work of creatives.

The creative brief is the most significant agency document. It is meant to constitute a bridge between strategists and creatives, shaping a common language, a mutual sense of understanding and, most important, the framework within which creative ideas will be assessed (de Waal Malefyt & Morais, 2010). First, we ensure that ideas respond well to the brief, that is if they are appropriate, and then we discuss whether these ideas are creative, are liked or not. Because creative work requires a lot of personal involvement and emotional effort, tensions are bound to arise and are also frequently welcome. Clear procedures and explicit criteria facilitate harmonious handling of such tensions.

Big agencies mostly have their own specially designed creative brief template. The way they cluster and organise information and requirements, dictates a thinking process that is supposed to constitute a source of competitive advantage. Agency members are trained into the particularities of their creative brief template.

Despite these particularities, however, most creative brief templates have a lot of similarities (indicatively: Henry, 2011; Mackert, 2012; Altstiel et al., 2023). This is because strategic thinking in advertising follows a specific path. We focus on these similarities because this is the best way to learn how to think strategically in the context of any agency. Creative strategy in advertising is all about answering the following questions:

1   Where are we now?
2   Where do we want to be after the campaign is over?
3   Whom should we talk to?
4   What should we tell them? Any extra information we should know, including deadlines or mandatory inclusions?
5   How could we tell them? How do we convince them?
6   Where / when will we find our target group?

The first question, as discussed, explains why a campaign is needed; what problems or opportunities are to be addressed. This should be evidence based. Knowing what we are trying to achieve will help the team plan more accurately. The second question is about campaign objectives. How will we know we did a good job? The better we understand the problem in all its dimensions, the better our response will be. If we rely on evidence, we will also be able to measure the results more efficiently and effectively.

- **Chapter 2 of this book covers the first two questions of the creative brief. Following the bridge metaphor, the chapter bridges advertising objectives with the effects of advertising on consumers.**

The third question is dedicated to people; human beings; individuals who buy or consider buying brands and goods to solve their own problems and enjoy life their own way. Beyond being just "targets", people are friends, colleagues, citizens, neighbours, family. We need to know how to address them, how to approach them, how to convince them, with strong arguments and consideration for their feelings, and with respect to their needs that may be different to ours. Some agencies that prioritise the need for ethical advertising, make sure to address any ethical implications around their audience or message in their strategy (Altstiel et al., 2023).

- **Chapter 3 is dedicated to people as target audiences for advertising, juxtaposing marketing-oriented consumer research with constructs and evidence from the social sciences, acknowledging that some of the theories presented require further reading.**

The fourth question focuses on the main message of each creative campaign. Often (but not necessarily) expressed through an end line or tagline[4], but always brought to life through the creative idea, the main message holds an entire campaign together, creates consistency across media, breeds new executions, boosts memorability and lies in the foundations of a strong creative idea.

What should also be addressed here is the overall language, style and tone of voice of a campaign, which ensures alignment with brand personality and thus allows each campaign to capitalise on past campaigns and to have a cumulative effect that strengthens further the brand.

Frequently, a creative brief also contains some practical information relating to the creative process. This is also addressed on Chapter 4 where we delve in everyday creative work and processes, in more detail. Such procedural questions often vary from one agency to another and mostly involve deadlines for meetings and presentations; allocation of key people in the process like approvers or consultants; budgetary constraints.

A creative brief also often mentions any mandatory inclusions. Such inclusions must be added on an ad, regardless of the main idea and the content of the ad. For example, in the EU, car advertising must include CO emissions; some companies want to always include their most recent awards or accolades; some products need to mention that they address those who are over 18 or 21 years of age; and some products come with health or moderate usage warnings. All this should be known from the beginning, so the creative team knows exactly how to develop their work correctly, instead of going back and forth, adding and removing elements.

- **Chapter 4 focuses on the main message, on creative ideas, and on the creative process as experienced within the creative department. The chapter draws from the advertising literature and from creativity theories, to define creativity, to explain the creative process and to provide insights on the everyday work and established practices of creative professionals in advertising agencies.**

The fifth question has to do with the content of advertising. A creative idea is developed to appear in different media. A creative idea becomes a story for TV or radio advertising; a single-minded visual for posters; a podcast; an article, or a series of articles for content marketing purposes; an infographic disseminated through social media; and so much more. How we take one key idea and turn it into great advertising is of great importance. Good ideas have failed because of poor execution, while mediocre ideas have skyrocketed because their execution was meticulous throughout. Every campaign idea must constitute a mix of information or rational arguments; of emotional stimuli and appeals; and of an overt or covert, stated or implied call-to-action. Every campaign idea must have the appropriate language, style, and tone of voice, which is relevant to the brand personality, and to the needs of the specific campaign. And every idea must be adjusted to make best possible use of each medium conveying it.

- **Chapter 5 of this book focuses on how to create multimodal advertising which uses text or combines text with image for posters, print ads, memes, and gifs.**
- **Chapter 6 focuses on how to create multimedia advertising using storytelling for video or audio ads.**

Arbitrarily, we make a distinction here: in Chapter 5 we use rhetorical tropes to discuss not only print and Out-Of-Home (OOH) advertising, but also any descriptive form of ad whether in multimedia or multimodal form. In Chapter 6, we use narrative theory and storytelling elements, to discuss whatever can be considered a story, whether this appears in multimedia or multimodal or plain textual form.

The last question is about media and touchpoints. Advertising is all about placing messages where people are and trying to captivate their attention. Choosing where to find the right people at the right time is by no means simple. Media planning is a separate function in the advertising industry; however, creatives and media planners must work in full alignment. Just imagine what would happen if planners book radio spots but creatives do not produce any radio commercials! Or think about how many ideas might emerge, for creative use of media, if creatives and media planners work together. Placing an ad is by no means just procedural. It's about allocating the client's budget in the best possible way, while maximising the potential of the creative idea.

- **Chapter 7 is dedicated to paid media, mass and digital, approaching media through the perspective of creative advertising.**
- **Chapter 8 delves in content marketing.**

These two chapters are separated based on one key distinction, addressed above: paid mass dissemination via web or social media platforms is covered in Chapter 7 as such activity aligns more closely with the definitions of advertising discussed above. Organic content dissemination, that is content that is uploaded, posted, but not promoted, is discussed separately in Chapter 8. These two chapters do not cover the broader realm of media and media planning. They only provide basic information on a need-to-know basis for creatives. Though, of course, everyone in the agency should be familiar with the entirety of operations across departments, further study is required for a more detailed and profound understanding of media strategy, planning, and buying.

- Chapter 9 describes ethical issues and the practice of self-regulation in advertising. The last chapter focuses on the emerging ethical challenges in the creative process, focusing on fair professional practice and social implications, and emphasising the immense importance of ethical decision making in creative advertising.

6 What is not in this book

Though the importance of viewing and studying older ads is highlighted in various chapters, this book does not provide an overview of the history of advertising which is fascinating and profoundly educational – an indispensable part of advertising studies. Students and young professionals are strongly encouraged to delve in the past of advertising, in their country and in the world.

The book mostly follows a European orientation. This orientation proves to be more significant in some chapters more than in others. In Chapter 9, regulatory issues are mostly approached through the frameworks and established practices of the EU, with some brief mentions in other countries. In Chapter 3, consumer behaviour is approached through the lens of western scholars. However, theories, tools, and best practices often seem to apply in broader contexts.

Discussing idea development, the book follows a media agnostic approach. We acknowledge that a good story can be executed as a TV advert or a video advert; that a great idea for print could also work (with some adaptations) as an outdoor poster or a social media post. Though specific tools are presented for conception, development and implementation of ideas, emphasising how ideas may take different forms or appear on different media, fosters an integrated approach to creative advertising, facilitating idea adaptation for different media and different purposes.

Furthermore, little emphasis is given in long form content and large texts. Such texts more likely appear in the context of content marketing and are quite frequently developed either by experts in certain areas or by specialised agency personnel that usually has a journalistic or media studies background. The traditional agency copywriter usually does not deal with long-form content and a transition in such a job position might require some further training.

When presenting theories from various fields, the book introduces and explains new terms. However, there are limits to the level of detail each new topic can be elaborated. Each chapter paves the way for further reading while providing an overview of key issues addressed, drawing from multiple disciplines. Savvy readers may recognise the need for further discussion in many instances or acknowledge that once multidisciplinary thinking is put into place, many more theoretical contributions than the ones discussed in this book could enhance the teaching and learning of advertising. Hopefully, such contributions will keep emerging.

Furthermore, though the book tries to combine traditionally accepted theories with current trends in practice, there are some significant challenges facing contemporary advertising that are not addressed in this book in detail:

- **Talent recruitment and retention:** unlike the past, there is recent evidence that creative advertising is no longer such a popular career path for many talented graduates[5] (indicatively: Gray, 2022). Maintaining the interest of youth is essential for the future of creative advertising, not only because of the fresh perspective young professionals bring in the agency; not only because of the strong social and environmental sensitivities of younger generations; but also, because agencies require a large pool of talent to find those that will fit in, stay and build a longer-term career path. Talent attraction requires further studying so that the advertising industry can understand and respond by providing appropriate incentives. No doubt creative advertising is challenging but it's also a very rewarding area of work, as discussed in Chapter 4.

- **Diversity and inclusion:** in various parts of this book, especially in Chapters 4 & 9, a brief argument is presented: that diversity and inclusion leads to more innovative and creative work because diversity of people generates diversity in ideas, multiplying perspectives, backgrounds, skillsets, and ways to inspiration. In Chapter 4, quite a few sources appear indicating the lack of diversity, especially gender and racial diversity, while there is evidence of ageism and more unconscious biases that negatively impact the agency environment. To document these challenges, we lack neither evidence nor reporting. What we are still missing is effective policies and measures to tackle these issues allowing for a more encompassing melting pot of minds, thoughts, and ideas. As argued, diversity and inclusion are not just "nice to have"; are not only "the right thing to do" morally; they are also indispensable for true creative innovation to emerge. Along these lines, the working conditions of creative professionals allow for further improvement to keep attracting talent as discussed above.

- **New media challenges**: in the early pages of this chapter, while discussing classic definitions of advertising, we mentioned some of the challenges agencies face today, to not only cope but also to innovate using interactive online technologies. This is a huge area of discussion with tremendous economic, political, and social implications. Polarisation, filter bubbles, microtargeting, mis-, dis-, and mal-information flood everyday conversations in the broader communication industry. Maintaining credibility through fair practice is still a huge challenge in this cluttered and unregulated landscape. This book does not address such issues and does not even attempt to cover all the parameters of the web and social media in relation to advertising. These alone require one book – or more. Instead, in a somewhat arbitrary manner we separate and focus on aspects of online advertising and content marketing that are most likely to involve advertising creatives – especially copywriters. Further research is needed on how the new media have impacted our understanding of creativity overall. The Cannes Lions engagement awards and the Titanium award could pave the way for further understanding of how new media re-shape traditional notions of creativity posing challenges to older as well as younger creatives.

- **The specifics of advertising design.** Aesthetics and visual appeals are an essential part of advertising. Good art direction elevates advertising to state-of-the-art artefacts that go beyond announcements and promotions to constitute great examples of artistic work. Advertising design must comply with the brand guidelines; must respond to user experience requirements – not only on the online environment; comply with media formats and limitations; accommodate textual information; and look nice... Just like copywriters who receive more support from this book, art directors need to possess a large cultural capital; to keep up with the trends; to keep monitoring not only great works of current and past advertising but also new developments in visual and interactive arts. Special tools around design are not covered in this book. On the contrary, there is an implicit assumption that even when strictly visual, advertising ideas are often conceived, discussed, and elaborated using words on the level of interpersonal communication between creative co-workers. Chapters 4, 5, and 6 however, might provide some insight on creative ideation, figurative thinking, and storytelling all of which might be developed with visual executions. The perspective of this book is more focused on language as a tool to breed ideas even if these ideas are expressed through visual-only content. Finally, another tacit belief is that imitation can lead to innovation and creativity; not in the sense that creatives should imitate each other's ideas. They should not. They might, however, imitate working rituals, thinking patterns, ideation techniques. Through imitation comes assimilation so that, eventually, each creative professional can create their own thinking patterns and modalities which, if combined with personal cultural capital, can breed unique ideas.

Most chapters of this book include a case study, while some include boxes elaborating on theory. All chapters include exercises to be attempted in class or at home, individually or in groups. This is meant to be a book combining theory with practice, addressing students and young professionals interested in creative advertising. There is no optimal way to combine theory with practice. What is for certain is that the younger one is, the more should they open to theory and abstract understanding, although it often seems that the haste for practical advice persists. Practice provides the "what". Theory provides the "why". In advertising, the "what" changes by the hour but the "why" remains surprisingly resilient in time. If one learns the "why", they can more easily navigate changes in "what" and "how", thus building a long-lasting career. Experience has shown that the opposite rarely works.

Time to practise!

- For as long as you study, you must watch, read, listen, or otherwise access at least 40 ads a day. Of these, 10 should be awarded; 10

should be over 20 years old; 10 should come from a market different than yours; and 10 should come from media you are less likely to prefer. The ads you would watch as an individual everyday do not suffice. On the contrary, they are part of your filter bubble. As an advertising student, you should burst this bubble and actively aim to acquire a more holistic view of advertising and a richer advertising experience.

- Find two definitions of advertising that are not discussed in this Chapter. Compare and discuss their similarities and differences.
- Take your favourite branded products and try to think which of these products you would be reluctant to repurchase from a different brand. Trace your preferences: are they shaped by habit? Reputation? Word of mouth? Personal knowledge? Do you have intense feelings about these branded products?
- Choose your favourite product and try to create the perfect advertising campaign for it; a campaign that you would not be able to resist.
- Consider three types of products you never buy, anything from private banking services, to hardware, to cosmetics. If you were to buy for the first time, which factors would matter to you? Do your answers vary per product category? Seek awarded ads for at least two of these products. Do you find these ads appealing? What would make you come up with similar or equally creative ads for a product you don't know or don't use?
- Consider personal branding: what are the benefits and pitfalls of approaching individuals as brands, if you are a recruiter, a colleague, or a celebrity fan? How would you set out to create your own personal brand? What would be your strategy? Which touchpoints would you select to reach out to your target groups? What would your main message be?
- Search online for different agency templates for creative briefs. Compare them. Can you trace how they answer the strategic questions discussed in this chapter?
- Trace three well-known successful campaigns and three well-known campaigns that backfired. Try to imagine what their creative brief included. Download a creative brief template and try to re-construct this brief.

Notes

1 https://www.ama.org/topics/advertising/.
2 https://gdpr-info.eu/
3 https://www.nativeadvertisinginstitute.com/blog/what-is-definition-native-advertising
4 https://adage.com/article/cmo-strategy/slogans-taglines-brand-s-battlecry/301217
5 see also: https://eaca.eu/industry/talent/

References

Altstiel, T., Grow, J., Augustine, D., & Jennings, M. (2023). *Advertising creative: strategy, copy, and design* (Sixth). Sage Publications.

Baviera, T., Cano-Orón, L., & Calvo, D. (2023). Tailored messages in the feed? Political microtargeting on Facebook during the 2019 general elections in Spain. *Journal of Political Marketing*, 1–20. https://doi.org/10.1080/15377857.2023.2168832.

Beard, F.K. (2017). The ancient history of advertising – insights and implications for practitioners: what today's advertisers and marketers can learn from their predecessors. (speaker's box)(report). *Journal of Advertising Research*, 57(3), 239.

Belch, G.E. & Belch, M.A. (2003). *Advertising and promotion: An integrated marketing communications perspective*. McGraw Hill.

Bell, D. (1978). *The cultural contradictions of capitalism* (Ser. Harper torchbooks, tb5040). Basic Books.

Bovee, C.L., & Arens, W.F. (1992). *Contemporary advertising*, Richard D. Irwin, Inc.

Conejo, F., & Wooliscroft, B. (2015). Brands defined as semiotic marketing systems. *Journal of Macromarketing*, 35(3), 287–301. https://doi.org/10.1177/0276146714531147.

Danaher, P.J. (2023). Optimal microtargeting of advertising. *Journal of Marketing Research*, 60 (3), 564–584. https://doi.org/10.1177/00222437221116034.

de Waal Malefyt, T. & Morais, R.J. (2010). Creativity, brands, and the ritual process: Confrontation and resolution in advertising agencies. *Culture and Organization*, 16 (4), 333–347.

Drewniany, B.L., & Jewler, A.J. (2014). *Creative strategy in advertising*. Boston MA: Cengage Learning.

Egan, J. (2015) *Marketing Communications*. London: Sage.

Fill, C., Hughes, G., & De Francesco, S. (2013). *Advertising: Strategy, creativity and media*. Pearson.

Gardner, B.B. & Levy, S.J. (1955). The product and the brand. *Harvard Business Review*, March-April, 33–39.

Gray, A. (2022, September 9). Advertising agencies ask "where are all the people?" in battle for talent. *Financial Times*. Available at: https://www.ft.com/content/d378ccad-d614-4dae-8c8f-753b2285c442.

Gurrieri, L., Tuncay Zayer, L., & Coleman, C.A. (2022). Transformative advertising research: reimagining the future of advertising. *Journal of Advertising*, 51 (5), 539–556. https://doi.org/10.1080/00913367.2022.2098545.

Henry, S. (2011). *Creative briefing: the creative perspective*. In: Butterfield, L. (Ed.) *Excellence in advertising: the IPA guide to best practice*. New York: Routledge, pp. 161–176 (first published in 1999).

Hesmondhalgh, D. (2007). *The cultural industries* (Second). SAGE.

Mackert, M. (2012). Account planning: Applying an advertising discipline to health communication and social marketing. *Health Marketing Quarterly*, 29 (3), 270–282.

Moore, K., & Reid, S. (2008). The birth of brand: 4000 years of branding. *Business History*, 50(4), 419–432.

Prummer, A. (2020). Microtargeting and polarization. *Journal of Public Economics*, 188. https://doi.org/10.1016/j.jpubeco.2020.104210.

Stuhlfaut, M.W. & Windels, K. (2019) Altered states: The effects of media and technology on the creative process in advertising agencies, *Journal of Marketing Communications*, 25 (1), 1–27, doi:10.1080/13527266.2017.1380069.

Turnbull, S. & Wheeler, C. (2017) The advertising creative process: A study of U.K. agencies. *Journal of Marketing Communications* 23(2) 176–194.

2 Objectives and effects

What advertising can (and cannot) do – and how to plan for results

1 Introduction

Every organisation operates trying to achieve goals and objectives. Businesses may strive for profit and added value to stockholders, or for viability, and sustainability. NGOs may strive for fundraising. Political or governmental organisations try to improve the lives of their constituents, and so forth. The broad aims are set by an organisation's leadership and then trickle down to different departments, functions, or teams who align their efforts and their suppliers accordingly. Thus, broader goals are translated to specific objectives on the team or departmental level, ensuring that what they aim at can be measured to prove success.

When an organisation engages in marketing and communication activities, the respective teams will ask themselves: "what can we do to help achieve organisational objectives?" For example, if an organisation's objective is to increase stock price, then the marketing department might choose to run a corporate image campaign or push to launch an innovative product. If an organisation's objective is to raise donations, then the communication's department might consider a fundraising event, and so forth. Business goals give the big picture and then, each function or department set their own specific objectives.

Marketing objectives stem from business objectives. Accordingly, advertising objectives stem from marketing objectives. These must be fully aligned but are not identical. Advertising can contribute to marketing objectives, might even increase sales just by being out there, but advertising cannot achieve all marketing objectives on its own. The full marketing mix needs to be optimized and advertising constitutes one part of this mix.

The marketing mix includes all activities around the famous 4Ps: product, place, price promotion (for a more detailed review: O'Kane, 2011; Belch & Belch, 2003; for a critique: Constantinides, 2006). These 4Ps have been questioned, revised, enriched, or even supplemented with the 4Cs, to indicate consumer-centrism versus market-centrism. The 4Cs are, respectively: consumer, convenience, cost, communication (Wasmer et al., 1997). Whatever the acronym, the marketing mix is a simple yet helpful tool, used extensively in marketing plans. The marketing mix indicates all aspects of a market offering that need to be managed, starting from the product per se, considering attributes, benefits, competitive advantages,

DOI: 10.4324/9781003330721-2

as well as branding and packaging. The second "P", pricing, addresses questions of consumer cost. Will the price be determined in reference to the competition? to production costs? to the product's lifecycle or switching costs? Then, the marketing team determines the appropriate places for this product to become available. For example, if this product is a facial cream, will it be distributed in pharmacies? Supermarkets? Cosmetic retail stores? Own stores? Online? Last comes Promotion (Communication) which may include distribution of samples, product placement, press releases, events, and more. Advertising is only one part of one part of the marketing mix.

Advertising cannot achieve marketing objectives on its own. If not well aligned with the marketing mix, it can prove to be ineffective, fragile, even unprofitable (Tellis, 2004, pp. 17–18). If the product does not cover the needs of its target audience and does not constitute a competitive solution; if it is not within reach; if the price is too high or too low, advertising alone cannot ensure success (Colley, 1961 as cited in Weilbacher, 2001, p. 21). There are numerous examples of companies who persisted in advertising their products while facing issues with distribution; of outdated products trying to push demand through advertising, and then blaming the agency for low sales. Imagine you watch an ad that makes you want to test-drive a car, and then you decide to buy it. If the dealer says the car will be available in six months, you might choose a competing model that is available. If you watch an ad and crave to buy a chocolate bar but can't find it in your local supermarket, then you might soon forget about it. In such cases, advertising might increase demand, and yet prove to be a waste of resources.

In this chapter, we will discuss what advertising can and cannot do; how advertising objectives are determined and measured. What advertising does, however, is much more. Beyond working (or not) for one brand, advertising impacts society at large, hence it has received intense criticism. Day-to-day work and KPIs focus on the success of one branded product or service, not on the cumulative implications of advertising overall. The impact of all ads together, of advertising in general, should not be ignored. A young advertising professional should understand this impact not only to develop a more socially responsible work ethic but also to avoid backlashes and tone-deaf creativity. Thus, the second part of this chapter will focus on the impact of advertising at large and present an overview of the way this impact has been approached.

Advertising belongs in the cultural industries (Bilton, 2017; Hesmondhalgh, 2007). The cultural industries are those industries whose primary function includes the production of social meaning (Hesmondhalgh, 2007). The cultural industries make and circulate products which we do not consume for functional purposes only, but more importantly, to express our aspirations, to contemplate on how to live, to shape our opinions, to exchange our preferences, to make sense of the world around us and our place in it, to enjoy and recreate ourselves. Advertising engages in the production of social meaning, but such meaning is means rather than ends. The advertising artefact is meant to achieve objectives for the brand that signs it, and these objectives guide the work of creatives.

In most creative industries, marketing helps the artefact. In advertising, the artefact helps marketing.

Objectives and measured results are the beginning and the end of each advertising campaign. In between lies creativity. On the outskirts lie budgets, business and marketing plans, on the inside lie ideas. Objectives are the starting point for an advertising strategy that frames creativity perhaps more so than in most of the other cultural industries and constitutes the key criterion to assess creative ideas.

2 Think – Feel – Do: How advertising sets its objectives.

To achieve marketing objectives, advertising is frequently a necessary but rarely a sufficient condition. Under specific circumstances, advertising can influence what people do, what they know or how they think, and how they feel.

Let us organise our thoughts around this, starting from what consumers could do, after exposure to an ad:

- Find out more. After watching an ad, consumers might seek information by visiting stores or websites or by asking consumers or experts online or off-line. This can be measured through website traffic and store visits while online tools help assess if the brand is talked about, proving the campaign managed to "**increase consideration**" – a prerequisite for most purchases. A consumer doing active research goes beyond just having a high regard for a product or brand (Keller, 2001, p. 118).
- Try a product. After exposure, consumers might try a new refreshment, chocolate bar, window cleaner, almost spontaneously; and then decide if they will buy again. For more expensive products, more steps are needed. To buy a new car, trial would be a test drive. This is a frequent objective usually defined as: "**induce trial**". Trial can be measured and usually appears as a spike in sales or store visits.
- Advertising can make consumers keep buying a branded product. This is defined as: "**increase loyalty**". Loyalty might signify an emotional connection or just a routine which is often encountered in low involvement products (Vaughn, 1980; 1986). We cannot reconsider every purchasing habit every time we visit the supermarket.
- Advertising can make people talk about the ad itself or the advertised offering. Talking about it increases its reach and makes others actively look for the ad or product. This is often described as: "**create word of mouth (WOM)**" or buzz.
- Advertising can also be ignored, forgotten, or hated.

It is somewhat simplistic to believe than one ad alone can directly make a consumer buy something. Beyond a few spontaneous, impulsive purchases, mostly concerning fast moving consumer goods, for advertising to lead to sales other factors are put into play (Lodish, 1997; Vakratsas & Ambler, 1999).

So far, we approached a cluster of possible objectives linked to behaviour and action, whether clearly or implicitly stated on the ad (as a call-to-action).

Such objectives are relatively easier to measure and to combine with broader marketing objectives.

To make people act though, advertising needs to influence their thoughts and emotions; their reasoning and their feelings; their knowledge and their affections. Action is the aftermath of thinking and feeling (Keller, 2013, p. 118).

What can advertising do to influence consumers' knowledge and reasoning?

- **Raise awareness**: provide facts and information about something consumers may not know:

  a A new brand or offering
  b A new product attribute or price or distribution channel or function
  c Competitive advantage
  d Brand values and personality
  e Social, environmental, political, or other causes which relate to a specific brand and its values.

- **Remind** consumers about a brand so they keep it top-of-mind when the time comes to buy. Too many products, especially those we are not emotionally attached to, are easily forgotten, or replaced when we reach the point of sales.
- **Educate** or train consumers around of all the above, providing reasons why and ways how a product can or should be bought or used. This goes beyond mere awareness or information. Imagine how the first hair conditioner was launched; or the first personal computer. Consider how advertising today embeds environmental information to assure consumers they are making responsible choices. When introducing an existing product to a new target group, training might be needed. This objective may impact creative work calling for more explanatory and demo- or text-based executions.

Whether cognitive objectives and appeals to reason have been successful, is harder to measure and requires tailored research, frequently designed to run pre- and post-airing to assess the difference -assuming this difference can be attributed mainly to advertising.

Such research often includes surveys exploring spontaneous recall (what are the first five [brands of] banks that come to mind?) or aided recall (from the banks listed below, which ones do you know?). An answer to the first question would indicate top-of-mind awareness; an answer to the second question would indicate awareness. There can also be questions like: "Have you bought this brand?" or "Would you buy this brand?" to measure intent; or questions like: "how is this brand different to others?" or "what does this brand do better?" to assess whether the consumer has learnt about the brand.

Every ad should have some appeal to reason, a logical argument, implicit or explicit. But reason alone rarely guides our actions and advertising has never been solely informative or factual. Even more so, the first reaction to an ad is frequently emotional, and then reason kicks in. "I like this ad" (or not) comes first, followed by an assessment on whether the ad is useful, relevant, or even appropriate.

However, for both business and ethical purposes, advertising should not neglect fact and information at the expense of feeling.

Ads appeal to emotion and frequently aim at eliciting specific emotions. Usually, a strategist works on a brief determining a desired emotional response as part of the campaign objectives: "We want to make the target group feel cheerful" or scared or angry or surprised or safe... To achieve this, creatives conceive, develop, and filter their ideas considering not only messages, imagery, and storytelling, but also the overall tone of voice of the ad or campaign.

Tone of voice is an elusive term that describes how a brand "talks" to consumers. For example, normally, we expect brands like Doritos to make us laugh, brands like Nike to elevate us, brands like Dove to boost our confidence, and so on. Usually, brands maintain a somewhat similar, or at least not contradictory tone of voice in their campaigns, unless they decide to make a radical shift which should be clearly defined in the brief.

Ideally, an emotion elicited by the ad should be transferred to the brand. Beyond feeling, let's say, excited when looking at an ad, the consumer should feel excited about the brand that signs the ad. Whether a consumer will develop some sort of brand affection after exposure; whether this affection will go in the consumer's brand jar and stay there; and whether this will also lead to a purchase, depends on factors beyond the control of advertising (Colley, 1961 as cited in Weilbacher, 2001, p. 21). Evidence suggests that emotional objectives yield more significant results when used to promote high-involvement products.

The FCB grid indicates that emotional arousal leads to sales of products that consumers tend to connect with, or for goods associated with self-indulgence, while informational campaigns are more appropriate for high-involvement products or services. Habit-formation campaigns are more appropriate for frequently purchased low involvement goods (Belch & Belch, 2003, p. 155; Vaughn, 1980; 1986). The FCB grid is more extensively discussed in Chapter 8, in connection to content marketing strategies.

We know that emotions influence consumers' choices. We know that advertising influences emotions and brand-consumer relationships (Chaudhuri & Holbrook, 2001) potentially leading to better marketing outcomes. Beyond that, there is no generalised, uncontested understanding of when, why, or how this happens (Weilbacher, 2001).

As expected, measuring the outcomes of emotional advertising is quite challenging. Quantitative research mostly indicates what people say they feel or plan to do, while filling out a form. Qualitative research findings are hard to generalise. Online tools measuring sentiment do not apply on all languages equally well, and the way these tools perceive context can be contested, as the case study in this chapter shows.

***

What we have just described is a free interpretation of the **"Think-Feel-Do"** model (Egan, 2015; Belch & Belch, 2003; Vakratsas & Ambler, 1999) frequently used to define advertising objectives, organise and assess creative work, even though one should always bear in mind the multitude of factors which affect consumer decisions, (Bruce et al., 2012).

The Think-Feel-Do model is associated with the hierarchy of effects, one of the oldest and prevailing approaches despite criticism (Belch & Belch, 2003; Vakratsas & Ambler, 1999; Barry & Howard, 1990). Some of this criticism involves sequence: do consumers first think or feel? Do they first do and then feel? And so forth. Here, we discuss this triptych as if sequence is not important. Some ads put emotion first, and then provide a rational argument. Some present a call to action and then give a reason why. "Think-feel-do" or "do-think-feel" or any combination is plausible under given circumstances and depending on each case. Impulse buying begins with "do". What is important is that all three aspects should be considered, albeit in different proportions, with different emphasis, and not in the same order.

The hierarchy of effects dates to the 19th century, with AIDA, an acronym for: Attention, Interest, Desire, Action. Notice the resemblance between AIDA and "Think-Feel-Do": Interest relates to reason, desire aligns with emotion, and action is the final step in both. AIDA was introduced as a tool for personal selling, but remains popular, especially in teaching, ever since (Belch & Belch, 2003; Altstiel et al., 2023). Criticism applies here as well, especially regarding sequence, but the first "A" is worth considering: attention grabbing is a key element of successful advertising, especially in cluttered environments or for highly competitive product categories. A scroll on your feed proves it eloquently.

One more approach is DAGMAR, an acronym for "Defining Advertising Goals for Measured Advertising Results" (Belch & Belch, 2003). DAGMAR connects goals to results, providing a framework for assessing what advertising achieved and, importantly, at what cost. DAGMAR identifies a list of goals communication can achieve, presenting communication as an attempt to make a difference: what was known or assumed or thought before and after an ad? What can communication change? The challenge for advertising ever since is to select appropriate, feasible goals and then compile evidence to assess their achievement as will be discussed below (Belch & Belch, 2003, pp. 205–210). DAGMAR suggests that the consumer-brand relationship goes through four steps: awareness, comprehension, conviction, and action (aka ACCA). This also reminds of the think-feel-do approach, where the first two steps are cognitive, followed by an emotional and an actionable objective / consumer response.

Creatives may not need to delve into the specifics of defining objectives, but they certainly need to adjust ideas, executions, and tone-of-voice to the given objectives, hence the importance of understanding how objectives are determined and how ideas contribute to the success of the ad and the brand. Objectives are a criterion to evaluate ideas and modify executions. If, for example, a retailer aims at a sharp increase in store visitations during the discount period, their advertising might need a loud, direct, hard-selling tone of voice whereas a brand targeting affluent segments might opt for elegance, abstract visuals, and low-key voice overs, if any.

3 From consumers to brands

Advertising aims at people, using media, but its effects are also measured on sales and on brands. The way consumers think or feel about a brand affects the brand in ways that go far beyond sales. Take, for example, a luxury item. A lot of people might know or even adore it, and yet might never buy it. The value of a luxury brand resides in consumers' hearts and minds. Thoughts and feelings matter.

Because advertising contributes largely not only to sales but also to brand value, advertising campaigns are designed to increase the importance of a brand to the eyes of the consumers, even if sharp increases in sales are not immediately evident or directly aimed at.

Brand management comes with useful constructs to explain and measure the connections between brands and consumers -and subsequently, the role of advertising in bridging these two. An extensive analysis goes beyond the scope of this book. To support creative work, we will discuss selective constructs in relation to the ability of advertising to elicit specific thoughts or feelings.

- **Brand image** is the sum of consumers' perceptions about a brand, reflected by the brand associations in their memory (Keller, 2013, p. 72; Keller, 1993). Successful advertising can improve brand image (Modig & Rosengren, 2014) which is the outcome of both knowledge and feeling associated with the brand but can also be impacted by changes in the marketing plans, the competitive environment, or broader sociocultural trends.
- **Brand affect** is the brand's potential to elicit an emotional response (Chaudhuri & Holbrook, 2001, p. 82). Advertising can strengthen brand affect (or not), combined with other initiatives in the context of brand management.
- **Brand personality** is the sum of human characteristics consumers attribute to a brand (Aaker & Fournier, 1995; Aaker, 1997; Fournier, 1998; Keller, 2013). This sum is elusive because different people would not necessarily associate a brand with the same attributes while existing brand personality measurement scales are often considered insufficient and confusing (Azoulay & Kapferer, 2003). However, we know that advertising helps build brand personality (Keller, 2013, p. 115). Personification and anthropomorphism of brands correlate to emotional rather than rational processes (Chen & Lin, 2021; Huang et al., 2020) which tend to increase attachment and brand loyalty (McManus et al., 2022). However, excessive anthropomorphism could lead to a reductionistic and oversimplified approach to consumer thoughts and decisions.
- **Brand equity** is the added value a brand gives its products (Keller, 1993; Keller, 2013). Brand equity resides in consumers' heads and hearts, in their individual brand jars. Adding meaningful content in the jar increases its weight and therefore the brand's weight and value. Keller has introduced CBBE – The Customer Based Brand Equity Model, trying to bridge the gap between what brands can achieve and how consumers are impacted by brand communication. Keller argues that each brand should start with introducing

itself, presenting its identity and standing out from competitors before moving on to start conveying meaningful communications, interacting with consumers, and gradually aiming at a reciprocal connection. CBBE aligns with DAGMAR.

The above constructs help explain the impact of consumer choices on brands and the role of advertising. The connection between them, however, is neither linear nor unidimensional (indicatively: Parris & Guzmán, 2023; Chaudhuri & Holbrook, 2001). Each construct provides an angle through which brands are examined, assessed, and built. Each construct requires a mix of measurements which involve consumer perceptions, feelings, and correlations with sales (Bruce et al., 2012) and market share, all of which can be measured with ad hoc or longitudinal periodic research.

There is a vast armoury of tools to measure brand equity (Keller, 2013, pp. 292–314) guiding decision making, yet all tools have limitations (Weilbacher, 2001, p. 76) both in their theoretic underpinnings and in practical implementation. The idea is that by affecting consumers, advertising also affects brands. Measuring effectiveness, then, should draw evidence from both.

The effects of advertising are approached via two paradigms (Tellis, 2004; see also: Eisend & Tarrahi, 2016). The behavioural paradigm studies consumers to see how advertising impacts their purchase choices, helping prove that the Think-Feel-Do objectives have been achieved, focusing on the effects of advertising on consumers. The modelling paradigm calculates data like budgets versus media exposure or sales, to assess campaign efficiency. The modelling paradigm seems to focus somewhat more on markets than on consumers and on quantitative rather than qualitative data, without of course excluding consumer research and campaign testing. Combinations of both types of measurements are needed as section 2.5 explains.

4 Arriving at sensible and plausible objectives

Before discussing measurements, we will first address all the effort preceding objective-setting. The list below compiles suggestions from various sources (indicatively: Belch & Belch, 2003; Vakratsas & Ambler, 1999; Egan, 2015) on what strategists should consider before determining advertising objectives.

It all starts with a basic question: where are we and where do we want to go? The first part involves an assessment of a brand or product's current situation (Belch & Belch, 2003; Vakratsas & Ambler, 1999) often with the use of tools like P.E.S.T., competitive analyses, and S.W.O.T. which constitute part of a marketing plan. Here is a non-exhaustive list of data and information that strategists need to consider during the situation analysis, tracing problems or opportunities advertising can address:

- **The target segments.** Who is our desired buyer? Which demographic segment(s) do they belong to? What are their psychographic characteristics? What have they been buying so far? What are their needs, fears, concerns, and aspirations? Their lifestyles? (Kelley & Jugenheimer, 2015; Bielby, 2021). We discuss this in detail, in Chapter 3. For now, it is important to remember that advertising builds bridges between brands and consumers and one should not try to cross the bridge without knowing what lies on the other side.

- **The product category and competitive landscape.** While a marketer reviews competition to adjust the marketing mix, the advertising agency reviews competition to seek creative benchmarks and opportunities towards a unique share in the consumer's mind (Kelley & Jugenheimer, 2015, Bielby, 2021, p. 102). By studying "what others do" advertising can pave the way for a distinctive positioning and tone of voice, a novel insight, or a unique supporting claim.
- **The Product Lifecycle (PLC).** Advertising differs depending on whether a product is new or established or maybe too old and obsolete, though this depends largely on the product category. Launching products might require training, factual selling propositions, more repetition of the brand name, etc. Established products may seek new reasons why consumers should buy, revitalise brand image or expand to address new target groups. Declining products may choose not to advertise at all or may try to preserve sales and reverse the declining trend by tapping on emotion, presenting competitive advantages, or offers (Belch & Belch, 2003; Kelley & Jugenheimer, 2015).
- **The media landscape.** Budget and choice of media define the appropriateness and feasibility of advertising objectives and can optimise the returns of the client's investment (Kelley & Jugenheimer, 2015). The media landscape might also offer opportunities to creatives to do innovative work.
- **Creative benchmarks.** To support the creative team, objective-setting should follow an extensive benchmarking which examines how competing products or similar products in other markets advertise. This can lead to better positioning statements and help creatives understand the task at hand: what to go for and what to avoid.

A brief note: some agencies expect the client to knock on the door with a specific request in mind. Other agencies prefer clients who come with a problem or even a mesh of information, without having necessarily predetermined that advertising is what they need. Also, some campaigns start from addressing a problem, while others start with a target group in mind and how to approach it.

Here is a non-exhaustive list of factors that strategists need to consider when determining advertising objectives:

- Relevance to marketing (and business) objectives without reiterating.
- Relevance to the media that will be used, and to key metrics such media provide.
- Relevance to a specific target group and respective research findings.
- Making a difference in comparison to the current situation and the competition.
- Measuring this difference combining data and metrics from different sources.
- Estimating the required resources to achieve these objectives – how realistic are they? A prevailing approach is that advertising needs SMART objectives – one more acronym standing for: Specific, Measurable, Attainable, Realistic, and Time-Bound (Doran et al., 1981; Altstiel et al., 2023).

The above help avoid the "tick the box" approach and generic objectives like: "create awareness; create a positive image; increase sales" etc. Generic is wrong. Objectives are the cornerstone of a campaign and a significant filter to assess creative ideas.

On a more theoretic note, how advertising defines objectives is influenced by how advertising conceptualises consumers. Do we assume that the consumer is a blank slate where advertising imprints its messages (Vakratsas & Ambler, 1999, p. 27)? Do we believe that consumers can be lured to make solely emotional or impulsive choices? Do we trust them to analyse the facts sufficiently? Consumer conceptualisation has significant ethical implications addressed in Chapter 9.

Case study: The Mouldy Whopper. Do not try this at home! (Consider trying it at work)

In 2021 Burger King released a 45-second timelapse video of a big whopper standing still in front of the camera for 34 days until it grows mouldy. Obviously, word of mouth skyrocketed. Obviously, the initial reactions were negative. Consumers called the ad gross, disgusting, weird, and unappetizing. According to the company's CMO, it's one of the most successful Burger King campaigns. How come?

To answer this, you need to consider the ad's objectives. The message at the end reads: "The beauty of no artificial preservatives". This is a piece of information that responds to a cognitive objective. And it seems that making viewers disgusted was an intentional, albeit controversial emotional objective for which the ad won the Top Bravery Award. The ad used the product to shock and, according to the Burger King CMO, it did not aim at quick sales. A discount would bring sales far more easily.

Burger King wanted to get the message across, loud and clear, addressing younger generations turning to healthier eating with fewer preservatives, who would be less likely to buy Burger King. A clean-cut statement might not have been persuasive. Copy-testing results showed that people were appalled but got the message. The team took the risk and the risk paid off.

The campaign generated significant word of mouth. Although the campaign sentiment appeared negative, a careful examination revealed that over 88% of what was written was either positive or neutral while consideration increased by 22.8% which is spectacular in this saturated category. People said they hated the ad, but they got the message which tells us a lot about advertising literacy and the consumers' ability to decode the intentions of advertisers.

This is a good example busting the myth that food advertising must always look yummy and indulgent, proving that if the objectives are set correctly, then there is room for controversial creative ideas.

5 Measurements and metrics

The measurement of advertising effectiveness has always been ambiguous, contested, and elusive (indicatively: Belch & Belch, 2003; Vakratsas & Ambler, 1999; Bruce et al., 2012). Ever since the famous quote attributed to Wannamaker: "Half my advertising spend is wasted; the trouble is, I don't know which half" the advertising industry has faced trouble trying to measure results proving the advertising budget was well spent.

"How much profit (or revenue or market share) do I get for every euro I spend to advertise?" The answer to this question is defined as ROI (Return on Investment). ROI helps when all goes comparatively well but does not help define areas for improvement and optimisation. More detailed measurements are needed, stemming both from the modelling paradigm focusing on markets and the behavioural paradigm focusing on consumers.

The effects of advertising are neither linear nor simplistic (Tellis, 2004; Weilbacher, 2001, p. 22–23). We do not assume "the masses" watch and ad and sleepwalk to the seller buying something they never needed. But we do know that, beyond impulse buying and fast-moving consumer goods, consumers contemplate on decision making and selectively respond to emotional calls of action under specific circumstances (Tellis, 2004, p. 152–154).

The focus here is on what creatives need to know, to be able to align their ideas with specific objectives, considering strategical parameters:

1 Creativity sells (Tellis, 2004, p. 22) leading to better recall, stronger brand image, and likelihood to purchase. A memorable, liked, discussed ad requires fewer exposures thus saving media budget. Creativity sells, but not unconditionally (Tellis, 2004, pp. 103–104) and on its own, does not guarantee efficiency or effectiveness.
2 It is essential for advertising to be able to prove efficiency, effectiveness, and contribution to the marketing mix. When results are negative or ambiguous, the blame game challenges client-agency relationships. The creative idea alone cannot save the day.
3 Advertising has both instantaneous and long-term effects. The carryover effects of advertising depend on factors beyond advertising (Tellis, 2004, p. 19; Belch & Belch, 2003, p. 199–200).
4 Measurements emerge after composite, tailored combination of available data and metrics.

Before new media, measurable data mostly emerged from three sources:

- evidence of sales or increased demand in the points of sales: this evidence would indicate that the entire marketing plan works, including advertising.
- evidence of media popularity, proving, statistically, how many times how many targeted individuals were exposed to the message.
- consumer research pre- and post-airing to check recall, likelihood, intent, and emotional responses. Consumer research requires time and money and is thus most likely to occur in larger campaigns.

Adding to these, the industry's reactions to new ads and comments that circulate around the agency world provide an indication of the campaign's potential impact even though research-wise these reactions may prove little.

In the new media environment, we have the above data sources, plus multiple new metrics some of which are presented in Table 2.1 Simple online metrics include user reactions usually manifested through clicks (and comments or shares where applicable) and impressions (how many times a page containing the ad loaded on a user's screen). Online user data measure user behaviour and reactions, then, but these are combined with big data available online via cookies or other features. Such data include browsing patterns, location, device, and more. Thus, advertisers can combine user behaviour with user analytics to create composite metrics (like, for example, how many inhabitants of a city "saw" an online ad). Advertisers can also combine online and offline data to create composite metrics.

Table 2.1 Aligning consumer objectives with simple, non-composite KPIs.

Objective	Mass media	Web metrics	Social media metrics
Learn about a new product feature. ("Think")	Statistically, awareness is measured by calculating viewership or readership. From a behavioural perspective consumer research is required.	Site & page visits (first-time or repeated); time on page. The number of impressions also indicates a user learned about the offering.	Clicks, comments, reactions, or questions on a post / page.
Feel excited by the new product feature. ("Feel")	Qualitative or quantitative consumer research	Sentiment analysis used with caution	Social media reactions (like, laugh, angry, sad) and shares. Qualitative content analysis of comments on the post / ad.
Find out more about the new product feature. ("Do")	Visits to the point of sales.	Click on banners or buttons with a call to action: ask, order, request, learn more, etc.; contact with messaging chatbots.	Clicks on posts, direct messaging (DM), contact with messaging chatbots.

For example, by combining clicks to sales an advertiser can calculate how much advertising money each click costs (CPC – cost per click).

Abundant data requires analytical and critical skills to cut through ambiguities. Even more so, platform metrics frequently seem to serve platforms' rather than advertisers' interests and priorities and there is still lack of transparency. Each platform determines on its own: how much an ad costs, how many people were exposed, and whether the brand's quantifiable goals have been achieved. In the EU, the quest for transparency and independent measurements is ongoing[1].

Best practice to measure advertising effectiveness is the alignment of objectives to available metrics. This requires thorough thinking. When a metric corresponds to a desired objective, it becomes a KPI, a Key Performance Indicator. By achieving a KPI the team knows they contribute to the overall objectives. Defining objectives that cannot be assessed is problematic. Describing improvements in metrics as an objective is insufficient. For example, increasing the number of a post's "likes" should rarely be an end in itself; "likes" should be a KPI for a communication objective like increasing brand image, engagement, or affect. Hitting the like button does not necessarily signify any of the above, especially if hitting like comes with contests and discounts. Self-serving metrics that do well without contributing to the campaign objectives are often defined as vanity metrics (Rogers, 2018; Hochuli, 2020). Accurate measurements require careful alignment of objectives to metrics; tailored composition of metrics; and customised measurement schemes for each campaign.

Try this as an exercise: determine clear objectives using the think-feel-do approach. Then define your KPIs by selecting the right metrics. Consider combining metrics where applicable. This will help you grasp the challenge and understand how KPIs are customised depending on the brand, the category, the objectives, and the media mix. Start with Table 2.1.

6 The unintended effects of advertising

Advertising objectives refer to one brand, one campaign, one ad. Even longer-term account planning refers to one brand, mostly in one market. Beyond having desired and planned effects, each ad might have unintended effects (Pollay, 1986), most of which come with ethical implications discussed in Chapter 9.

Each ad might aim at things it does not do and do things it does not aim at. And even more so, each ad is part of all the ads consumers are exposed to.

As Goddard (1998) has pointed out, it is easier to deconstruct or dismiss one ad, but it is much more difficult to cut through the entire mesh of ads surrounding us. We cannot afford the critical processing of each of the hundreds of ads we are exposed to every day. And as Pollay (1986, p. 23–24) notes, those who claim to be immune to advertising naively assume that because they dismiss one ad, they are not affected by the pervasiveness of all ads together.

Ignoring the effects of advertising is not an option for students, scholars, and professionals. Beyond the micro-level of one-ad-at-a-time, we need frameworks which allow the understanding of advertising as a social phenomenon (Pollay, 1986; Gurrieri et al., 2022) often considered negative and harmful to society.

The social consequences of advertising are usually not in the professionals' scope. However, advertising contributes to the weaving of the broader socio-cultural context we live in. Advertising is not alone in this process. Some even doubt its power in comparison to other industries and institutions (Tellis, 2004). This highlights the need to study the interplay of advertising with other factors influencing society but does not qualify as an argument against the need for a thorough understanding of the consequences of advertising (Pollay, 1986; Zayer & Coleman, 2015; Gurrieri et al., 2022). Pollay (1986) offered one of the first reviews of the criticisms facing advertising, calling for more and new research approaches. An extensive literature review goes beyond the scope of this chapter but the attempt here is to provide a bird's eye view, inspiring for further reading.

6.1 Shopping for meaning in the symbolic marketplace

People consume ads just like they consume products. They appropriate ad meanings and messages (Baudrillard, 1972) and use them to express their sense of self and social identity. Advertising mediates not only between consumers and brands but also between the self and others (Goldman & Papson, 1996), hence the criticism going back decades, that advertising trivialises language and dehumanises personal relationships (Pollay, 1986, p. 23; Jhally, 1987). Jhally (1987) argues that advertising fragments the self to countless tiny needs, all to be satisfied by branded products, while Goldman & Papson (1996) argue that, in mature markets, advertising is all about creating meaningful signs in an excessive attempt to create distinctions among parity products, for audiences who play an active role in decoding and re-encoding these messages, and who use these distinctions to define and describe themselves in relation to their selected peers.

Ads are also consumed in our social interactions as cultural references, signifying not only who we are but also where we belong. Brands and ads often revolve around communities or sub-cultures of consumption that help us define our social identity. Each ad is made to mean something *to you* or *for you*. Our needs are socially constructed (Baudrillard, 1972; Sahlins, 1976; Douglas & Isherwood, 1979; Jhally, 1987) and culturally embedded (Bourdieu, 1984), apprehended and realized in interaction. We may try to keep up with the Jones, but the Jones are not the same for everyone. We have sight of what there is to have, by looking in but also by looking out; by assessing what others have, or do, or want. Advertising portrays the Jones for each of us, impacting our views on a vast array of topics that go far beyond the advertised product.

By making products "mean" something more than what they will be used for (Baudrillard, 1972), advertising creates further classifications and distinctions (Goldman & Papson, 1996) that connect peers and separate others. Advertising makes products signify not just affluence but also lifestyles, environmental awareness, care for animals or third world prosperity, pride, diversity, inclusion, self-confidence, and more, often engaging in identity politics. Advertising fills the brand jar with meaning to be shared and exchanged. Being ubiquitous and repetitive, advertising harvests and borrows from media, culture, art, history, and everyday experience, combining products with themes which then return to public discourse (Jhally, 1987).

This is quite close to what creatives do when they ideate, as will be discussed in Chapter 4. They use their entire cultural context as a point of reference to cherry pick stimuli, put them in a melting pot and bring them back as stories or symbols or both, designed to serve the need for extra meaning.

Thus, when we consume, we do not just consume the product. We also consume the ads and the symbolic value that exists in both products and their ads. And when we buy products, even our most rational choices are affected by the implicit or explicit meanings we assign.

If marketing distributes goods, advertising distributes meaning.

6.2 *Who's in, who's out? Advertising representations*

Advertising misrepresents. Advertising idealizes and distorts. Ads never aim to show the world as it is. They are not about reporting the facts. An ad is not a documentary. And consumers know. But if one counts the thousands of ads consumers are exposed to each day and then considers the know-how and resources invested in advertising, then it is easy to apprehend how the tiniest misrepresentations of each one ad multiply to heavily impact our sense of self and otherness.

Advertising misrepresents by including and by omitting; by including stereotyped representations of the ideal consumer, or idealised parodies; and by omitting anyone or anything unfamiliar or less than perfect. Even if, on the macro-level, we acknowledge this excess, on the micro-level, a creative who finds herself deciding on casting or setting will opt for the most attractive alternatives and try to create the perfect ad, the perfect ambience and surroundings for the product. Furthermore, as will be discussed in Chapter 3, the way target groups are defined and profiled often combines myopic quantitative data with presbyopic insights leading to an idolised consumer whose representation finds a way in the ad.

By cherry-picking what suits the needs of a brand or a creative idea; by adding in a melting pot, by developing, and airing, advertising acts like a distorting mirror (Pollay, 1986) reflecting prevailing themes and topics. Advertising does not invent; advertising borrows (Goddard, 1998; Holbrook, 1987) but then returns something different (Schroeder and Borgerson 2005). In the representational system of advertising, stereotyping and misrepresentation exclude minorities and perpetuate discrimination, alienating, dramatizing otherness, preventing inclusion, and creating stigmatizing environments (Nolke, 2018; Kearney et al., 2019; Gurrieri et al., 2022). Acknowledging that ads are abstractions (Jhally, 1987) and that authentic character building is not part of their objectives; accepting that for the sake of creativity sometimes people are reduced to props (Williamson, 1978), does not justify or nullify misrepresentations and their negative effects.

Though there are signs of a movement towards more inclusive advertising (some examples in: Gurrieri et al., 2022), it is worth noting that to tackle the issue of misrepresentation, one must go back to the beginning of the brief, back to the objectives. Addressing issues of misrepresentation and stereotyping during production is far too late, barely suffices, and established practice rarely leaves room for thinking of such issues at a late stage and beyond the task at hand, as will be discussed in Chapter 9.

We still have a long way to go to interweave considerations about the impact of all ads in the planning for each ad.

Time to practise!

- Consider similarities and differences between Think-Feel-Do, AIDA, and ACCA.
- Seek similarities between ACCA & CBBE in the context of advertising.
- You are about to run a campaign launching a new product, aiming to create awareness, excitement, and trial. Create a basic questionnaire that will run before the launch and one that will run after the launch, which will help you measure the success of the campaign. Which questions would you ask? Look for examples or templates on the web and compare.
- Which online and social media metrics could you combine to measure if consumers are more favourable toward your brand than they were before your campaign?
- Write down 10 taglines or jingles from ads you remember from your childhood. Try to describe these to your classmates explaining what resonated. Which brand were they promoting? Do you buy the brand? Watch these ads and try to trace the think-feel-do sequence.
- Ask people that are over 20 years older than you, for ads they remember and try to locate them online. Discuss whether they appeal to reason or emotion or both. Discuss whether they have a clear call-to-action. Compare to ads you are exposed to everyday.

Dissections

Looking at ads who have aired already and guessing the brand's objectives is a useful exercise. We may not have been there when objectives were defined, but a careful examination can give plausible answers.

- Check out the Colin Kaepernick poster Nike released for the 30th anniversary of "Just do it". Does this ad have an explicit call-to-action? Does the call-to-action reflect the ad's advertising objectives? How would you describe these objectives?
- Watch the ad titled: "How to look your best the morning after" (https://www.youtube.com/watch?v=d-XHPHRIWZk). Apply the think-feel-do approach to discuss the sequence of appeals. How would you describe the objectives of the ad?
- Watch the Doritos "Try another angle" Superbowl 2023 ad. The ad appears to have a direct call-to-action. Does this reflect the action that the brand wants the consumer to preform? How would you define the objectives of the ad using the think-feel-do approach?

Note

1 These reports provide insight on the debated issues of platform transparency and need for regulation:

-https://eaca.eu/wp-content/uploads/2022/07/The-DMA-Impact-on-agencies-EACA-.pdf

-https://www.europarl.europa.eu/RegData/etudes/STUD/2021/662913/IPOL_STU(2021)662913_EN.pdf

-https://assets.publishing.service.gov.uk/media/5dfa0580ed915d0933009761/Interim_report.pdf

References

Aaker, J., & Fournier, S. (1995). A brand as a character, a partner and a person: three perspectives on the question of brand personality. *Advances in Consumer Research*, 22(1). Available at: https://www.acrwebsite.org/volumes/7775/volumes/v22/NA-22/full.

Aaker, J.L. (1997). Dimensions of brand personality. *Journal of Marketing Research*, 34 (3), 347–356.

Altstiel, T., Grow, J., Augustine, D. & Jenkins, J.L. (2023) *Advertising creative: Strategy, copy, design*. Sage.

Azoulay, & Kapferer, J.N. (2003). Do brand personality scales really measure brand personality? *Brand Management*, II(2), 143–155.

Barry, T.E., & Howard, D.J. (1990). A review and critique of the hierarchy of effects in advertising. *International Journal of Advertising*, 9 (2), 121–135. https://doi.org/10.1080/02650487.1990.11107138.

Baudrillard, J. (1972). *Pour une critique de l'économie politique du signe*. Gallimard.

Belch, G.E. & Belch, M.A. (2003). *Advertising and promotion: An integrated marketing communications perspective*. McGraw Hill.

Bielby, L. (2021). *Super strategist: the art and science of modern account planning*. Figure 1 Publishing.

Bilton, C. (2017). *The disappearing product: marketing and markets in the creative industries*. Edward Elgar Publishing.

Bourdieu, P. 1984 [1979]. *Distinction: A social critique of the judgement of taste*. Trans. Richard Nice. Cambridge, MA: Harvard University Press.

Bruce, N.I., Peters, K., & Naik, P. A. (2012). Discovering how advertising grows sales and builds brands. *Journal of Marketing Research*, 49(6), 793–806. https://doi.org/10.1509/jmr.11.0060.

Chaudhuri, A., & Holbrook, M.B. (2001). The chain of effects from brand trust and brand affect to brand performance: the role of brand loyalty. *Journal of Marketing*, 65(2), 81–93. https://doi.org/10.1509/jmkg.65.2.81.18255.

Chen, K.-J., & Lin, J.-S. (2021). Revisiting the effects of anthropomorphism on brand relationship outcomes: the moderating role of psychological disposition. *European Journal of Marketing*, 55(8), 2174–2200. https://doi.org/10.1108/EJM-07-2018-0471.

Constantinides, E. (2006) The Marketing Mix Revisited: Towards the 21st Century Marketing, *Journal of Marketing Management*, 22(3–4), 407–438, doi:10.1362/026725706776861190.

Doran, G.T. (1981). There's a s.m.a.r.t way to write management's goals and objectives. *Management Review*, 70, 35–36.

Douglas, M. & Isherwood, B. (1979). *The world of goods: towards an anthropology of consumption*. London: Routledge.

Egan, J. (2015). *Marketing Communications*. Sage.

Eisend, M., & Tarrahi, F. (2016). The effectiveness of advertising: A meta-meta-analysis of advertising inputs and outcomes. *Journal of Advertising*, 45(4), 519–531.

Fournier, S. (1998). Consumers and their brands: developing relationship theory in consumer research. *Journal of Consumer Research*, 24(4), 343–353.

Giddens, A. (1991). *Modernity and self-identity: Self and society in the late modern age*. Cambridge: Polity Press.

Goddard, A. (1998). *The language of advertising*. London: Routledge,

Goldman, R., & Papson, S. (1996). *Sign wars: the cluttered landscape of advertising* (Ser. Critical perspectives). Guilford Press.

Gurrieri, L., Tuncay Zayer, L., & Coleman, C. A. (2022). Transformative advertising research: Reimagining the future of advertising. *Journal of Advertising*, 51(5), 539–556. https://doi-org.acg.idm.oclc.org/10.1080/00913367.2022.2098545.

Hesmondhalgh, D. (2007). *The cultural industries* (Second). SAGE.

Hochuli, D. (2020, February 10). The right and wrong ways to use vanity metrics. *Content Marketing Institute*. Available at: https://contentmarketinginstitute.com/articles/vanity-metrics-marketing-goals/.

Holbrook, M.B. (1987). Mirror, mirror, on the wall, what's unfair in the reflections on advertising? *Journal of Marketing*, 51(3), 95–103. doi:10.1177/002224298705100307.

Huang, R., Zhou, X., Ye, W., & Guo, S. (2020). Think versus feel: two dimensions of brand anthropomorphism. *Journal of Product & Brand Management*, 29(7), 955–969. https://doi.org/10.1108/JPBM-11-2018-2125.

Jhally, S. (1987). *The codes of advertising: fetishism and the political economy of meaning in the consumer society*. St. Martin's Press.

Kearney, S., Brittain, I. & Kipnis, E. (2019). "Super Disabilities" vs "Disabilities"? Theorizing the Role of Ableism in (Mis)representational Mythology of Disability in the Marketplace, *Consumption, Markets and Culture*, 22 (5–6),545–567. doi:10.1080/10253866.2018.1562701..

Keller, K.L. (1993), Conceptualizing, Measuring, and Managing Customer-Based Brand Equity, *Journal of Marketing Research*, 29, 1–22.

Keller, K.L. (2013). *Strategic Brand Management: Building, Measuring, and Managing Brand Equity* (Global Edition). Pearson.

Kelley, L.D., & Jugenheimer, D.W. (2015). *Advertising account planning: planning and managing an IMC campaign* (Third). Routledge/Taylor & Francis Group.

Lodish, L.M. (1997). J.P. Jones and Blair, M.H. (1996). On measuring advertising effects – another point of view. Response to Jones and Blair. *Journal of Advertising Research*, 37 (5), 75.

McManus, J.F., Carvalho, S.W. & Trifts, V. (2022). The role of brand personality in the formation of consumer affect and self-brand connection, *Journal of Product & Brand Management*, 31(4), 551–569. https://doi-org.acg.idm.oclc.org/10.1108/JPBM-08-2020-3039.

Modig, E., & Rosengren, S. (2014). Can advertising creativity affect product perceptions and retailer evaluations? *Journal of Product & Brand Management*, 23(6), 452–461. https://doi.org/10.1108/JPBM-06-2014-0651.

Nolke, A.-I. (2018). Making Diversity Conform? An Intersectional, Longitudinal Analysis of LGBT-Specific Mainstream Media Advertisements, *Journal of Homosexuality*, 65(2), 224–255. doi:10.1080/00918369.2017. 1314163.

O'Kane, B. (2011). *Marketing basics*. NuBooks.

Parris, D.L. & Guzmán, F. (2023). Evolving brand boundaries and expectations: looking back on brand equity, brand loyalty, and brand image research to move forward, *Journal of Product & Brand Management*, 32(2), 191–234. https://doi-org.acg.idm.oclc.org/10.1108/JPBM-06-2021-3528.

Pollay, R.W. (1986). The Distorted Mirror: Reflections on the Unintended Consequences of Advertising, *Journal of Marketing* 50(2), 18–36. doi:10.1177/002224298605000202.

Rogers, R. (2018). Otherwise engaged: social media from vanity metrics to critical analytics. *International Journal of Communication*, 12, 450–472.

Sahlins, M. (1976). *Culture and practical reason*. University of Chicago Press.

Schroeder, J.E., & Borgerson, J.L. (2005). An ethics of representation for international marketing communication, *International Marketing Review* 22(5), 578–600. doi:10.1108/02651330510624408.

Tellis, G.J. (2004). *Effective advertising: Understanding when, how, and why advertising works* (Ser. Marketing for a new century). Sage Publications.

Vaughn, R. (1980), How advertising works: a planning model. *Journal of Advertising Research*, 20(5), 27–33.

Vaughn, R. (1986), How advertising works: a planning model revisited. *Journal of Advertising*, 26 (1), 57–66.

Vakratsas, D., & Ambler, T. (1999). How advertising works: what do we really know. *Journal of Marketing*, 63(1), 26.

Wasmer, D.J., Williams, J.R., & Stevenson, J. (1997). A reconceptualization of the marketing mix: using the 4 c's to improve marketing planning in higher education. *Journal of Marketing for Higher Education*, 8(2), 29–35.

Weilbacher, W.M. (2001). Point of view: does advertising cause a "hierarchy of effects"? *Journal of Advertising Research*, 41(6), 19.

Williamson, J. (1978). *Decoding advertisements: ideology and meaning in advertising*. Boyars.

Zayer, L.T., and C.A. Coleman. 2015. Advertising professionals' perceptions of the impact of gender portrayals on men and women: A Question of ethics? *Journal of Advertising* 44 (3), 1–12. doi:10.1080/00913367.2014.975878

3 Audiences and consumers

How people read products and consume ads.
How ads read people

1 How people read products and consume ads

People read ads in ways that are individually unique and socially constructed. We perceive using our senses, we assimilate, and interpret depending on our personality, mental structures, mood, and context. We read using language, which is constructed and taught, but we also read using images and we think by constructing mental images. We read ads, but we also read products, whose meaning we appropriate and use in daily interaction to establish relevance or convey our values and idea(l)s. Advertising becomes a point of personal and social reference (Goldman, 1992). Consumption is a way to belong and stand out; to express both similarities and differences (Ritson & Elliott, 1999), and to experience pleasure (Campbell, 2018).

Cultural anthropology shows that products are used in the construction of self-narratives and identities; as ways to belong in a community or society (Douglas & Isherwood, 1979) and as parts of ritualistic consumption (Arnould & Thompson, 2005). Some objects define us, the way Linus is defined by his blanket and Colonel Mustang by the white gloves. We use brands and ads to build and convey our sense of self (Ritson & Elliott, 1999). Brand culture and consumer culture are part of the fabric shaping our identities and personal points of reference (Berger, 2019; McCracken, 1986; Goldman, 1992, 2000). We also "read" and interpret each other's objects and brands in similar ways. People have always used objects to convey messages about themselves, as the seminal work of Ervin Goffman (1959) has shown. Consumption is more than just use and gratification – it's a form of communication and a way of belonging.

Through brands, we see a parallel process, of meaning exchange through symbols. In the western world at least, beyond just possessing an object, we also intend to possess its signifying value signalled by the brand, which we use to signal about ourselves (Bilton, 2017; Goldman, 1992; see also: Gardner and Levy, 1955; Holbrook & Hirschman, 1993). We use some brands, in some cases, as building blocks for the construction of our social identity. Brands create their own vocabulary (Goldman, 1987; Goldman & Papson, 1996; 1994). We can assume something different for two people when one carries a Samsonite and the other carries an Adidas backpack to work. Some brands mean nothing to *you* but might mean something to someone else; and vice versa.

DOI: 10.4324/9781003330721-3

So, when people read ads, beyond being informed or convinced, they see these ads as part of their vocabulary for statements of self-expression; for differentiation and belonging – whether tokens of meaning are acquired through the possession of the product or through the ad's content – catchphrases, jingles, images, or memes.

Reading ads helps us understand the consumption of meaning and the meaning of consumption. Analysing ads helps us develop critical skills. In the following chapters we proceed with the making of ads. First comes analysis, then synthesis. Critical and creative thinking work in tandem.

2 Basic semiotics

Semiotics tells us that we do not actually exchange thoughts and ideas. We exchange signs that carry the meaning we wish to convey. Language and images are such signs. Semiotics is the study of how we use signs and symbols. This section reduces the vast, stimulating field of semiotics (for a more thorough reading: Nöth, 1995; Chandler, 2002; Beasley & Danesi, 2010; Berger, 2006; 2010; 2019; Oswald, 2011) to a few key terms, constructs, and tools that help focus on advertising as a semiotic artefact. Though "making" and "reading" ads are different processes; and though a meaning is frequently lost, one cannot make ads if they cannot read ads; one cannot create meaning if they do not know what meaning is made of.

2.1 The sign

Growing up we learn that things "mean"; that <3 means "heart" and thereafter "love", so we attach meaning to this drawn object, thus turning it to a symbol, often forgetting that it may mean nothing (or something different) to those who come from a different country or culture. Think of slang and the generations; of jargon; of medical terms…

We learn that "o" means the sound we make when our lips form a circle. We learn language – our first and perhaps most complex system of signs. At home we learn how to speak, at school we learn how to write and read. What we learn is how to exchange (visual and auditory) signs to convey meaning. We are literate, not only when we can put signs together, but also when we realise that these signs are not universal. We are literate, when we know that "x" reads "z" in the beginning of a word; that "x" stands for an unknown number in equations; or that "π" is 3.14 in math but reads "p" in Greek. We learn that signs might have different meanings in different contexts and that most signs are arbitrary – the result of convention, not of a natural connection. Thus, red "means" danger on road signs and passion on roses; and a bell sound means the break is over, but only when we are at school. At work, a bell might signify we need to evacuate.

A sign is the combination of a signifier, that is what triggers our senses, and of its agreed meaning (Nöth, 1995; Chandler, 2002). The study of signs emerged in the realms of philosophy (Peirce, Russel) and linguistics (Saussure) who distinguished between the sign as a whole; the signifier as a sensory stimulus; the signified meaning which is denoted and the referent which is connoted and subjectively constructed in the eyes of the beholder. A cross means something different to a Christian and a Pharmacist.

2.2 Denotation & connotation

Denotation is the literary, obvious, commonsense meaning of the sign, as discussed above. A sign might also have connotative meaning, that is socio-cultural or personal associations relevant to emotion or ideology (Chandler, 2002; Nöth, 1995, pp. 100–103; Berger, 2010, pp. 15–16). A bell might denote school breaks and connote a playful childhood.

Signs are polysemic (Nöth, 1995, pp. 337) because their meaning varies depending on context and on the reader's perspective. Signs make sense next to other signs, not in isolation. Combining and comprising signifiers creates new connotations and meaning emerges through implicit syntheses. Advertising masters such syntheses for the purposes of persuasion, obscures the semiotic arbitrariness and reveals a world that appears real and plausible even when we know it is purposefully constructed. Signs and their combinations lead to connotations which, put next one to the other, create brand narratives.

Consider the yellow, curvy capital M. It could denote the letter of the alphabet, or McDonalds. It could connote French fries or kids' parties, or a familiar place to eat when in a foreign country; or the yellow arches; or the drive through; or an old birthday celebration… All brands are symbols. They denote a product or company, but they are designed and promoted to connote much more. A bird might stand for a bird; or for Dove or Hollister and most probably you will be able to find more brands whose logo has a bird. We know which bird stands for which brand, not because we are taught but because we learn. A brand is a symbol that we learn to "read" using both denotation and connotation (Berger, 2019; 2010, pp. 75–80; see also: Beasley & Danesi, 2010, pp. 44–45).

Brand awareness, recognising a branded product, is denotation. Every other objective advertising can achieve, requires the formation of connotations. This is always an imperfect process, though. The brand jar includes more than just advertising, which is always interpreted in context. Other factors also come into play, from personal experience to negative publicity.

Advertising adds connotative meaning to brands, and to do so, it borrows from other signs, from the cultural domain. Advertising turns meaningless products to symbols. Take a pen, for example, and place it next to gold cufflinks and a leather briefcase. Take a soda can and place it on the sand next to a beach towel. Take a perfume and place it in the hands of a celebrity. Now, take a step back. This sounds familiar, not creative. Creativity is about the uniqueness of connotations in the eyes of the targeted consumer.

2.3 The metaphor

To create connotations, the brand transfers meaning from other signs to itself. There is a term for this transfer, it's called metaphor. According to Chandler

(2002) a metaphor occurs when a signifier of one sign and the signified of another, form a new sign. This metaphor is about the product but also its context and the understanding of reality at large. For example, when Lady Gaga promotes Dom Perignon rosé, Lady Gaga symbolises female glamour and transfers this glamour to the product so when one looks at the bottle, they denote the product and connote female glamour. There is no resemblance or evident reason why these two are similar or relevant, yet advertising brings them together in seamless connection (see also: Berger, 2019; Beasley & Danesi, 2010, pp. 118–119). This lack of natural or anticipated resemblance that can create new meaning, is what sets metaphor apart from other tropes that will be discussed in Chapter 5. So, when you see a Red Bull, you might recall wings and connote energy, though there is no natural resemblance.

Not a single dot appears on an ad by accident. It's all part of meticulous, multiply reviewed writing and design. Strategy frames the court where creativity can play. Each ad works in context, is temporary and easily outlived by the next one, which is impressive considering the effort and resources dedicated to get each mere detail right. The ads we recall years later are a drop in the ocean of ads we are exposed to every day. Advertising captures its time, and then flies away with it, which is why analysing old ads is a remarkable way of discovering how people produce different contexts and how contexts produce different people.

Though the chapter uses examples from print advertising and performs semantic analysis, all ads can be analysed using semiotics. The more complex the ad, the more elaborate the tools we need. Paradigmatic analysis examines the position of one sign next to alternative signs. Syntagmatic analysis examines the position of one sign next to complementary signs. All these help approach advertising critically, though their discussion goes beyond the scope of this book.

2.4 Encoding and decoding

When we put symbols together, we encode. When we analyse them, we decode (Nöth, 1995, pp. 207–209). When encoding, we create a total that is larger than the sum of its parts and hope that others will understand it as we intend them to. When decoding, we do not just recognise and comprehend; we also interpret and assess (Chandler, 2002) the signified meaning as well as the connection with its signifiers.

Creatives encode, consumers decode. This is the process of communication. Similar notions are expressed from the Shannon & Weaver model all the way to the Luhman systemic thinking that examines communication as a synthesis of three steps: information, utterance (encoding), and understanding (decoding). The more media savvy consumers become, the more creatives need to push the envelope (Goldman & Papson, 1994), otherwise ads seem naïve or pushy. Just compare an ad from the 1950s with a contemporary one and see how creative advertising (in)tends to become more subtle, covert, and aligned with current aesthetic preferences.

Judith Williamson (1978) described the interaction between consumers and ads as a four-step process. First, we see the signs and create the meaning of the ad. Meaning lies only in the eyes of the decoder. The ad selects but the reader processes. Second, we are created by the ad. The ad calls us in its world, and we choose whether to respond to this calling. There is always a place for the reader in the ad. So, during the third step, the reader responds and recreates themselves in the ad, becoming part of the ad before owning the product. Advertising is meant to create a sense of lacking and then fulfil it, according to Williamson (1978). If the reader engages with an ad, then the fourth step is to take its meaning away, appropriate it and use it to convey messages about themselves. This is what Williamson calls Totemism, and this is how she considers the role of advertising as ideology. Quite a long paragraph to describe our exposure to an ad which might last a split second, and this is a key takeout: even when we skip or ignore advertising, something stays in our memory. We thus learn about products that we may never use, or develop a desire for something new, and so forth. The un-noticed is still there to shape our context, even when we seem to ignore it (Jhally, 1987; Williamson, 1978).

But then, meaning does not stay confined between the "maker" and the "reader". Meaning travels through social exchange. Are *my* connotations of Nike compatible with *yours*? Do we have the same image of the brand and what it stands for? Would we feel more similar, hence maybe more intimate, if we discovered we use the same personal care brand? Would we jump to similar stereotyped conclusions if we saw a person carrying a Penguin tote bag? We engage in an implicit dialogue when we decode what the brand "says" for its owner.

The semiotic functions and cultural implications of advertising have attracted a lot of attention (indicatively: Goldman, 1992; Goldman & Papson, 1994; 1996; Berger, 2006; 2010; 2019; Beasley & Danesi, 2010; Oswald, 2011). Starting from the work of Barthes (1977) who took semiotics from up the shelf of high culture down to the trivial world of popular culture, a lot of scholars have used semiotics to study advertising. Semiotics might appear too abstract at times, but it's the only way to render the implicit explicit and thus approachable from a critical perspective.

A semiotic approach has been useful in explaining not just advertising but also the symbolic aspect of a lot of our consumption patterns (Baudrillard, 1972), rituals (de Certeau, 2011), tastes (Bourdieu, 1984), and constellations (Baudrillard, 1968). Older analyses focused a lot on consumption as a signifier for social status (Baudrillard 1972; 1970; Barthes, 1977). Later, consumption has been associated with sub-cultures and tribalism (Maffesoli, 1996; Veloutsou & Moutinho, 2009); with identity politics (Banet-Weiser, 2012); with individual lifestyles (Beasley & Danesi, 2010, pp. 10–15) and attitudes to social issues (Williamson, 1978; Berger, 2010). Combining these perspectives with more business-oriented perspectives has led to the construct of transformative consumer research (Davis & Ozanne, 2019; Mick, 2006) that adopts an intradisciplinary approach through integrative frameworks.

This brief introduction on semiotics is useful to creatives because it renders tacit processes more explicit, both from the creator's and from the recipient's perspective. Creative work appropriates symbols from the social and cultural realm and uses them to transfer their meaning to the brand. This is what creatives do, even when it is not articulated that way. And although aesthetics and design are not emphasised in this book, do remember that an artful blending makes symbols make sense, appearing intuitive and attractive (Barthes, 1977). Semiotics explains how we make ads and how we read ads.

3 How to read through an ad

When we look at an ad, we think we get it. But we don't; not until we use words to articulate clearly and explicitly what the ad shows and says; what the symbols are and what their meaning is. Deploying language to make the implicit explicit makes all the difference. This is fundamental when examining ads. Before articulating the ad idea or message, this ad works without our critical participation. Critical thinking needs understanding, manifested through language and utterance.

Below is a five-step process to analyse print advertising that combines text with image.

- Step 1: observe. Forget about everything else and write down (or circle) everything you see on the ad. Nothing is self-evident or trivial, and nothing should stay tacit. Our initial response to advertising is always emotional. We should leave it aside and put every detail down on paper because no detail is randomly chosen on the ad.

  a Start with words. Determine the headline and the tagline. Write down keywords that are repeated in the body copy, the text of the ad.
  b Proceed with the visual: is it a photo, a sketch, an illustration, or clip art?
  c List all the objects that appear on the ad, regardless of size or prominence.
  d Note all key colours: black and white? Saturated? Pale? Sepia? Is there evidence of colour alignment between objects? Are there any dominant brand colours?
  e Continue with the design elements: dominant shapes, objects out of pro- portion... what captures our attention first? Follow the course of the eye.

- Step 2: analyse & deconstruct. Trace the signifiers. Start considering what they may mean. Question the obvious: why this shape? this colour? this object or word? Dismantle the ad. But most of all, ask these questions:

  a How does the text relate to the visuals? Is it complementary? Contra- dictory? Explanatory?
  b Which metaphors can you trace? What are the exchanges between sig- nifiers? Which meaning is transferred to the brand?
  c What is missing? Something always is.

- Step 3: Expand. Try to grasp the context of the ad: trending topics; social concerns; values and lifestyle elements. Check for comments the ad might have on social media. The more accurate and relevant your search, the more plausible and accurate your interpretation. Signifiers should never be considered self-evident.

- Step 4: Assess. At this point you should start reaching to conclusions. You can see the ad from a distance to trace any ethical considerations. You can start discovering the strategy behind the ad by considering whom this ad appeals to and what its aims at. Thus, you reconstruct the ad in a way that may explain or contradict your initial emotional reaction. All interpretations are accepted when they rely on accurate observation.

Time to practise!

- Study the "Bird, Shark" 2010 WWF campaign. Identify signifiers and write their meaning.
- Study the "Show mustn't go on" print ad. Identify the visual signifiers. Discuss the headline in relation to popular music and whether this relation transfers meaning from the song to the ad. Consider the connection to the logo.
- In 2019, Budweiser remade two of its 50's print ads to celebrate Women's Day. Choose one pair of ads and note all the signifiers that change. Discuss how this differentiates the meaning of these two ads. Carefully trace all the similarities.
- Use semantics to analyse at least three print ads of your choice. Make sure one comes from a different country whose language you can understand, and one comes from a different decade. Apply this model and share your conclusion with a classmate. See whether you agree on your observations and assessments.
- Trace the signs and the metaphor in the "Lego airplane" ad.
- Study the McDonald's "Wi-Fries" ad. What are the signifiers? Is there a transfer of meaning?

---

4 How ads read people

As symbols and signs are open to interpretation, the process of communicating through the media is bound to be incomplete and imperfect, which is also what makes it so exciting. After having defined communication objectives, reading into people is the next step in campaign planning. We need to read into people, to make sure we deliver a relevant, appropriate, and original message. This section examines how planners "read" into consumers.

4.1 STP

STP stands for: Segment, Target, Position. Proposed by Philip Kotler (1999), this model creates a sense of order around the chaos of fragmented audiences.

- **Segment**: Imagine you open your Google maps application, and you look at the flattened globe. You want to see Brisbane. You start zooming in, until the city appears on your screen. You keep zooming until you find your hotel or the restaurant somebody recommended. This is one way a target group can be defined: first, we need an overview of the market. Do we focus on a national market, like the Australian or the UK market? Or on a big city because we run a local store? This market is our flattened earth. We have just segmented geographically, Now, within the chosen market, we segment further: we use demographic filters to include and exclude, for example minors; or men; or those with a very high income, and so on. Segmentation, however, can also work backwards: making observations about people's attitudes or lifestyles or buying patterns, a planner can define a cluster ad hoc, profile it and then set it as a target group (Lawson & Todd, 2002, p. 298).
- **Target:** Once we isolate a segment, we focus on studying this segment. Research evidence helps build a profile which also requires a good understanding of psychographic and lifestyle elements. At this stage, we know enough of our target group's needs and wants, we can move to the next stage.
- **Position:** to create a connection between the branded offer and the specific target group, we write a message, a proposition, a promise that will link this particular product to this particular target group. The same product might be positioned somewhat differently to address a different target group (often at a later stage). The positioning is one sentence. A sentence that states how a branded offering differs from competing ones and what it promises to the specific target group (Keller, 2013, p. 79–93; Belch & Belch 2003, p. 51–58). Positioning a brand appropriately to each target group in a clear and single-minded way is neither easy nor simple. The brand remains the same, but the positioning needs to be tailored. What a branded product does might appear easy to describe. What this product does *for you* is a different story. Packaged orange juice might promise energy and wholesomeness to mothers or cool-ness to teenagers or refreshing breaks to office employees. The product is the same but the reason why *you* would buy it depends on who *you* are. The positioning is the skeleton of a bridge connecting two ends: the product and the consumer. Both should be reflected. A good positioning is not creatively written but should lead to a creative insight, tagline, or idea. A good positioning must be simple, intuitive, and clear, but a lot of work is needed to explore complex issues and countless possibilities before arriving there.

4.2 *Dividing and classifying*

Demographic information helps the planning team divide a market and then focus on a selected segment. Frequent demographic "dividers" are **age, gender, income, education, area of residence, and family status** (Belch & Belch, 2003, pp. 46–47; Keller, 2013, p. 114). However, depending on the product, special dividers might be used like religion or political affiliations, or even more precise demographically known information like, for example, house owners versus house renters. Finally, a cohesive segment is selected, i.e., "35–44, primarily women, who earn less than 50.000 a year and raise children below 10yo alone or with a companion".

Demographics are important not just for profiling but because they help with media planning: media release information about who consumes their content, allowing better media selection without wasting budget. A vast demographic requires huge media investment. Some think that if a media plan covers a wide range, then a branded product will reach more people, hence have more sales. The truth is often the opposite as the campaign runs the risk of spreading itself too thin and offering a generic message that does not resonate.

The key question for creative advertising though is: "how do I 'talk' to these people? What do I have to say to them?" beyond demographics, a lot more is needed.

4.3 Psychographics and lifestyles

Consumer research has attempted to study differences among people, by observing psychographic elements and lifestyle elements. Psychographics refer to consumers' personal characteristics which may impact their buying decisions (Lawson & Todd, 2002, p. 297; Wells, 1975), mostly drawing from psychology. Lifestyle is defined as the set of personal choices individuals make (Lawson & Todd, 2002, p. 305) within a social context, mostly drawing from sociology, as will be discussed below.

There are overlaps between these two constructs which reflect different theoretic underpinnings (Lawson & Todd, 2002) but at the level of everyday work, both psychographics and lifestyles can be used (Altstiel et al., 2023, p. 147) to define and profile a target group in two ways: first, by applying forward thinking, meaning that one defines a segment and then collects and processes information examining individual needs, uses, and gratifications; second, reversely, by first examining the social forces shaping individual choices and then creating ad hoc clusters of consumers who are likely to follow similar choices (Lawson & Todd, 2002).

Consumer research has tried to define steady psychographic and lifestyle parameters which can apply in different contexts and be quantified using scales, so that each target group comes with scientifically confirmed characteristics thus helping campaign planning. Models like VALS[1] or Hofstede's cultural dimensions (Hofstede, 1983) have been used in the past but have also received a lot of criticism especially around replicability (indicatively: Beatty et al., 1988; Yankelovich & Meer, 2006; Minkov & Kaasa, 2021) in different contexts or on a longitudinal basis. Assuming there will be a way to classify consumers in a handful of everlasting clusters seems somewhat elusive. Currently the model of the generations appears to be more popular (indicatively: Chaney et al., 2017) but comes with its own weaknesses and can be of help only when combined with local and product-specific research.

Psychographic information seems to more frequently refer to the targeted individuals' emotional traits and buying motivators: **aspirations, needs, fears, hopes, desires, ideals** (Moore et al., 1995). Starting from the tangible needs and benefits of a branded product, the team might proceed to explore the feelings and emotions associated with these needs. For example, if an agency wants to promote baby formula, they may appeal to parents' need for safety, trust, and reassurance. If these psychographic characteristics are overused, especially by competitors, then the team might go further and consider issues of convenience or focus on the joys of upbringing; the memories of sleepless nights after their baby has grown up; the sacrifices involved when raising a child, and so forth.

The role of advertising is to achieve persuasion by combining reason with emotion – logos and pathos, in the Aristotelian sense. Advertising should also appeal to ethos, our sense of morality. The more emotional an ad, the stronger the need for an explicit or implicit underlying rational argument, to avoid misleading exaggeration. There is evidence that emotional appeals work more when promoting value-expressive products, those that are important to the sense of self and identity (Johar & Sirgy, 1991), and that individual differences influence the response to emotional versus rational appeals (Moore et al., 1995) however, seeking balance is important.

Advertising convinces some people, sometimes, because advertising appeals (Belch & Belch, 2003; Keller, 2013, p. 182) to their needs and wants and aligns these with a branded offering in a specific cultural context (Zhang & Gelb, 1996). In the western world, needs and wants do not usually lay at the bottom of the Maslow's pyramid. Instead, they are more about being and belonging, about self-expression, acceptance, and self-actualisation. But it's not that simple. Promoting car tyres using half-naked girls, appealing to the desire for sexual gratification might have worked a few decades ago. Today audiences are savvier and more demanding, rejecting the idea of being emotionally manipulated and / or objectified.

To understand how people feel, we need at least two things: evidence and empathy. To assume that others feel the same way we do because it's "natural" or "self-evident" or "the right thing" is the worst mistake one can make in advertising. Whoever the "other" is or however similar they may seem; we need to study their viewpoints and attitudes carefully. Research provides evidence, then empathy comes to put us in their shoes. Reading research requires critical skills. Empathy requires emotional intelligence. To become more empathetic, an advertising professional needs more than reading stats. They need to be able to see things from different perspectives. The way to become more empathetic goes through art and cultural capital from diverse sources. The arts open the door to the soul of the "other", aligning feelings and inspiring. Art helps a creative professional delve in people and be able to talk to them and with them; not at them or down on them.

Lifestyle is also important to planners and creatives alike, often proposed instead of a psychographic analysis (Lawson & Todd, 2002). Lifestyle is by no means a simple or shallow term. In his early writings, Anthony Giddens (1991) approached lifestyle as a trait of late modernity, arguing that the modern era is the most complex ever experienced: action, interaction, information as well as the possibilities of "who" or "what" to be, are tremendously augmented in relation to pre-modern societies. For the first time ever in late modernity, mobility, urbanisation, education, and institutions allowed individuals to forge their identities rather than being bound by their family ties or birthplace. According to Giddens, modernity gave the "self" unimagined possibilities. Gradually, the self becomes a reflexive project, a result of constant negotiation between alternatives, flexible and receptive to changes. Many sociologists express similar views. The self being formed in cooperation, in narration, in discourse, in interaction and in sociality is a common theme. Accepting oneself as well as being recognized and accepted by others is what identity politics is all about (Calhoun, 1998, p. 212–213 & 221; Woodward, 1999, p. 24) and brands today engage actively in identity politics, either to take a stance on social issues or to follow trends or to piggyback and go with the flow. Either way, brands affect **lifestyle which is the entirety of personal decisions on how to live and who to be;** it's how each individual composes life phases, preferences, roles, and relations in a coherent narrative.

The self becomes a reflexive project and consumption is an integral part of this process which also involves instability, complexity, and information impossible for anyone to possess, so as to make important decisions about self-identity, life planning and lifestyle. To make all these decisions, the modern subject heavily relies on expert systems and symbolic tokens.

According to Giddens, symbolic tokens (like money, for example) are means of exchange which proliferated in late modernity and are used in a variety of contexts. Symbolic tokens incorporate commonly accepted meanings standardized via repetition, providing security and predictability in our daily routines. Symbolic tokens reduce complexity, regulate our decisions, and aid self-reflection (Giddens, 1991).

From a broader perspective, brands can be seen as symbolic tokens containing appropriated meaning and exchanged in interaction. Brands regulate our decisions (indicatively: Bahn, 1986; Rudd & Kohout, 1983), make our choices feel safer, less complex or risky (Matzler et al., 2008) and contribute to our self-reflection and sense of self-identity (Elliott & Wattanasuwan, 1998). Brands transcend localities (Akaka & Alden, 2015), become part of our everyday routines (indicatively: Cowan & Spielmann, 2017), and help express our beliefs (Lan Nguyen & Roedder, 2005; Reingen et al., 1984; Ritson & Elliott, 1999; Goldman & Papson, 1994).

Baudrillard (1972, p. 86, also referring to Riesman) argued that for individuals to be a part of society, an entrance fee is required; a "standard package" of socially constructed needs, covered by a set of goods and services which compile an ideal minimum, a standard model of middle-class life. Today, the standard package contains not only products but also brands. Brands state not just what we have but also where we belong, what our values are, who we are (Goldman, 1992; Goldman & Papson, 2000; Oswald, 2011). Lifestyle is profoundly personal and social at the same time.

Advertising mediates between the personal and the social, adding meaning to our choices (Mitchell et al., 2007). Brand equity derives by large from the fact that consumers consider, discuss, and share such choices. As information regarding brand choice is too much, it is hard to imagine an adequately informed consumer who has the time and energy to process all available information regarding every choice, thus brands as symbolic tokens provide indispensable shortcuts. Subtle differences between brands can be far more telling than the possession of the product they sign.

Social Network Theory explains how each consumer is a decision-making center accepting stimuli from the other consumers in their social network, and processing these to make important decisions. Our family, social, professional, community network influences our choices (Brown & Reingen, 1987) and consequently, our identity (White, 2012). Our choices and desires are not shaped in a vacuum. The better connected we are, the better the choices we make and the richer our social capital (Burt, 2000).

Studying lifestyles, then, goes far beyond creating TV commercials with happy families or flirting couples. It is about understanding everyday acts of self-repre-sentation and self-actualization; acts by people who seem, or not, like us but are not us, and whose choices might seem irrational at first but are always the result of more thinking and feeling than one can tell at first glance. Studying lifestyles requires and fosters respect. As advertising becomes strategic; can benefit from big data; addresses literate audiences; and cannot easily rely on standardised scales, studying lifestyles becomes one of the most important skills in the agency. Good planners and creatives must be empathetic ethnographers, studying "others" daily. People-watching should become a lifelong hobby as it is the only way to con-tribute to an original and appropriate positioning and creative idea. If you haven't already, start exploring your own "otherness".

Understanding how people want is more important than understanding what people want.

4.3 The STP challenges

STP is mostly a planner's job, but creatives should have a good understanding of the process. Delving in people is something every single person in an agency should practise doing. By no means is STP a "tick the box" procedure.

STP can go deep into exploring sub-groups within a demographic like, for example, 18–24 winter sport fans as opposed to 18–24 hip hop fans, and so forth. Lifestyle patterns can also be used for as primary dividers for segmentation, like when we distinguish between pet owners and non-pet owners, to promote cat food. Especially in large markets, very small clusters of consumers (niches) might not only allow a product to succeed but also to acquire a distinctive personality. Ocean Pacific apparel, Warby Parker sunglasses, or Santa Cruz skateboards could be such examples and we should study how such brands started from a well-chosen niche.

Segmentation is a process of exclusion and inclusion. As discussed in Chapters 2 & 9, exclusion has significant social and ethical implications. A lot of people feel misrepresented, under-represented, or marginalised. Each ad is bound to include and exclude. This is what targeting is all about in the first place. On the level of strategic planning professionals should show awareness and consideration of the need to target and portray groups in ethical and professionally efficient ways, avoiding backlashes and social media storms of wrath.

Furthermore, consider the importance of semiotic literacy and fluency for an account planner: they could find insightful ways to symbolise common psychographic traits; to read into the symbolic importance of consumption trends; to visualise elements which define sub-cultures; to understand design elements that appeal to specific segments; and to convey all the above to the creative team, thus making research data more relevant, palatable, and creatively useful.

5 Tools to understand people.

5.1 *Customer journeys*

AIDA and DAGMAR (Chapter 2) showed us how consumers go through stages to buy something. Based on these, the theory of the customer funnel explores from a brand's perspective how campaigns raise awareness to many, attract the interest of fewer prospect buyers, then instigate desire to even fewer who will undertake some action – buying or checking out a branded offer and its competitors.

The advent of the world wide web gave new directions to the study of consumer research. Cookies have enabled a detailed understanding of the process consumers follow. We know when an ad instigates a set of clicks that lead a user to an e-shop, how many clicks, to which websites, for how long, what else the user bought, and if they shared this experience online. Of course, we do not buy all products following the same process. Buying bottled water or a summer walk is quite different than installing a new heating system at home – a much longer and more challenging journey.

The mapping of a consumer's steps demonstrates common patterns for products and product categories; and for specific consumer clusters (Tueanrat et al., 2021). By combining online with offline data like store visits or sales, a marketer or planner can thus customise a campaign and assess its success in detail. This is the customer's journey, and it becomes longer and more complex when the purchase is costly and requires knowledge (Kuehnl et al., 2019). More effort is needed to buy your first car, than any other car after that, though cars require more searched, compared to fast moving consumer goods (FMCGs) like snacks or supermarket products. But even your first bottle of detergent might take you through a brief journey where you think and balance aspects like price, perceived cleaning power, environmental aspects and shelf discounts.

So, here is what we know about customers in general: an initial stimulus like an ad or a friend's comment, grabs their attention and triggers their interest on a product – this is the stage of acquiring awareness, the pre-purchase process (Lemon & Verhoef, 2016) in which curiosity and interest prevail. Once a consumer creates a short list of alternatives, research begins for the final decision to be made. You may have experienced this when you bought your first smart phone: within a given price range, trying to determine if a triple camera is more important than saving space, if speed is a basic requirement, if the operating system is compatible with your other devices and so forth. This is the painful part, then.

Excitement often goes away as the best possible choice is not always affordable or available and compromises have to be made, while the outcome depends largely on the overall experience of every branded touch point (Lemon & Verhoef, 2016). Our choice is not the end of this journey (Kuehnl et al., 2019). For the company that we chose, a new adventure begins, the post-purchase phase (Lemon & Verhoef, 2016): will we stay loyal? Will we buy more products from the same company (cross-selling)? Will we write a positive review? Will we recommend this product (ambassadorship)?

Each customer journey is unique, ranging from instant gratification to months of research. Different people allocate different amounts of time and effort for the same product and reach the point of purchase having followed different paths (Rosenbaum et al., 2017). A planner should be able to map and customise this journey per target group and branded offer, focusing on the touchpoints that matter (Rosenbaum et al., 2017) while a creative should understand the needs and the emotional state prevailing on each touchpoint, when working on headlines and visuals for marketing and re-marketing purposes. Paid advertising instigates interest and desire, while rich web content supports active research.

5.2 Customer personas

Bringing your consumer to life is frequent advice to both planners and creatives, to achieve a customer-centred output (Zhou et al., 2021). Sometimes it feels reassuring to talk to a person that feels real and try to convince them to choose an offering. A persona, then, is like a descriptive identity card which contains the selected demographics of a target group, enriched by key psychographic and life-style elements (Chatzopoulou et al., 2022), usually including tech savviness and habits, which may be connected to the product but not too narrowly. Add a picture and you almost feel you can engage in dialogue.

However, personas are frequently gross generalisations of idealised consumers, like "John, 35, earns €70000 annually, lives alone in a loft and loves to exercise, has accounts in all social media", which feels more like a Tinder profile than an outcome of informed consumer research.

To be helpful, a persona must:

- generalise but not idealise; we do not target the handsome, successful, self-accomplished.
- contain the unpleasant: John's challenges, anxieties, concerns, compulsions – not just everyday routines or gratifications.
- contain or lead to a unique insight that will pave the way for unique, tailored creative ideas.
- not be too broad. Visualising demographics is hardly of any use.
- not be too narrow or too specific or expanding in areas of an imagined personality that is of limited interest.
- constitute part of a broader segmentation effort and stand next to other personas without significant overlaps (Pires et al., 2011; Jansen et al., 2021; Cruz & Karatzas, 2020).

It takes critical skills and a combination of data from many different sources to include and exclude when creating a persona, to inspire and frame creative thinking, without limiting it too much.

***

Every model or framework of thinking comes with tacit assumptions and requires a level of abstraction. So, each model can help navigate through complexity but should be supported by tailored evidence. Otherwise, models can lead to gross overgeneralisation, stereotyping, or under- and misrepresentation undermining the success of a campaign.

Hopefully, this section has convinced the reader that "others" are not like "us" and that few, if any, are the things we should take for granted. As individuals, we often stereotype others, even if tacitly, to be able to build on experience and cut through complexity. As advertising professionals though, we should be able to break through stereotypes, delve in patterns and traits of people and study them from scratch. Assumptions around sex, gender, age, parenthood, success, area of living, or occupation are always inevitable and yet always there to obscure our professional understanding. Imagine a 50-year-old copywriter who tries to come up with unique ideas to promote ice cream to a foody millennial whose body is their temple; imagine a 25-year-old copywriter trying to promote station wagons with baby seats. Imagine an art director who listens to heavy metal, trying to promote a jazz club. Learn how to change shoes.

Time to practise!

- Explore your own otherness: Join an open group or forum on a controversial topic like vaccination or flat earth. Spend half an hour daily, for at least two weeks, observing respectfully what people say and how they interact. Take a few notes in bullets every day. Write down your conclusions and discoveries. Empathise even if you do not accept their views. Work like a digital ethnographer.
- Try to imagine at least two personas targeted with the NIKE "What will they say about you?" advert.
- Invite at least three friends from different regions of the world in a group discussion on "how do you choose". Select at least three types of products like cosmetics, cars, snacks, colleges and discuss the steps each one takes before finalising their choice. Focus on similarities and differences. See if culture plays a role. Map your journeys and compare them.
- Select and observe three awarded ads or campaigns. Try to assume what the product positioning might be. Try to assume how the target group was described in the brief. There is no right or wrong answer. Reverse engineering helps the mind get in the shoes of professionals and improves forward thinking.

6 Insights

Those who have a digital background, tend to confuse insights with data. Insights are more than meaningful data. Accordingly, a lot of strategists tend to confuse insights with creative ideas.

Defining an insight is as challenging as finding it. You know when you don't have it, you know when you have it, and you don't know exactly how to describe it. As elusive as this mind sound, the advertising industry tends to use the term "insights" in a very specific way.

According to the Oxford dictionary, insight is a clear, deep, and sometimes sudden understanding of a complicated problem or situation. In advertising, the problem is always the same: how to create meaningful, unexpected ads connecting a specific branded product to a specific target group, in a unique, memorable way.

Beyond data and research, the first key that unlocks insights is observation of even the most menial human behaviours. Observing people curiously and restlessly, what triggers them, what hurts them, how they respond to everyday occurrences, what are their special moments and routines, who are their significant others, how they express their feelings and more, is essential. Observations stay with us latently until a moment comes when they can be of use, combined with research evidence or analytics. As Campbell (1992) noted: "little clues often lead to big insights". Insights may be value-driven, lifestyle-driven, behaviour-driven, or just plain rational. But once an insight has emerged, it appears simple, almost self-evident, as if it had been there all along but nobody noticed.

An insight frames creative thinking meaningfully, paving the way for a great advertising idea (Koslow, 2015, p. 6; Parker et al., 2021). Sometimes, by definition, an insight feels like an a-ha moment. When strategists experience such a moment, they set the stage for creatives to experience an a-ha moment a bit later. Insights are, or should be, creative, even if typically, they are created by planners (Parker, Ang, & Koslow, 2018).

An insight is appropriate when:

- Working as a bridge between a consumer and a product.
- Inspiring creatives to come up with unexpected yet relevant ideas.
- Competitors have not exploited a similar territory.

Perhaps one of the most interesting attempts to understand insights from an academic perspective, comes from the work of Douglas Holt who demonstrated through extensive, longitudinal content analysis: "How brands become icons" and coined the term: cultural branding. Holt developed the idea that brands can truly become significant tokens in the cultural sphere, when they bring to life a cultural contradiction people experience but have not articulated. Campaigns like the Marlboro Cowboy or Budweiser's "Whasssup" as well as brands like Coke and Corona were examined under this light showing that people felt understood and represented by brands who acknowledged, portrayed, and made explicit the cultural contradictions of their time. Cultural contradictions are or lead to insights which can be brought to life through a combination of observation and research. Not all insights qualify as cultural contradictions, but cultural contradictions are or breed insights. Here are some examples:

- The insight for #likeagirl by Always is that girls' confidence plummets as they enter their teen years and experience changes in their bodies. Empowering them is important.
- The insight for #Equality by Nike, also a major cultural contradiction facing the USA, is that equality should have no boundaries, just like in a sports court where fair play ensures people are defined by their actions and can progress and contribute to the best of their abilities.

One way to define an insight is to consider it as a bridge between a piece of consumer research evidence, and a specific observation or experience relevant to the targeted consumer.

From a research perspective, significant contributions on insights come from a team around Scott Koslow who studied how advertising account planners work on unlocking insights to then convey these to creatives and clients who may feel somewhat reluctant to aim at highly creative and unpredictable executions (Koslow, 2015, p.6). Advertising insights emerge from a combination of research, personal knowledge domains (including cultural capital), challenging conventions, borrowed sources, and a narrative approach (Parker, Ang, & Koslow, 2018). Account planners consider the key elements of good insights to be originality, relatability, usability, and vision (Parker, Ang, & Koslow, 2018). The first three of these elements are very closely associated with the criteria used to assess creative advertising as will be discussed in Chapter 4.

Planners, just as much as creatives, should be great observers and great ethnographers. To some extent, everyone involved in creative advertising, including clients, should be an ethnographer. And in the agency, "otherness" should be part of the everyday work and routine. This is one of the key reasons why diversity of personnel on all levels is of paramount importance. There is still painful evidence that advertising is not an inclusive industry documented more extensively in Chapter 4. Although diversity and inclusion are studied mostly from an ethical lens (indicatively: Gurrieri et al., 2022) their contribution in targeting and in creativity is essential. Women, older ages, different races, the disabled, all are severely underrepresented, and the "Mad Men" line up still stars in most western agencies. Diversity is not just nice to have or the ethical thing to do; it's the only way towards great ideas.

Case study: Dumb ways to die

In 2012, an Australian campaign on train safety smashed all the awards. Meanwhile, in Greece, kids were downloading an app game where they had to save tiny little creatures from dumb deaths and accidents. Most of these Greek kids will never know that this game was part of an effort to prevent railroad accidents.

In Melbourne, a bunch of funny creatures somewhat resembling Happy Tree Friends or Little Mrs & Misses, appeared on a video, each dying in a very dumb way: pocking sticks on grizzly bears, using their private parts as piranha bates, or dressing like a mousse during hunting season. For three minutes, a playful, childlike song described these morbid moments only to present the three last creatures who die from being careless or reckless around trains. "Be safe around trains. A message from Metro" said the voice over at the end. The video was accompanied by a website, by merchandise, by the app-game and more.

To the old school advertiser, this campaign might have sounded weird, as advertising on social issues, especially safety issues, would usually take a dramatic or even shocking approach: "please be careful, come home safe, we love you", and the like. This combination of morbid and mocking was unseen until it became one of the most successful ads of all time.

To find out how come this campaign reduced railroad accidents by at least 20% (Allagui & Breslow, 2016), you really must think of the target group. Try some reverse engineering: whom did this campaign appeal to? Research had showed that teens forming gangs around the rails and performing dangerous stunts, were those most frequently involved in railroad accidents. And then came public suicide attempts. Did these people know they were in danger? Obviously. Thus, an awareness campaign was not needed; an attitude change campaign was needed. To achieve this change, the agency de-dramatised stunts and public demonstrations of bravery or despair, dismissing these as dumb – as dumb as keeping a rattlesnake as a pet. Teens responded by turning this ad to a huge viral success.

Excellent targeting and profiling made the difference here, as well as a great strategic decision on tone of voice and the focus on multiplatform content. What this campaign also taught us is that dramatic advertising is not the only way to change attitudes and that fun can more easily go viral. Dumb dying proved to be one of the most successful insights.

- Read more about the campaign, here: https://dumbwaystodiecases tudy.wordpress.com/ and here: https://www.theguardian.com/media/ 2013/jun/22/cannes-lions-advertising-awards
- Watch the ad here: https://www.youtube.com/watch?v=IJNR2EpS0jw
- Visit the website and download the games here: https://www.dumbwa ystodie.com/
- See also: Allagui & Breslow, 2016.

7 The role of big data in creative advertising

Big data contributes to the understanding and clustering of web users and consumers, helping study behaviours, attitudes, and values expressed online (Erevelles et al., 2016; Hofacker et al., 2016). Big data can help advertisers target and profile more efficiently, assisting planning, measurements, real-time optimisation, and Return on Investment (ROI).

Although it is frequently argued that big data can also boost creativity, there is no blueprint to follow (Goor et al., 2022; Chen et al., 2019; Barnet, 2013). If a curious creative or an inspired planner are asked to swim in a sea of data, they are quite likely to fish great insights – combined with personal observation. However, data does not speak creatively by itself. To spark creativity, big data helps when it's raw, used for random queries rather than filtered searches. The interesting thing about insights is that you never know what you are looking for, until you find it. Data should be presented in a way that allows creatives to explore, wander around, play, combine, and experiment.

Time to practise!

Following the examples in this chapter, try to write down one sentence explaining the insight for:

- The Nike – Colin Kaepernick campaign
- The Mayo – Hellmans Superbowl ad
- The Passat – Darth Vader Superbowl ad.

Note

1   https://www.strategicbusinessinsights.com/vals/about.shtml

References

Akaka, M.A. & Alden, D.L. (2015) Global brand positioning and perceptions, *International Journal of Advertising*, 29 (1), 37–56, DOI: doi:10.2501/S0265048709201026.

Allagui, I., & Breslow, H. (2016). Social media for public relations: Lessons from four effective cases. *Public Relations Review*, 42 (1), 20–30. https://doi.org/10.1016/j.pubrev.2015.12.001.

Altstiel, T., Grow, J., Augustine, D., & Jennings, M. (2023). *Advertising creative: strategy, copy, & design* (Sixth). SAGE Publishing.

Arnould, E.J., & Thompson, C.J. (2005). Consumer Culture Theory (CCT): twenty years of research. *Journal of Consumer Research*, 31 (4), 868–882. https://doi-org.acg.idm.oclc.org/10.1086/426626.

Bahn, K.D. (1986). How and when do brand perceptions and preferences first form? A cognitive developmental investigation. *Journal of Consumer Research*, 13 (3), 382–393. https://doi.org/10.1086/209077.

Banet-Weiser, S. (2012). *Authentic tm: the politics and ambivalence in a brand culture* (Ser. Critical cultural communication). New York University Press.

Barnet, M. (2013, April 10) Data vs Creativity, *Marketing Week*. Available at: https://www.marketingweek.com/data-vs-creativity/.

Barthes, R. (1977) *Image, Music, Text. London*: Fontana Press

Baudrillard, J. (1968). *Le système des objets*. Paris: Gallimard.

Baudrillard, J. (1970). *La société de consommation*. Paris: Gallimard.

Baudrillard, J. (1972). *Pour une critique de l'économie politique du signe*. Paris: Gallimard.

Beasley, R., & Danesi, M. (2010). *Persuasive signs: the semiotics of advertising* (Ser. Approaches to applied semiotics, 4). Mouton de Gruyter. https://doi.org/10.1515/9783110888003.

Beatty, S.E., Homer, P.M., & Kahle, L.R. (1988). Problems with VALS international marketing research: an example from an application of the empirical mirror technique. *Advances in Consumer Research*, 15 (1), p. 375.

Bejou, D., Keiningham, T., & Aksoy, L. (Eds.). (2006). *Customer Lifetime Value: Reshaping the Way We Manage to Maximize Profits* (1st ed.). Routledge. https://doi.org/10.4324/9780203826126.

Belch, G.E. & Belch, M.A. (2003). *Advertising and promotion: An integrated marketing communications perspective*. McGraw Hill.

Berger, A.A. (2006). *50 Ways to understand communication: a guided tour of key ideas and theorists in communication, media, and culture*. Rowman & Littlefield.

Berger, A.A. (2010). *The objects of affection: semiotics and consumer culture* (1st ed., Ser. Semiotics and popular culture). Palgrave Macmillan.

Berger, A.A. (2019). *Brands and cultural analysis* (1st ed. 2019). Springer International Publishing. Retrieved July 9, 2023, from https://doi.org/10.1007/978-3-030-24709-6.

Bilton, C. (2017). *The Disappearing Product: Marketing and Markets in the Creative Industries*. Cheltenham: Edward Elgar.

Bourdieu, P. 1984 [1979]. *Distinction: A Social Critique of the Judgement of Taste*. Trans. Richard Nice. Cambridge, MA: Harvard University Press.

Brown, J.J. & Reingen, P.H. (1987). Social ties and word-of-mouth referral behaviour. *Journal of Consumer Research*, 14 (3), 350–362.

Burt, R.S. (2000). The network structure of social capital. *Research in Organizational Behavior*, 22, 345–423. doi:10.1016/S0191–3085(00)22009–22001.

Calhoun, C. (1998). *Critical Social Theory: Culture, History and The Challenge of Difference*. Oxford: Blackwell.

Campbell, C. (2018). *The romantic ethic and the spirit of modern consumerism: new extended edition* (2nd ed. 2018, Ser. Cultural sociology). Palgrave Macmillan. https://doi.org/10.1007/978-3-319-79066-4.

Campbell, L.F. (1992). *Consumer Insight Workbook: How Consumer Insights Can Inspire Better Marketing and Advertising*. Copy Workshop

Chandler, D. (2002). *Semiotics: The basics*. London: Routledge.

Chaney, D., Touzani, M. & Slimane, K.B. (2017) Marketing to the (new) generations: summary and perspectives, *Journal of Strategic Marketing*, 25 (3), 179–189, DOI: doi:10.1080/0965254X.2017.1291173.

Chatzopoulou, E., Poulaki, I., & Papatheodorou, A. (2022). Effective airline market segmentation: The case of Singapore airlines group. In: Aktaş Gürhan, & Kozak, M. (Eds.) *International case studies in tourism marketing* (Ser. Routledge international case studies in tourism). Routledge. https://doi.org/10.4324/9781003182856.

Chen, G., Xie, P., Dong, J., & Wang, T. (2019). Understanding programmatic creative: the role of AI, *Journal of Advertising*, 48 (4), 347–355. https://doi.org/10.1080/00913367.2019.1654421.

Cowan, K., & Spielmann, N. (2017). The influence of rituals on luxury product consumption: implications for brands. *Journal of Brand Management*, 24(5), 391–404. https://doi.org/10.1057/s41262-017-0045-5.

Cruz, A. & Karatzas, S. (2020). Understanding your Buyer Persona. In: Heinze, A., Fletcher, G., Rashid, T., & Cruz, A. (Eds.). *Digital and social media marketing: a results-driven approach* (Second). Routledge, Taylor & Francis Group.

Danesi, M. (2017). Visual rhetoric and semiotic. *Oxford Research Encyclopedia of Communication*. Retrieved 1 Feb. 2022, from https://oxfordre.com/communication/view/10.1093/acrefore/9780190228613.001.0001/acrefore-9780190228613-e-43.

Davis, B., & Ozanne, J.L. (2019). Measuring the impact of transformative consumer research: The relational engagement approach as a promising avenue, *Journal of Business Research* 100, 311–338. doi:10.1016/j.jbusres. 2018.12.047

de Certeau, M. (2011). *The practice of everyday life*. Translated by Steven F. Rendall, (3rd). California: University of California Press.

DeBode, J.D., Haggard, D.L., & Haggard, K.S. (2020). Economic freedom and Hofstede's cultural dimensions, *International Journal of Organization Theory & Behavior*, 23 (1), 65–84. https://doi.org/10.1108/IJOTB-11-2018-0124.

Douglas, M. & Isherwood, B. (1979). *The world of goods: towards an anthropology of consumption*. London: Routledge.

Elliott, R., & Wattanasuwan, K. (1998). Brands as symbolic resources for the construction of identity, *International Journal of Advertising*, 17 (2), 131–144.

Erevelles, S., Fukawa, N., & Swayne, L. (2016). Big Data consumer analytics and the transformation of marketing, *Journal of Business Research*, 69 (2), 897–904.

Gardner, B.B. & Levy, S.J. (1955). The product and the brand. *Harvard Business Review*, March-April, 33–39.

Giddens, A. (1991). *modernity and self-identity: Self and society in the late modern age*. Cambridge: Polity Press.

Goffman, E. (1959). *The presentation of self in everyday life*. New York: Anchor Books.

Goldman R. (1987) Marketing Fragrances: Advertising and the Production of Commodity Signs. *Theory, Culture & Society*, 4 (4), 691–725. doi:10.1177/026327687004004007.

Goldman, R. (1992) *Reading ads socially*. London: Routledge.

Goldman, R., & Papson, S. (1996). *Sign wars: The cluttered landscape of advertising*. New York: Guilford Press.

Goldman, R., & Papson, S. (1994). Advertising in the Age of Hypersignification, *Theory, Culture and Society* 11 (3), 23–53.

Goor, P., Kerr, G., & Jin, H. S. (2022). How has the digital environment affected advertising creativity? digital's impact on the creative process, person, and product: A Delphi study, *Journal of Advertising Research*, 62 (2), 118.

Gurrieri, L., Tuncay Zayer, L., & Coleman, C.A. (2022). Transformative advertising research: reimagining the future of advertising, *Journal of Advertising*, 51 (5), 539–556. https://doi.org/10.1080/00913367.2022.2098545.

Herskovitz, S., & Crystal, M. (2010). The essential brand persona: storytelling and branding. *Journal of Business Strategy*, 31 (3), 21–28.

Hofacker, C.F., Malthouse, E.C. & Sultan, F. (2016), Big Data and consumer behavior: imminent opportunities, *Journal of Consumer Marketing*, 33 (2), 89–97. https://doi.org/10.1108/JCM-04-2015-1399.

Hofstede, G. (1983). National cultures revisited. *Behavior Science Research*, 18 (4), 285–305. https://doi.org/10.1177/106939718301800403.

Holbrook, M.B., & Hirschman, E.C. (1993). *The semiotics of consumption: Interpreting symbolic consumer behavior in popular culture and works of art* (Ser. Approaches to semiotics, 110). Mouton de Gruyter.

Holt, D.B. (2004) *How brands become icons: The principles of cultural branding*. Boston, MA: Harvard Business School Press.

Jansen, B.J., Jung, S.-gyo, Ramirez Robillos, D., & Salminen, J. (2021). Too few, too many, just right: Creating the necessary number of segments for large online customer populations, *Electronic Commerce Research and Applications*, 49. https://doi.org/10.1016/j.elerap.2021.101083.

Jhally, S. (1987). *The codes of advertising: Fetishism and the political economy of meaning in the consumer society*. St. Martin's Press.

Johar, J.S. & Sirgy, M.J. (1991) Value-expressive versus utilitarian advertising appeals: when and why to use which appeal, *Journal of Advertising*, 20 (3), 23–33, doi:10.1080/00913367.1991.10673345.

Keller, K.L. (2013). *Strategic brand management: Building, measuring, and managing brand equity* (Global Edition). Pearson.

Kotler, P. (1999). *Kotler on marketing: How to create, win, and dominate markets*. Free Press.

Kuehnl, C., Jozic, D., & Homburg, C. (2019). Effective customer journey design: consumers' conception, measurement, and consequences, *Journal of the Academy of Marketing Science*, 47 (3), 551–568. https://doi.org/10.1007/s11747-018-00625-7.

Koslow, S. (2015). I love creative advertising: What it is, when to call for it, and how to achieve it, *Journal of Advertising Research*, 55 (1). https://doi.org/10.2501/JAR-55-1-005-008.

Lan Nguyen, C. & Roedder, J.D. (2005). The development of self-brand connections in children and adolescents, *Journal of Consumer Research*, 32, 119–129.

Lawson, R., & Todd, S. (2002). Consumer lifestyles: A social stratification perspective. *Marketing Theory*, 2 (3), 295–307. https://doi.org/10.1177/1470593102002003278.

Lemon, K.N., & Verhoef, P.C. (2016). Understanding customer experience throughout the customer journey. *Journal of Marketing*, 80 (6), 69–96. https://doi.org/10.1509/jm.15.0420.

Luhmann, N. (1995). *Social systems* (Ser. Writing science). Stanford University Press.

Maffesoli, M. (1996). *The time of the tribes: The decline of individualism in mass society* (Ser. Theory, culture & society). Sage.

Mannheim, K. (1952). *Essays on the sociology of knowledge* (1st ed.). Routledge. https://doi.org/10.4324/9781315005058.

Matzler, K., Grabner-Kräuter, S., & Bidmon, S. (2008). Risk aversion and brand loyalty: The mediating role of brand trust and brand affect. *Journal of Product & Brand Management*, 17(3), 154–162. https://doi.org/10.1108/10610420810875070.

McCracken, G. (1986). Culture and consumption: A theoretical account of the structure and movement of the cultural meaning of consumer goods. *Journal of Consumer Research*, 13 (1), 71–84.

Mick, D.G. (2006). Meaning and mattering through transformative consumer research, *NA—Advances in Consumer Research*, 33, 1–4.

Mick, D.G. (2005). Consumer research and semiotics: Exploring the morphology of signs, symbols and significance. *Sage Library in Business and Management*, Vol. 1 (2005), P. 207.

Mitchell, V.W., Macklin, J. & Paxman, J. (2007). Social uses of advertising: An example of young male adults. *International Journal of Advertising*, 26, 199–222. doi:10.1080/10803548.2007.11073007..

Minkov, M., & Kaasa, A. (2021). A test of Hofstede's model of culture following his own approach, *Cross Cultural & Strategic Management*, 28 (2), 384–406. https://doi.org/10.1108/CCSM-05-2020-0120.

Moore, D.J., Harris, W.D., & Chen, H.C. (1995). Affect intensity: An individual difference response to advertising appeals, *Journal of Consumer Research*, 22 (2), 154–164.

Muñiz, A.M., Jr & O'Guinn, T.C. (2001), Brand community, *Journal of Consumer Research*, 27 (4), 412–432.

Nöth, W. (1995). *Handbook of semiotics* (1st paperback, Ser. Advances in semiotics). Indiana University Press.

Oswald, L.R. (2011). *Marketing semiotics: signs, strategies, and brand value*. OUP Oxford.

Parker, J., Koslow, S., Ang, L., & Tevi, A. (2021). How does consumer insight support the leap to a creative idea?: Inside the creative process: Shifting the advertising appeal from functional to emotional, *Journal of Advertising Research*, 61 (1), 30–43.

Parker, J., Ang, L., & Koslow, S. (2018). The creative search for an insight in account planning: An absorptive capacity approach, *Journal of Advertising*, 47 (3), 237–254. https://doi-org.acg.idm.oclc.org/10.1080/00913367.2018.1474146.

Pires, G.D., Stanton, J., & Stanton, P. (2011). Revisiting the substantiality criterion: From ethnic marketing to market segmentation, *Journal of Business Research*, 64 (9), 988–996. https://doi.org/10.1016/j.jbusres.2010.11.022.

Reingen, P.H., Foster, B.L., Johnson Brown, J., & Seidman, S.B. (1984) Brand congruence in interpersonal relations: A social network analysis. *Journal of Consumer Research*, 11, 771.

Ritson, M. & Elliott, R. (1999). The social uses of advertising: An ethnographic study of adolescent advertising audiences, *Journal of Consumer Research*, 26 (3), 260–277, https://doi.org/10.1086/209562.

Roschwalb, S.A. (1992). *The consumer insight workbook. how consumer insights can inspire better marketing and advertising* (Book). Journalism Educator, 47(2), 93.

Rosenbaum, M.S., Otalora, M.L., & Ramírez, G.C. (2017). How to create a realistic customer journey map, *Business Horizons*, 60 (1), 143–150. https://doi.org/10.1016/j.bushor.2016.09.010.

Rudd J. & Kohout F.J. (1983). Individual and group consumer information acquisition in brand choice situations, *Journal of Consumer Research*, 10, 303.

Stampfl, R.W. (1978), The consumer life cycle, *Journal of Consumer Affairs*, 12, 209–219. https://doi.org/10.1111/j.1745-6606.1978.tb00884.x.

Strauss, W. & Howe, N. (1991) *Generations: The history of America's future, 1584 To 2069*. William Morrow & Co.

Strong, C. (2015). *Humanizing big data: Marketing at the meeting of data, social science and consumer insight*. London: Kogan Page.

Tueanrat, Y., Papagiannidis, S., & Alamanos, E. (2021). Going on a journey: a review of the customer journey literature, *Journal of Business Research*, 125, 336–353. https://doi.org/10.1016/j.jbusres.2020.12.028.

Veloutsou, C., & Moutinho, L. (2009). Brand relationships through brand reputation and brand tribalism. *Journal of Business Research*, 62(3), 314–322. https://doi.org/10.1016/j.jbusres.2008.05.010.

Wells, W.D. (1975). Psychographics: A critical review. *Journal of Marketing Research*, 12 (2), 196–213. https://doi.org/10.1177/002224377501200210.

White, H.C. (2012). *Identity and control: how social formations emerge (second edition)*. Princeton University Press.

Williamson, J. (1978) *Decoding advertisements: Ideology and meaning in advertising*. Boyars.

Woodward, K. (1999). Introduction, In: Woodward, Kathryn (ed.) *Identity and Difference*. London: Sage in association with the Open University.

Yankelovich, D., & Meer, D. (2006). Rediscovering market segmentation. *Harvard Business Review*, 84 (2), 122.

Zhang, Y., & Gelb, B.D. (1996). Matching advertising appeals to culture: The influence of products' use conditions, *Journal of Advertising*, 25 (3), 29–46.

Zhou, J., Wei, J., & Xu, B. (2021). Customer segmentation by web content mining, *Journal of Retailing and Consumer Services*, 61. https://doi.org/10.1016/j.jretconser.2021.102588.

4 Ideation in practice and in theory

1 Introduction

The creative idea is the cornerstone of advertising success. Ideas are generated and gradually developed to full scale campaigns. Advertising agencies develop know-how and best practices which help breed great ideas and should be perceived as the creative soil in which talent will flourish. Individuals, on the other hand, should foster and manage their personal skills in alignment with organisational requirements, to be able to deliver good work. Creativity matters in advertising because it increases memorability, awareness, resonance, and salience thus increasing likelihood to purchase and decreasing airing costs (indicatively: Reinartz & Saffert, 2013). Even if clients and agencies do not always share the same views on what creativity is, whether and when it is needed, (Sasser et al., 2013), creativity remains the cornerstone of advertising (Precourt, 2013).

This chapter approaches creativity both as an area of knowledge and as a skill. Knowledge is power and a creative professional who understands principles of creativity can manage herself or himself and find ways to improve creative output, acknowledging and handling challenges. A mature understanding of both individual and environmental factors affecting creativity can help a creative professional develop their potential. Balancing between theory and practice, we will examine creative work in advertising starting by defining creativity and proceeding with discussing advertising ideas and the processes that help generate such ideas.

2 Creativity: A context-specific definition

Creativity studies are mostly associated with psychology and the areas of cognitive, developmental, social, or differential (Simonton, 2006). Children and education attract a lot of attention, particularly fostering creativity in the classroom both as means to learn and to express oneself. The creative industries have also attracted a lot of interest and have yielded significant knowledge on the barriers facing creative professionals and all involved stakeholders (Powell, 2008). Organisations are also a fruitful area of creativity research. From employee well-being to innovation and product development; from team building to problem solving, creativity finds its way in organisation studies facing opportunities and barriers (Andriopoulos, 2001).

DOI: 10.4324/9781003330721-4

In advertising, the first contributions to the understanding of creativity initially came from agency founders like Ogilvy, Burnett, and Osborn. Significant contributions emerged from the collaboration of Osborn with Parnes (Parnes, 1985). Today, creativity is widely discussed from many perspectives: as an individual skill, as organisational culture, and as advertising product (Smith & Yang, 2004). The industry also focuses on the need to attract young talent (Gray, 2022).

As creativity is a vast and multifaceted topic, we need to frame it properly for the purposes of this book. To proceed, we adopt the following definition:

> Creativity is the production of a novel and appropriate response, product, or solution to an open-ended task. Ultimately, a response or product is creative to the extent that it is seen as creative by people familiar with the domain in which it was produced.
>
> (Amabile, 2013).

This definition focuses on the outcome rather than the process; on the product rather than on individual experience and gratification, thus Amabile's approach would hardly apply in the case of a toddler who draws, for example. But such an approach is needed to discuss creativity in organisational environments, as means rather than ends, where every individual attempt is never solely individual and undergoes organisational processes to fruition.

Furthermore, this definition focuses on open-ended tasks and ill-defined problems whose solutions always have advantages and disadvantages and therefore entail risk of success or failure, especially in advertising (El-Murad & West, 2003). Some great solutions might be less feasible due to restrictions; others might be predictable and, thus, less compelling; others might appear promising but fail along the way or even backfire. Marketing and advertising are full of such examples. Creative directors often narrate stories of great ideas that never saw the light of day due to the lack of appropriate budget; ads which appeared very promising but were treated very negatively by consumers. Whatever the case, it is important to understand ill-defined problems sometimes lead to ill solutions, for reasons that are easier to understand retrospectively rather than proactively. This also applies in the case of success.

Going back to the definition, another significant aspect is subjectivity. Ultimately, who decides what is creative and what is not? This is a question most young creatives have asked at some point, seeing their ideas being rejected or modified. Expertise and experience provide the answer. Decision making is assigned to those who have proven track record of previous success. There is no clear path to become a decision maker in most creative industries. Also, when the focus is on the outcome, the process can sometimes become painful, especially when one's ideas are rejected or twisted.

Amabile's definition further explains that creativity is always context specific. One might have the skills to be creative, but one must learn to be creative within a certain domain or industry. A depth of understanding of that domain (Boden, 2003, p. 22) is required before one can contribute with solutions that are not just creative but also original, meaningful, relevant, and feasible.

The following sections will focus on advertising creativity as both product and process. Each aspect is discussed separately. Then, techniques are presented to help creative professionals conceive and express interesting advertising ideas. At the end of this chapter, we revisit broader aspects of creativity as a skill and a challenge, examining what is needed for a professional to foster and maintain their creativity in the agency environment.

3 Creative advertising: the product

There is no universally accepted definition of what constitutes creativity in advertising and the reason why must have become clear so far. Originality and appropriateness combined (Koslow, 2015) lead to what marketers and advertisers accept as creative but, yet again, these terms are somewhat elusive and can only be assessed per case. Elements of originality include memorability, aesthetics, the element of surprise, and the evoking of strong emotions. Elements of appropriateness include brand-specificity, target-group resonance, and the potential to keep creating more executions out of one main idea.

Frequently though, when a rough advertising idea is first conceived, it has none of the above elements, just a promise and some potential that an experienced creative can discern. A big idea is like a peach kernel. At first glance it feels stiff and dry, but a great tree can blossom out of it, with the contribution of the entire agency. Thus, having a great idea; recognising a great idea; and executing a great idea are completely different things.

As stated, a creative idea is a bridge between the consumer and the branded offering; a bridge strong enough to handle pressure from competitors and from content overload; powerful enough to hold the weight of all the different executions; attractive, so people want to cross it; a bridge that blends with the landscape, its context, while standing out – so it becomes a landmark. This is the checklist, then. When a new idea emerges, while it is still rough and unmoulded, the questions to ask are:

- Does it only connect the specific product with the specific target group?
- Can it pave the way for multiple executions in multiple media?
- Will it be unexpected, attractive, yet clear to those it targets?
- Could it become a landmark?

Every bridge has two ends. The brand and the consumer. On the one hand stands the branded offer with an objective, a positioning, competitors, and current communication needs; with its own personality or style guide; with attributes and benefits. On the other end are consumers with their individual everyday needs, concerns, and desires; with their cultural references; with insights waiting to be discovered. A bridge needs solid grounds to hold its foundations. One end of the bridge is cemented in the business world, the other is cemented in culture (Bilton, 2016).

For big ideas to emerge, more than creative thinking is required:

• A strong client-agency relationship that includes trust and generous sharing of information, even when such information is considered less important
• A strong strategy that goes beyond the trivial and the mundane
• A creative team that comprises diverse professionals in terms of background, social context, and lifestyle, which works openly, resiliently, demonstrating tolerance
• A set of steps to follow toward a great outcome.

Time to practise!

Reverse engineering:

• Choose several campaigns you are fond of and reverse-engineer them. Observe carefully as many executions as possible. Try to find the main idea underlying and holding together these executions. Put down on paper, in fewer than 100 words, including the end-line, if there is one.
• Try to pinpoint what exactly it is you like the most about these ideas – or not. Can you discern between production values, use of celebrity, resonating messages or twists in storytelling? Do you appreciate this idea when you see it plain on a piece of paper?
• Then, think how the creatives could have come up with this idea? What is the key insight? What could be written in the brief that helped them towards this direction?

This is a process that will appear extremely difficult at first but can grow to become habitual. Walking along paths defined by someone else, might help you imitate and assimilate their thinking styles, thus broadening your creative explorations.

4 From an idea to a campaign: elements of synergy & integration

Early in the process of first ideas, a key question emerges: "Is this idea campaignable?" a frequently used piece of jargon indicating that this idea can support multiple executions in multiple media for multiple purposes and, perhaps, for more than one advertising burst. "Campaignable" ideas have a cumulative effect and create important marketing synergies. The more a consumer is exposed to an idea, the more media and touchpoints they experience the message in, the more are they likely to remember the campaign message. Thus, the effect of advertising lasts longer. Integrated communication campaigns need big ideas that allow for multiple executions. From a creative perspective, we know when we have such an idea if we can trace the 4Cs of integrated campaigns. These are:

- Coherence: are all executions tied together? If one were exposed to more than one execution, would they know these are parts of the same campaign? Do they all convey compatible messages, with the same style and tone of voice? The "Dove Real Beauty" campaign is such an example.
- Continuity: can our idea lead to many different executions consecutively? Can we keep using it to develop more stories and follow up campaigns? The "Nike. Just Do It" campaign is such an example.
- Complementarity: do the different executions complement one another so that they offer a complete experience? The "Dumb ways to die" campaign is such an example.
- Consistency: are there common elements, visual, verbal, or design elements, which help the audience recognise each execution as part of a main, larger campaign? These elements must be seen or read or heard; must be observed on an ad and not relate to inferred assessments on strategy like, for example that the same objective is pursued (Pickton & Broderick, 2005, p. 28–30 & 533; Pickton & Hartley, 1998).

From a creative professional's perspective, then, consistency can be achieved through the use of common elements in language, design, and imagery. These elements are often broadly outlined in the brand guidelines that should inform every advertisement as much as every full-scale campaign. Brand guidelines mostly revolve around design elements and, less so, around textual elements but overall, they help define a look & feel and a tone of voice that creatives must adhere to, to ensure compatibility of each proposed idea and campaign to the overall brand personality and image. Beyond brand guidelines though, campaign specific guidelines – explicit or implicit – help an idea grow properly, last longer and reach its maximum potential.

Case study: It's a Tide ad

Imagine you gather with friends to watch your favourite sports final game. You know ads will get in the way. Perhaps you imagine beer or cars or snacks, but, seriously, detergent? Couldn't they find a better time?

Tide rode the USA Superbowl finals' night in 2018, won an Effie Award among other distinctions, gathered millions of likes on YouTube and hijacked the most celebrated night of advertising on the mass media worldwide.

According to the agency input, the creative team first started working on ideas around stains but then came up with the idea to reverse this (remember reversal when you read section 8.4 in this chapter) and focus on cleanliness.

Other than a very interesting idea demonstrating how cleanliness is ubiquitous – and not only in advertising; other than a great execution featuring David Harbour from "Stranger Things"; other than the spoofs that came later where Tide blended with Old Spice and more, this idea is a master class in look & feel, style, and tone of voice.

The ad features separate instances all of which are associated with specific product advertising. People laughing on the beach equals soda. A man driving toward a glorious sunset landscape equals car advertising. A bunch of friends laughing in a bar equals beer advertising. Two men giving a handshake in the middle of a nowhere street equals insurance advertising and the yellow ribbon with a fake 0800 number helped a lot... Each scene was meticulously crafted to play with our advertising literacy and familiarity, with our implicit understanding of advertising functions.

As creatives, however, what we can learn from this ad is not only how to reverse our predictable ideas but also how to create ideas that break the rules while following the rules. On the one hand, we must conform to length, production values, and brand look & feel. On the other hand, we have to be original, unpredictable, and fresh. How can one comply with established, recognizable norms, stereotypes and codes while also defying established patterns, stereotypes, and codes? What kind of thinking exactly leads to ideas that are mainstream advertising without being trapped in the confinements of mainstream advertising?

The more we know the rules, the more we explicitly state the rules, the more do we become able to break these rules, to innovate, to create something that is both original and appropriate for the brand and for its target group. Try to reverse the idea of the Tide Ad all the way back to the client's brief. Try to create a follow up campaign for next year's Superbowl, without becoming repetitive and ruining the surprise element. It takes a lot of untidy thinking to create such an outcome.

Find out more here:

- https://www.effie.org/legacycases/case/US_2019_E-4397-528
- https://www.dandad.org/en/d-ad-tide-ad-campaign-case-study-insights/
- https://www.thedrum.com/creative-works/project/saatchi-saatchi-tide-its-tide-ad
- https://www.madmarketingpro.com/blog/tide-ad-super-bowl-2018-commercial-ad-analysis
- https://www.adweek.com/brand-marketing/every-ad-is-a-tide-ad-inside-saatchi-and-pgs-clever-super-bowl-takeover-starring-david-harbour/
- https://adage.com/videos/tide-its-a-tide-ad/1435
- https://adage.com/creativity/work/super-bowl-2018-tide-its-tide-ad/53806
- https://www.wsj.com/articles/the-making-of-the-tide-ad-that-scored-in-the-super-bowl-1529285099

*** *

Time to practise!

Reverse engineering

- Select a recent national scale campaign that spans across media. Locate as many executions as possible and note the observable visual, verbal, and design elements of consistency between executions.
- Find one product launch campaign and monitor it while it is running, including its accounts on social media. Trace the visual, verbal, and design elements of consistency.
- Find an Entry Kit for a creativity competition and download it. Select a campaign and fill in the required text so that your submission has a chance to win. Present the strongest aspects and the unique qualities of this campaign.

5 Creative advertising: The agency process

This section describes the process that usually leads to creative campaigns within an advertising agency. Beyond individual thinking patterns and processes, the way the agency organises creative work has a significant impact on both people and their creative product.

Each agency might boast a unique way to deliver creative work, however most agencies follow similar paths based on best practice and on human pollination as people move from one agency to another carrying around tacit knowledge and ways to work. There is room for more research in this area. Turnbull & Wheeler (2017) address this gap presenting a series of stages leading to a creative campaign while Stuhlfaut & Windels (2019) delve in the changes new media have brought in the processes around creative advertising.

There are two basic tendencies. The first, which is more traditional and applies to smaller markets or smaller scale projects, is to follow a linear approach starting from the client request, which is transferred to planners, who will write the creative brief and pass it to the creative department. Once the creatives have completed their work, a deck will be combined and presented back to the client who might approve or reject or request modifications.

The second tendency is more recent but not necessarily prevalent. Each of the participants in the process described above, participates in various steps to ensure alignment and collaboration. Planners discuss with clients and creatives before passing the creative brief; creatives discuss with planners before seeking approval from the creative director; the agency copy-tests ideas with client representatives or consumer representatives (via focus groups or other small-scale research) before sharing with the client's senior management (Turnbull & Wheeler, 2017; Stuhlfaut & Windels, 2019). The second approach is less linear, more complicated and, of course, more time consuming but alignment is achieved between all parties, surprises are avoided, and the final approval does not involve too much risk.

The former, linear process feels like baton passing (Ostwal, 2020). A devil's advocate could argue that agencies try to be creative albeit following an assembly line not much different than putting together a car, with each one of the workers involved tightening one screw. Especially during the framing of a project and the outlining of what is needed (Altstiel et al., 2023; Henry, 2011; Simmons, 2006), ensuring that all parties are aligned is of importance. Involving different parties also fosters a shared understanding and avoids intra-agency compartemtalisation.

Whether linear or meander-like, the creative process involves certain types of creative thinking and creative output which are examined in this chapter. After receiving the brief, creatives do not simply work until the day of the presentation. Instead, they share their work in stages (Stuhlfaut & Windels, 2019; Turnbull & Wheeler, 2017; Bilton, 2009; Henry, 2011; Mackert, 2012; Altstiel et al., 2023) and through yardsticks for alignment and approval, whether this involves the creative director or the planners or anyone else.

In all the models research has traced, there is a first yardstick after the brief which involves creating and sharing "first" or rough ideas. The team works for some days and tries to come up with many alternatives which are, however, underdeveloped, abstract, and incomplete. They might include a story or a sketch or an end line or a reference visual along with a rationale. These ideas are presented to the creative director or the planners. Upon discussion, some ideas are given the "go ahead" while others are thrown in the bin, which is always full as more ideas are rejected than accepted. Articulating, sharing, understanding, and assessing draft ideas for something that does not exist is extremely difficult but necessary so that creatives do not waste time on an idea that might have a flaw or be less compatible with the brief. Furthermore, the process of discussing first ideas creates precious alignment between strategists and creatives, making people feel they are on the same page.

After this process is over, creatives will work toward the second yardstick, by developing the ideas that have been agreed or approved. When all ideas have been fully developed, the whole team will meet again, delving in each proposal and discussing areas of strength or elements that need improvement. Fine tunings might be needed in some cases, or a fully developed campaign might be rejected even at this stage because it is too mundane or incompatible with the strategy or out of budget.

This leads to the next yardstick which involves a review of all the finalised proposals and a preparation to receive the final sign-off from the client or the client's senior management.

These yardsticks, "first", "second", and "finalised" ideas help understand how creative work takes place, but also how employees, managers, and entire teams can manage and adjust their skills and styles, participating in this process in fruitful ways (Bilton, 2007; 2010).

Theoretic viewpoints: Exploratory, combinational, and transformational creativity

Studying creativity, Boden discerned three different types: exploratory, combinational, and transformational creativity. The three types of creativity differ in the psychological processes involved in generating the novel ideas but also in understanding or appreciating these once they have arisen (Boden, 2010, p. 42). So, novelty, according to Boden, may be understood both psychologically and historically, from the individual's perspectives and within the organisation's constraints. Boden's contribution can enrich the understanding of creative processes in advertising thus leading to better organisational practice and, importantly, more self-awareness on behalf of creative individuals. A rough alignment with advertising is attempted here, though further tailored research is required.

Exploratory creativity is closely related to ideation, the chase for new concepts or ideas which will then be developed and deployed in different media. Exploratory creativity is adventurous (Boden, 2010, p. 4), yet the most highly constrained (Boden, 2010, p. 7). Exploratory creativity generates novel structures from the existing rules and conventions, and it is valuable because it can enable someone to see possibilities they had not glimpsed before (Boden, 2010, p. 33). In exploratory creativity, one works within a culturally accepted style, or conceptual space (Boden, 2010, p. 73), and processes its rules or constraints to generate new alternatives. (Boden, 2010, p. 99). This is exactly what ideation in creative advertising is all about. Culture constitutes the established space. Brand guidelines, style, and tone of voice, as well as client requirements and media specifications constitute the established structures and constraints that creatives should be aware of, early in the creative process.

Combinational creativity is the generation of unfamiliar combinations of familiar ideas (Boden, 2010, p. 2, also citing Sternberg, 1988; Boden, 2003, p. 51). This is one of the most popular and frequently discussed approaches to creativity even among experts. Combinations can lead to creativity in every domain of human activity often involving complex cognitive processes and domain specific know-how (Costello & Keane, 2000). Conceptual combinations also help creative problem solving (Kohn et al., 2011). Print advertising relies on compelling combinations. A sliced tomato and a ketchup bottle are combined in the famous "No one grows ketchup like Heinz" print ad by McCann Erickson. All forms of multimodal advertising (print, outdoor, social media posts, memes or gifs) combine words and / or images; and all types of stories combine events or patterns to deliver memorable and unanticipated outcomes, as will be discussed in Chapters 5 & 6. Beyond hard skills and domain knowledge, combinational creativity requires acute observation skills, a very rich store of knowledge, and the ability to create links of many different types (Boden, 2010, p. 36–37). Especially in advertising, there is no substitute for a rich, diverse cultural capital. Combinational creativity relates to thinking with analogies or structural similarities (Boden, 2010, p. 166).

Transformational creativity occurs once someone traces and then breaks culturally sanctioned rules thus leading to "impossibilist surprises" (Boden, 2004, p. 75) within the context of an accepted cultural style or conceptual space. Transformational creativity amends or ignores normally respected constraints (Boden, 2010, p. 2) allowing for otherwise inconceivable ideas (Boden, 2004, p. 3; 2013, p. 43). Transformational creativity, then, is about context, not just content and its outcomes pave new ways for what can be thereafter conceptualised (Boden, 2004, pp. 3–6, chs 4–6). As an example, in advertising, transformational creativity involves unconventional, creative use of media that changes the advertising landscape permanently. The first advergame; the first branded mini-series; the first branded meme; or even, going back, the first advertorial, the first 30" commercial, the first scratch-and-sniff print ads were transformative ideas that brought pervasive changes even if, soon after, these ideas became part of the mainstream.

6 Connecting practice to theory

6.1 Divergent and convergent thinking in creative advertising

First and second ideas, often come from divergent and convergent thinking, respectively. Divergent thinking is the generation of a variety of ideas and alternative solutions to problems, while convergent thinking brings together disparate pieces of information attempting to solve a particular problem (Guilford, 1957). Divergent thinking helps the mind open up, take different directions, ignore limitations, think "out of the box" and test a variety of ideas. Convergent thinking delves deeper, relies on focus and attention to detail, combines, and deepens the efforts to deliver a complete outcome.

When a creative team first starts exploring a brief, they are supposed to take different directions and provide as many ideas as possible. They apply divergent thinking in the sense that they seek alternatives to what has existed already in advertising, in terms of message and, sometimes, even in terms of media. Exploratory creativity (Boden, 2004) at this stage looks for new stories, new metaphors, new analogies, new ways to express insights, new opportunities to borrow from popular culture and trends, new touchpoints. This type of exploration will not only breed unexpected ideas but will also create a context in which ideas will be assessed against each other. Creatives go broad but don't go deep, not just yet.

When a creative team starts developing selected ideas, convergent thinking more likely applies; less looking around, more looking in. Each member delves in an idea trying to develop it in full detail, adding elements of surprise, perfecting, fine-tuning, ensuring the brief is followed, solving problems, and considering the broader media context. Exploration at this stage looks for plot-twists, unexpected expressions, design variations and so forth; anything that can enhance or elaborate an idea, making it original, memorable, and unpredictable. If the process of ideation involves a lot of exploration, the process of development involves a lot of combinational creativity (Boden, 2004). However, procedures and thinking patterns are not and should not be rigidly aligned. Kilgour & Koslow (2009) found that non-creative advertising professionals performed very well using divergent thinking tools but not as well when using convergent thinking tools. This may be because convergent thinking during idea development requires a lot of tacit knowledge of techniques and experience that copywriters and designers acquire by the years and appears to be domain specific (Simonton, 2015).

Few are the attempts to study advertising creativity using tools from the creative studies (Smith & Yang, 2004; Precourt, 2013; Reinartz & Saffert, 2013) and even fewer are the attempts to discuss individual and team processes in the agency. This is significant because creative professionals need more than just talent to be able to deliver good results. They need awareness of what they do, how and why they do it, so they can consciously allocate skills and develop ways of effective work. So far, we have connected divergent and convergent thinking with the process of ideation. But, within the organisational setting, we must focus on the outcome. So, what comes out of all these different ways of thinking?

6.2 Fluency, flexibility, originality

According to Guilford (1957) divergent thinking yields creative outcomes that may differ in terms of fluency, flexibility, and originality. Fluency describes the quantity of alternatives generated in a limited amount of time. Flexibility describes the ability to approach the task at hand through different perspectives, generating ideas that are different and diverse one from the other. Originality describes the ability to generate ideas that have not existed before – to the extent those involved in the process can know and assess (Guilford's work has been extensively used and somewhat modified over the years. Indicatively: El-Murad & West, 2004).

This is exactly how different creatives perform in advertising as well. Some tend to be more fluent, delivering too many ideas within a given brief and timeframe. Others tend to deliver fewer ideas, but distinctively different one from the other. Then, there are those who might come up with one idea and fixate on it until it becomes perfect, converging too early in the process. Finally, there are those who tend to demonstrate not only flexibility but also originality in their thinking, by exploring less anticipated thinking paths.

To have great and original ideas, the creative team needs to start with plenty of ideas (Simonton, 1998). In advertising, fluency and flexibility are prerequisites for originality because, during the creative process, an original idea shines within its context and among its alternatives, not in a vacuum and rarely in an absolute manner. In the creative process, then, different types of thinking and different types of creative output contribute to the outcome. Starting on the job, creatives tend to be either inclined toward fluency or toward flexibility and elaboration. Originality comes with experience.

Individual differences, then, must be combined with organisational procedures. At the same time, such differences must be preserved because diversity in thinking leads to diversity in ideas. And, of course, in the creative department nobody works in isolation. Creatives work both individually and in groups, throughout the process. Moments of interaction and collaboration alternate with moments of intense self-concentration. The exchange of ideas and feedback is like an ongoing game of table tennis where multiple players hit the same ball, the idea. Some people seem to think that all this interaction can easily conceal any individual weaknesses and that one can hide just be providing feedback or incremental contributions. The opposite is true. When time comes to contribute, one cannot pass.

6.3 Preparation, incubation, illumination, verification

There is one more contribution to consider when it comes to creative thinking. This came from Wallas back in 1926 and has resurfaced recently in the broader context of creative studies (indicatively: Sadler-Smith, 2015). Wallas argued that there is a four-stage mental process one follows to come up with novel thinking. Acknowledging and managing this mental process can help deliver optimal outcomes. These four stages are: preparation, incubation, illumination, and verification. During the first stage, we immerse in learning, reading, searching, benchmarking, delving in the topic of interest, finding out all there is before attempting to contribute with something new. Then we must incubate. Incubation prevents us from passive reading and paves the way for creativity. During the stage of incubation, we must forget the task at hand. However, as preparation has occurred, thinking continues latently and we become more intimate with the task, even if not actively thinking about it. This is how illumination comes, the third stage, which a lot of people experience as an a-ha moment, out of the blue. Once we enter the illumination stage, we can develop the idea and then move on to the fourth stage, verification. During the final stage, we examine how applicable or suitable or feasible our novel thought is.

So, illumination is never random or sudden or spontaneous. Illumination is the result of preparation and incubation, whether that be deliberate or not. "A-ha" moments have antecedents. Wallas then explains what lies behind moments of inspiration creatives often experience, in the shower or while sleeping, as the urban legend goes. He also explains why some of the greatest ideas come, unfortunately, right after the presentation: because at this point, we let go. When we do not consciously allow ourselves to incubate, to get some distance from an urgent project, then illumination will not come. Even during pressing times, one must actively seek moments of distancing and there is evidence that in advertising those who engage in incubation tasks which involve brain areas different from the creative task, perform better (Schütmaat et al, 2022). So, if you walk in the creative department and see people chatting or swiping or snacking during working hours, beware they are not lazy or laid back. They might as well claim they are incubating!

Preparation, for the advertising creative, is also important. Such preparation goes beyond reading the brief and includes reading consumer research or analytics, delving in the product and, of course, benchmarking: looking for similar campaigns in different markets, keeping up with the trends of creative advertising, and exploring case studies. Furthermore, verification in creative advertising takes place as described above in section 5. Every time an idea passes on to the next level, it has gone through verification, and this is reiterated until the idea airs.

This model also allows us to consider diversity in thinking, but within a pattern. Individuals go through the four stages, but not at the same pace. Some prefer frequent short breaks (Leroy et al., 2020; Lu et al., 2017); others read faster; some go into passive reading earlier than others and so forth. All aspects of how we live our everyday life, our habits, our routines, our rituals, our mental state affect our thinking one way or the other. Thus, if we know about the four stages, we can learn to manage our performance and output seeking alignment with the team and organisational requirements. We can observe ourselves in comparison to our team. We can ensure we acknowledge which stage we are in. We can improve how we experience work, simply by understanding and managing those stages.

Time to practise!

○ Form a group of peers and work on first ideas for a brand campaign, for exactly one hour. You should select the same brief but work individually. Work on four rounds:

1   Prepare: browse, read, do research, study. Keep notes and end this stage using automatic writing.
2   Incubate.
3   Return to your initial ideas: write down the initial concept and a rough tagline for each.
4   Share your ideas and exchange feedback on each idea.
5   Exchange feedback on your experience during the first three stages:

    a   How much time did you allocate in each?
    b   How much time would you allocate if you tried this again?
    c   When did you experience fatigue or mental blocks?
    d   Were you more or less productive compared to your peers? Remember that this exercise is for fluency, not for originality. Self-reflection and self-discipline are tested.

You may continue with this exercise and test convergent thinking, if each team member chooses to develop an idea developed by another member.

○ Read the Turnbull & Wheeler (2017) and the Stuhlfaut & Windels (2019) paper. Which of the steps described in each paper would more likely require divergent thinking? which would require convergent thinking? document your responses acknowledging that both convergent and divergent thinking may occur in all the steps.

7 Creative advertising compared to creative problem solving and design thinking

Beyond advertising, similar steps are proposed in more general frameworks for what is defined as Creative Problem Solving (CPS). Parnes (1985; see also:

Osborn, 1963; Noller, Parnes & Biondi, 1976) introduced a structured approach on creative problem solving which breaks the creative process into concrete steps that lead to more and better results. These steps are: 1. Mess finding / definition of objectives; 2. Fact finding; 3. Problem finding; 4. Idea finding; 5. Solution finding; 6. Action finding. The most interesting aspect of CPS is that it does not start with a problem that needs to be solved. Defining the problem is the third step which follows a stage of exploration and a stage of data gathering. These allow for a re-definition of what constitutes a problem, call for a different framing and understanding of the problem and thus pave the way for more innovative solutions. Keep in mind that Alex Osborn was the "O" in BBDO, a successful advertising man who not only did the creative work but also contemplated a lot on how he did it and how he could transfer this knowledge. Collaborating with Parnes, he contributed significantly in the understanding of advertising creativity and creative studies.

Novel or creative thinking is also the backbone of design thinking defined as a methodology, or simply put, a set of steps, which lead to design solutions. Different authors provide somewhat different steps (Razzouk & Shute, 2012; Dorst, 2011; Kimbell, 2011) but all of the methodologies have considerable elements in common: design thinking leads to an applied or applicable output. Therefore, though design thinking is a process, the focus is on the outcome. Design thinking methodologies also allow for divergent thinking in the beginning and convergent thinking toward the end of the process.

There are significant similarities between Creative Problem Solving (CPS), design thinking and ideation in creative advertising. All three start with some type of learning or preparation which leads to a deeper understanding; all three combine different types of thinking collaboration; all emphasise the outcome. Their steps run in parallel. Their main difference is context: the setting and the requirements in which these methodologies are put to use. Table 4.1 presents a comparison of three different approaches.

Table 4.1 Comparing creative problem solving, design thinking, and creative advertising

Creative problem solving (Noller, Parnes, & Biondi, 1976)	Design thinking (Plattner et al., 2010)	Creative advertising (Turnbull & Wheeler, 2017; Altstiel et al., 2023).
Mess-Finding: Exploring a Situation / defining objectives	Empathise	Account planning
Data-Finding: Gathering Information		
Problem-Finding: Defining the Problem	Define	Strategy
Idea-Finding: Generating Possible Solutions	Ideate	First ideas
Solution-Finding: Choosing a Solution	Prototype	Approved idea
Action-Planning: Developing a Course of Action	Test	Production

8 Tools & techniques for advertising creativity – towards a modus operandi

We have discussed creative ideas in advertising, and then we have put creativity in a broader context to better explain some of its key dimensions. We have discussed processes that lead to creative outcomes. Now we will discuss the role and importance of tools that help creative thinking. Such tools can be used by an individual or within a group.

However, tools have limitations. First, no tool in the world can replace the need for cultural capital and for spontaneous, unstructured thinking, especially during the first stages of the creative process, after someone has delved in the mess and mesh of a situation getting prepared to define and address a problem. Second, many tools are context specific. A copywriter, an engineer, and an organisational expert might not necessarily benefit from the same tools, though such tools might be able to fit in many different tasks. Third, tools can also be classified by their contribution in divergent or convergent thinking and by their contribution in different stages of the creative process. Fourth, not all tools are for all people. However, the more tools you can use, the more fluent and flexible your thinking becomes, thus increasing your chances to come up with something original. Fifth, all tools require practice and learning before being put to good use. Applying tools is not always intuitive. Openness and patience are required for the creative person to learn to stream their thinking toward different directions.

Here, we discuss tools which allow for divergent thinking, taking for granted that before using the tools, one has gone through the stage of preparation, so they know all there is to know, and they can empathise with the situation. Tools for convergent thinking tailored to creative advertising are presented in Chapters 5 & 6.

8.1 Automatic writing – free associations

Automatic writing is perhaps the best place to start if one aims at fluency and originality. Automatic writing helps blend the writer's cultural capital, influences, and experiences with the task at hand. Automatic writing should occur after meticulous preparation which involves reading, benchmarking and personal research. All you need is a notepad and a time slot for uninterrupted, concentrated work. Turn everything off and spend 10–30 minutes simply putting down on

Table 4.2 A list of tools that help creative thinking.

	Divergent thinking	Individual work	Group work
Automatic writing	x	x	
Forced connections (verbal or visual)	x	x	
SCAMPER	x	x	x
Consumer props	x	x	x
Brainstorming or brainwriting	x		x

paper whatever comes to mind: phrases, sketches, keywords, short stories, questions, rhymes, song or movie titles, etc. The goal is to keep writing, unstoppably, without assessing, thinking, or in any other way revisiting what you have written. You just keep going, until you are completely drained out. There will be peaks and valleys in this process. Some people have a hard time starting but then experience a good flow, while others start easily but then get stuck earlier, and / or more than once in the process. Don't stop the first time you feel stuck or dry. Just keep going for as long as you promised yourself to. Once the time has passed, take a break, forget about this, and revisit your notes after a break for incubation. You might realise that a lot of what you have written is irrelevant and must be deleted. Nobody is watching, though. Delete and organise the rest: create clusters of similar ideas, set an order of preference, and start working on whatever is left on your pad at this stage. Use techniques described below to shape each idea which may be roughly discussed or exchanged in a brainstorming session. Whatever type of creative work you do, automatic writing is the perfect start, providing raw material and stretching the capacity for fluency. The outcome is rich but neither deep nor eloquent yet. However, after preparing for the brief, a round of automatic writing can help you expose a series of thoughts through keywords or images and start creating associations and combinations before any other tool is put to use.

8.2 Forced connections

This is a book about bridges between brands and consumers and about combined elements that may lead to a great idea. So, place a representation of the task at hand on your left. Then, choose a completely irrelevant object or word or image and put it on your right; anything from a sentence to an object like a baseball cap or an eggplant or a spaceship. Try to connect these two by writing down sentences or stories, or even by sketching similar forms or items. Every step which brings one item closer to the other must be written down. Do this for 10–30 minutes and then take a break. You may repeat, using a different right-hand stimulus. This helps flexibility because it forces you to explore unimagined possibilities (Mauzy, 2006).

8.3 Consumer and brand prompts

Prompts might feel a bit like third grade, but they can certainly help individuals and teams delve in the consumer insights and empathise with their target audience. You may create your own prompts depending on what triggers you or on the brief. Simple things like: "If I were_____ I would_____" or "If I had_____ I could_____" or "I would like to_____" or "I hate it when_____" might help you get in the shoes of another person whose needs or desires or hopes or aspirations you do not share. Understanding others is the best way to create ideas for consumers. Your thinking diverges beyond what you take for granted, thus feelings or thoughts or even stories start emerging. Hold on to these and, most of all, hold on to the emotions. Compare these prompts to what has emerged from your automatic writing and focus on possible matches.

Similarly, use the game of metaphors to find alternative ways to describe the brand and its benefits or promises by playing the "what if" game or by asking: "If it were_____ what would it be?" this can help you re-imagine the object of your work and describe it in different ways that pave the way for interesting visuals and stories.

8.4 SCAMPER

SCAMPER helps both create and edit ideas, bringing them to an abstract but eloquent and clear form. Though SCAMPER can hardly substitute for the lack of automatic writing, it can help you take your automatic notes and convert them to clear ideas: one sentence with a couple of bullet points or sketches, still abstract but easy to assess versus the brief and easy to realise how it can grow to appear in different media. Alex Osborn is the one who introduced SCAMPER whose use, therefore, is most relevant in advertising. SCAMPER is an acronym for: Substitute, Combine, Adapt (or Adjust), Magnify (or Modify), Put to other uses, Eliminate, and Reverse. Take any sentence or visual. Start thinking how you can change it or any part of it, using the SCAMPER verbs. Do not exclude anything too early in the process. Be patient, write everything down and apply more than once for each idea. A lot of trivialities will appear, but some possibilities or impossibilities might help you move forward and give you the feeling you have got something good. There is plenty to discard with every tool once the process is over. But in a handful of sand, you will always have grains of gold, you just need to be able to identify these. Remember that SCAMPER can be used to analyse existing ideas and try to imagine how these were conceived, but there is more than one plausible way to go back.

4.8.5 Brainstorming / Brainwriting

Osborn, again, first defined and introduced brainstorming that, along with SCAMPER and CPS, are now widely used in many professional settings beyond advertising. Brainstorming is easy to understand, but not simple. Too many teams get it wrong (McPolin, 2018; Byron, 2012; Rossiter & Lilien, 1994) so it's important you understand its basic principles and rules of thumb. First, brainstorming is not a substitute for individual thinking. On the contrary, the best way for creative teams to do a great job is alternate sessions of individual thinking with sessions for brainstorming in which people exchange ideas or fragments of what could be an idea, seeking team input. Second, brainstorming is not a last-minute solution because our ideas do not work well. It should be integrated in the early stages of the creative process to allow for divergent input. Third, brainstorming does not breed ideas. Brainstorming gives you amazing raw material that could lead to ideas (McPolin, 2018), but this raw material requires a lot of processing (Mumford, 2000) after the brainstorming. "A-ha" ideas during a brainstorming session, do not always pass through the verification process.

To conduct a successful brainstorming, here is what you need: first, a concrete timeslot of about 30–60 minutes. Brainstorming is not meant to last forever. The thought that "we will all gather in a room and won't leave until we nail it" rarely proves right. You need as much, or much more time later, to sort the outcomes out and develop or assess ideas that emerged from divergent thinking. Then, you need a dedicated group of 6–12 people, all having read the brief and being prepared, but some less exposed or into the project than others. Pollinating the group with colleagues who do some homework beforehand but have not spent days or weeks into the same topic, helps bring new ideas on the table. If the same people try to brainstorm repeatedly, they will end up in a group-think process reiterating and going around in circles. Third, you need a facilitator (Byron, 2012) who may or may not participate but who must write everything down. Everything. Fourth, you need peers. People who feel equal. Put a CEO in a room of juniors or a junior in a room of C-suite executives and you realise that they moderate their contributions too much, opposing the basic principle of brainstorming which is the uninhibited utterance of any thought that comes to mind. In a non-peer environment, self-awareness prevails, and people might talk much more or much less than what they would if indeed they were uninhibited. Some may feel constantly assessed from the senior participants (McPolin, 2018). Fifth, in a brainstorming there is no room for assessment. One might utter a new thought or contribute to somebody's thought but is not supposed to "like" or "dislike" or approve or disapprove any contribution on the spot. At the end of the meeting, the note keeper will distribute the notes, and this will be the time for each member to contemplate on each idea. To avoid getting off focus or engaging in small talk, a brainstorming should be intensive and time constrained pushing everyone to their limits. Most good ideas will emerge toward the end (McPolin, 2018). You will know it went well when it finishes, before you even read the notes, because you will need a long break.

Brainwriting can be conducted in the same way, but participants exchange their ideas in notes which are collected and read out loud, anonymously. This is less lively, of course, but may allow introvert or self-aware participants to contribute. Usually, brainwriting is conducted in "rounds" where people write, exchange notes, and then write again. At the end, all the elaborated notes are read out. Mind-mapping (Rowley et al., 2011) is also a way to combine brainstorming with notetaking or brainwriting and the way participants connect ideas creating mental maps might help create new associations and bring combinational creativity (Boden, 2004) on the table thus leading to more or more appropriate ideas.

***

These tools facilitate divergent thinking and exploratory creativity in response to a given brief. The outcome is a list of raw ideas in the form of a sketch, a paragraph, a tagline or a story pattern, underdeveloped but promising. How this will finally become an ad will be discussed in the following chapters.

Always remember that being up to date and having a rich cultural capital is essential and can be substituted by no tool. On the contrary, tools will work better if the person who uses them possesses a rich palette of stimuli and experiences, and after a lot of practice.

A good way to assess your first ideas, is to return to the brief requirements and use them as a checklist: Will the idea achieve the specific objectives? Does it address the right target group? Does it convey the right message clearly? Are insights well used and skilfully conveyed? Can this idea be developed for different media? Does it allow for multiple executions? Can it be produced within budget? Within the deadlines?

Time to practise!

- In 10 minutes, find at least 30 different ways to use a pair of tweezers. Try this with friends and compare notes. How many of the ideas appeared only once?
- Find one campaign you are fond of and consider you have to create a follow up.

  - First prepare by studying the brand and the campaign
  - Then, use automatic writing for 20' to and write down all the words, phrases, or images that come up.
  - Take a 10' break.
  - Revisit your initial notes: discard, enrich, link. Organise a list of rough ideas.
  - Use forced connections to come up with new ideas or stronger metaphors for your campaign.
  - Use SCAMPER to develop new messages or new stories.

- Try all the above for every new campaign you get exposed to.
- Select a campaign you like, write down the main idea and try to imagine how the creatives could have used SCAMPER to arrive to this idea. Consider this reverse engineering approach with other techniques, too.

---

9 The everyday life and the clichés of the creative advertising professional

So, what does it feel like, working in the creative department? How does everyday life unravel? It can't be all fun and games, after all. In this section, we will briefly discuss several topics that relate to the experience of the creative advertising professional.

In other creative industries, more often than not, creative contributors are not usually employees but tend to freelance or work under flexible contracts. In advertising, however, most creative professionals are meant to be creative daily, 9–5 and beyond, going to the same office, talking to the same colleagues, and working for the same clients. This might appear contradictory, and one needs to foster their own creativity in and out of the office, on and off working hours (Mumford, 2000). This is one of the particularities facing creative professionals in the advertising agency.

9.1 *The creative genius and the team*

In the agency, the stereotype of the creative genius is widely spread (Bilton, 2007; 2010). A stereotype is neither true nor false, but it's always partial and myopic. Based on Amabile's definition, one can easily infer that creativity is never just about the individual. Individual contributions are the cornerstone of any creative idea. However, one's idea will more likely flourish if acknowledged, supported, and promoted by others.

An entire team comprising different skillsets can help creative ideas grow. Each talented person needs open ears, and nobody is equally good at everything. A great creative director needs to have and breed a strong team of copywriters and art directors. A good copywriter needs someone who will convert a message to a poster. A good script writer needs a great film producer. A good designer needs a good copywriter and so forth. Big talents might go astray if the soil they are cast in is not fertile. Relying too much on individual charisma does not always ensure a steady agency output (Bilton, 2007; 2010).

Putting the right people together, ensuring diversity and fostering compatibility is needed in order to have fluent and flexible ideas with a strong potential for originality (Luecke, 2003). Beyond creativity, domain knowledge also matters, meaning that professionals will become more creative when they learn more about advertising and more about their clients' business.

A lot of young professionals feel they are constantly put down or fear that someone "takes their ideas" which become "ruined" or "appropriated" by others during execution. This is the wrong mindset. Good advertising only comes out of teamwork. Each job-role has something to add or change. There is no such thing as "my idea". People should feel they own your idea as much as you do, because it's the only way they will invest in it and work all the way to perfection. And this is what you are supposed to do for other people's ideas. So, the person matters; but not one talented person; each person. Credit is due not only to those who generate ideas but also to those who contribute to ideas generated by their colleagues.

Teamwork, on the other hand, can also be challenging, and not only for introverts. Sometimes the team calls when you would rather focus on your own thoughts. In other cases, you need someone to exchange ideas with, but they are not available. Sometimes you get lost when everyone brainstorms, or you feel that others "don't get it". In advertising, teamwork takes time and blending in, requires effort, especially in the beginning. Individual work and teamwork alternate multiple times during every working day, challenging our flexibility, openness, and ability to concentrate.

9.2 *The Ps of creativity in the agency*

Rhodes (1961) argues that process, press, and product significantly impact individual creativity and the output of a creative person.

Process is mostly understood individually and mentally: what are the thoughts, steps, stages a creative thinker goes through before their idea is fully grasped and shared. Process matters because without it ideas cannot stand out and cannot be successfully executed. Creativity needs a flow of work to lead to innovative advertising (broadly speaking, the difference in the use of the terms "creativity" and "innovation" is addressed in Anderson et al., 2014).

Press is approached as the sum of environmental constraints which affect the likelihood, scope, and aim of creative thinking. Advertising agencies combine individual thinking processes with organisational processes, as discussed above, thus combining personal skills with business needs. This often puts pressure on individuals who need to demonstrate both divergence and alignment with procedures and deadlines. Such alignment comes with experience. Being aware of this dipole helps professionals mature, adjust, and manage their needs and capabilities.

Product, according to Rhodes, refers to an embodied manifestation of the conceived idea, which frequently differs significantly from the original concept. As discussed above, in the agency where product matters the most, combining divergent with convergent thinking, breadth with depth and openness with discipline leads to good ideas. Creatives must develop complementary skillsets, and this might require special, targeted effort, hence the need for good creative management and professional support.

Kristensen (2004) adds the importance of physical space and its impact on creative productivity. In advertising, room is needed both for group work and for isolation. Open space offices allow for collaboration but not for self-concentration and the opposite goes for traditional office arrangements. Having ample room for people to get in a different mindset during the day is important. A young professional learns to adjust and make as good use of space as can be allowed.

The "Ps" of creativity then, explain that beyond the "person", a lot of environmental factors impact creative output (for a more systematic review and measurement of such factors, see: Amabile et al., 1996).

9.3 Soft skills

Kover (2016) argues that in advertising more people than acknowledged can be creative and that demonstrating self-assurance to keep overcoming hurdles is what makes some stand out. This is partly true. Along with self-assurance, several complementary soft skills are needed for a creative person to navigate the agency world (Windels et al., 2013). To begin with, a creative person should demonstrate eloquence and persuasion. Especially during the stage of first ideas, what you have in mind is so abstract and fluid, that sharing it in a convincing manner to demonstrate its potential is very important. A creative thinker must be both inspiring and convincing for their idea to take the go-ahead. Communication skills and presentation skills also help a creative professional bring an idea to life. Acting out or letting an idea speak for itself both require practice and experience.

Resilience is also a very important skill. One must not only work long hours in intensive and mentally exhausting ways, but also cope with rejection. Although easier said than done, rejection should not be taken personally. Nine out of ten ideas never see the light of day in an advertising agency. Staying positive and productive, eliciting feedback, and trying again is what makes a creative professional progress in the agency world.

Creatives should also be up to date (Barroso et al., 2021) in matters other professionals need not be. New technologies, campaign benchmarks, cultural trends from art to cuisine and from social media to theatre and series should be at their fingertips. Being up to date allows them to reach out to diverse audiences and to be able to draw ideas and raw material from a variety of stimuli. The cultural capital and the technology capital required in this job, require significant investment to acquire and maintain. To the list of soft skills needed not only to succeed but also to enjoy everyday life in the creative department, add empathy, emotional intelligence, self-discipline, and tolerance to ambiguity (Mumford, 2000).

9.4 Deadlines, stress, risks, and incentives

Creatives often face pressure because of deadlines (Wang et al., 2017) or rejections or have this feeling that more time could have led to better work. This is partly accurate. In small doses or for a limited amount of time, pressure can help people stay agile and alert, and intensify their creative efforts, even more so when they acknowledge the importance or the urgency of a task. If, on the other hand, conditions of pressure are prolonged or seem to revolve around projects of less importance, then, eventually, creativity is obstructed. Even if people feel more alert and creative, their output is most likely not (Amabile et al., 2002; Amabile, 1996; Amabile et al., 1996). Different people have different perceptions of what constitutes too much pressure (Luecke, 2003). Indeed, some pressure usually helps, preventing idleness (Mumford, 2000). But if stress takes over, people often experience signs of burning out or even an over-reliance on personal skills that may prove to be detrimental (Bilton, 2014), becoming less capable of assessing the outcome of their creative efforts, usually overestimating their output (Amabile, 1996). Stress may have beneficial effects on creativity, if stressors are perceived positively as challenges. When perceived as hindrances, stressors obstruct creativity (Ren & Zhang, 2015).

Risk-taking is found to increase creativity yet is linked to smaller clients and younger creatives. The riskier an idea the more likely the rejection from peers, seniors, or clients, in any of the stages of the creative process. However, younger creatives are not only more likely but also expected to take risks, to "go wild", to bring the unexpected in their team, especially during the first stage of divergent thinking, idea generation and exploration. Even if their ideas don't pass to the next stage, having them and sharing them matters. So, especially during your first years in the agency, rejection is OK. It's better to have an idea rejected because it is too bold than because it is too mundane.

Being creative is primarily an intrinsic motivation (Amabile, 1990). We experience gratification when engaging in creative tasks, even more so when we engage successfully. The key questions for young advertising professionals is: do you enjoy doing creative work, even when facing stress, pressure, deadlines, and rejections? And so far, many have been answering "yes" though recently recruiting new creative talent in advertising has become more challenging (Gray, 2022). Extrinsic incentives also play a key role in the professional arena. Good compensation, recognition of our efforts, distinctions are essential to keep us eager and positive.

There is a complex relationship between incentives and creativity (Amabile, 1990; Hennessey & Amabile, 1998). In educational settings, intrinsic incentives are considered more important and extrinsic incentives have been found to have a negative influence on creativity. At work though, an appropriate mix of intrinsic and extrinsic incentives is needed for creative advertising professionals to maintain their motivation, especially after years on the job. There is no one-size-fits-all mix. Everyone has their own preferences and expectations, which is why human resource management can play a crucial role in fostering a creative working culture and creative directors should be trained to be able to manage people showing consideration of what they actually need to stay motivated. Because more money is not always the answer, try to figure out what it is you may need other than money to be able to perform better, and seek ways to claim it after the first few years in the industry. A 20% increase in salary will not bring a 20% increase in creativity.

Here are some tips to develop self-awareness and the ability to manage challenges facing creative professionals:

- Instead of procrastinating or postponing the undertaking of a new brief, start the preparation process for it as early as possible, while incubating over a current one (Schütmaat et al., 2022). Using more work to get our mind off work might seem counter intuitive but it helps.
- Observe yourself: do you work better if you take more, shorter breaks or fewer and longer ones? Claim the pace that helps you, within the limitations you face. Creative work has moments of immense exhilaration and moments of intense depression and frustration. Learn to welcome both but keep a safe distance.
- Manage stress that may emerge from factors beyond time pressure: rejection, criticism, self-doubt (El-Murad & West 2004; 2003) and try to foster an environment in which you feel you can take risks while you acknowledge that feedback and the contribution of others in your work is a positive element for creative success.
- Discuss with peers or seek training and consultation where available, especially if you are an introvert. You may find that others have experienced the same concerns.
- Don't fear to present risky ideas. Avoid playing safe, especially as an entry level creative professional.
- Reflect on the mix of incentives that will make you perform better and claim this mix as you gradually progress in the agency.
- Seek praise (Bilton & Cummings, 2009) but, most of all, seek feedback and feed-forward input that will help you improve.

9.5 The need for diversity and management

Though the benefits of diversity are more than obvious in creative teams, advertising is not famous for being inclusive. Ever since the time of the Mad Men glass walls and glass ceilings block the way for people who represent otherness in terms of sex, gender, age, race, and more, while homosociability is observed, especially in the creative department. (Miliopoulou & Kaparcliotis, 2021; Brodmerkel & Barker, 2019; Roca et al., 2016; Windels & Mallia, 2015; Scanlon, 2013; Windels & Lee, 2012; Pueyo-Ayhan, 2010; Mallia, 2009; Broyles & Grow, 2008). Being culturally open and striving for diversity is essential in advertising. Beyond the ethical implications lurking in homosociability and lack of inclusion, (indicatively: Gurrieri et al., 2022; Boulton, 2013; Gregory, 2009; McLeod et al., 2009) it is clear by now that authentic, unique, and appropriate ideas can only emerge by diverse teams who mingle and exchange viewpoints with or without a task at hand. Advertising people carry their own stereotypes at work. To be able to create outside of the labels and the boxes, a truly diverse environment is necessary to broaden their horizons (Thompson-Whiteside and Turnbull 2021).

Furthermore, one of the challenges facing creative departments is the combination of creative skills and managerial skills (Bilton 2009; 2014; 2015; Mallia et al., 2013). When art directors and copywriters get promoted, they acquire an enhanced role in idea development and decision making. However, a managerial position also requires knowledge and competencies that creatives are not necessarily familiar with. Managing people, fostering diversity, creating a spirit of inclusion and tolerance, leading teamwork, resolving conflict, inspiring and mentoring, allocating work, monitoring timesheets and budgets, and much more, are skills to be acquired and lifelong learning should be at the top of a promising creative executive's list.

9.6 Compartmentalisation

One of the popular themes in the everyday life of the agency is the rivalry between creatives and the client service department (Koppman et al., 2022; Robbs & Llovd, 2016; Grant et al., 2012; Vanden Bergh et al., 1986). According to the intense stereotyping from both sides, creatives are procrastinating, disorganised, wasting time, always blaming it on the requests, the deadlines, and the briefs; while client service people are stingy, always siding with clients, who do not give good ideas a fair chance, and ignore important aspects of creative work, constantly asking for edits and changes (Precourt, 2013). Nicknames, memes, and stereotypes might bring a smile here and there but if taken too seriously they lead to unfruitful compartmentalisation. Though this rivalry is intensely observed in advertising, it is also found to occur more broadly in the creative industries (Bilton & Leary, 2002).

Yes, there is a department called "creative", but in an advertising agency everyone must be creative. Creativity is both a privilege and a burden, not exclusive to any department, while account planning is recently being considered the cornerstone and the meeting point of strategy and creativity, a significant yardstick on the road to creative work, as it combines "what" we have to say, expressed in strategy with "how" to say it, relying on creativity (Bilton, 2009; Bilton et al., 2022). Creatives should acknowledge novelty, input and feedback wherever it may come from while account managers should acknowledge the particularities of creative work and stand up for the ideas of their colleagues. Risk taking to promote unconventional ideas should be of concern to the whole agency. Otherwise, what is lost in the tension is great creative work.

Time to practise!

- Try to assess your own soft skills. Can you trace your strengths and weaknesses? Which would help or obstruct your career in an advertising agency? Which ones could you improve, and how? Consider using techniques like the Johari Window.
- Write five reasons why one should use tools for creative thinking, and five reasons why one should not.
- Watch the old film: "Modern Times" and try to discern the pitfalls of assembly lines and serial production. Transfer these in the context of the advertising agency as it emerges from your readings. Trace opportunities and difficulties in the process of creative advertising.

References

Altstiel, T., Grow, J., Augustine, D., & Jennings, M. (2023). *Advertising creative: Strategy, copy, and design* (Sixth). SAGE Publishing.

Amabile, T.M. (1990): Within you, without me: The social psychology of creativity. In: Runco, M.A. & Albert, R.S. (Eds.) *Theories of Creativity*. Sage.

Amabile, T.M. (1996). *Creativity in context*. Westview Press.

Amabile, T.M., Conti, R., Coon, H., Lazenby, J., & Herron, M. (1996). Assessing the work environment for creativity, *The Academy of Management Journal*, 39 (5), 1154–1184, https://doi.org/10.2307/256995.

Amabile, T.M., Hadley, C.N., & Kramer, S. J. (2002). "Creativity under the gun." special issue on the innovative enterprise: Turning ideas into profits. *Harvard Business Review* 80 (8), 52–61.

Amabile, T.M. (2013) Componential theory of creativity. In: Kessler, E.H., ed., *Encyclopedia of management theory*, Sage Publications, London, 134–139. http://dx.doi.org/10.4135/9781452276090.n42.

Anderson, N., Potočnik, K. & Zhou, J. (2014) Innovation and creativity in organizations: A state-of-the-science review, prospective commentary, and guiding framework, *Journal of Management*, 40 (5), 1297–1333.

Andriopoulos, C. (2001), Determinants of organisational creativity: A literature review, *Management Decision*, 39 (10), 834–841. https://doi.org/10.1108/00251740110402328.

Barroso, L.C., Abad, V.M., & Solís, M.F. (2021). Essential skills in current creative advertising: University vs. professional reality, *ICONO 14, Revista de comunicación y tecnologías emergentes*, 19 (2), 1–26. Available at: https://www.redalyc.org/articulo.oa?id=552567897005.

Bilton, C., & Leary, R., (2002), What can managers do for creativity? Brokering creativity in the creative industries, *International Journal of Cultural Policy* 8 (1), 49–64.

Bilton, C. (2007). *Management and creativity: From creative industries to creative management*. Blackwell.

Bilton, C. (2009) Relocating creativity in advertising: From creativity versus strategy, to creative strategy, and strategic creativity? in A. Pratt and P. Jeffcutt (eds.) *Creativity, innovation and the cultural economy*, London, Routledge, pp. 23–40.

Bilton, C. (2010) Manageable creativity. *International Journal of Cultural Policy – Special Issue on "Creativity and Cultural Policy"* ed. C. Bilton, Vol. 16 no. 3 (July 2010), pp. 255–269.

Bilton, C. and Cummings, S. (2014) ed. *Handbook of management and creativity* (Cheltenham: Edward Elgar)

Bilton, C. (2014) Uncreativity: The shadow side of creativity. *International Journal of Cultural Policy* 21. 2: 153–167.

Bilton, C. (2015) Management in the cultural industries. In: Oakley, Kate and O'Connor, Justin, (eds.) *The Routledge companion to the cultural industries*. Routledge Companions. Abingdon: Routledge, pp. 283–295.

Bilton, C. (2016): A Creative Industries Perspective on Creativity and Culture. In: V. Glaveanu (ed.). *The Palgrave Handbook of Creativity and Culture Research* (London: Palgrave Macmillan), pp. 661–679.

Bilton, C., Cummings, S., & ogilvie, dt. (2022). *Creativities: The what, how, where, who and why of the creative process*. Elgar.

Boden, M. (2003). *The Creative mind: Myths and mechanisms 2nd*. London: Routledge.

Boden, M. (2010). *Creativity and art: Three roads to surprise*. Oxford University Press.

Boulton, C. (2013). The ghosts of mad men: Race and gender inequality inside American advertising agencies. In: McAllister, M. & West, E. (Eds.) *The Routledge companion to advertising and promotional culture*. Routledge, pp. 252–266.

Brodmerkel, S., & Barker, R. (2019). Hitting the "glass wall": Investigating everyday ageism in the advertising industry. *Sociological Review*, 67 (6), 1383–1399.

Broyles, S.F., & Grow, J.M. (2008). Creative women in advertising agencies: Why so few "babes in boyland"? *Journal of Consumer Marketing*, 25 (1), 4–6.

Byron, K. (2012). Creative reflections on brainstorming. *London Review of Education*, 10 (2), 201–213. Available at: https://acg.on.worldcat.org/oclc/802919101.

Costello, F.J. & Keane, M.T. (2000), Efficient creativity: Constraint-guided conceptual combination. *Cognitive Science*, 24, 299–349. https://doi.org/10.1207/s15516709cog2402_4.

Dorst, K. (2011) The core of "design thinking' and its application, *Design Studies*, 32 (6), 521–532. https://doi.org/10.1016/j.destud.2011.07.006.

El-Murad, J. & West, D.C. (2003). Risk and creativity in advertising, *journal of marketing management*, 19(5–6),657–673, doi: doi:10.1080/0267257x.2003.9728230.

El-Murad, J. & West, D.C. (2004). Definition and measurement of creativity: What do we know? *Journal of Advertising Research*, 44, 188–201. doi:10.1017/S0021849904040097.

Grant, I., McLeod, C. & Shaw, E. (2012), Conflict and advertising planning: consequences of networking for advertising planning, *European Journal of Marketing*, 46(1/2), 73–91. https://doi.org/10.1108/03090561211189248.

Gregory, M.R. (2009). Inside the locker room: Male homosociability in the advertising industry, *Gender, Work & Organization*, 16 (3), 323–347. doi:10.1111/j.1468-0432.2009.00447.x.

Guilford, J.P. (1957). Creative abilities in the arts. *Psychological Review*, 64 (2), 110–118. https://doi.org/10.1037/h0048280.

Gurrieri, L., Tuncay Zayer, L., & Coleman, C.A. (2022). Transformative advertising research: reimagining the future of advertising. *Journal of Advertising*, 51 (5), 539–556. https://doi.org/10.1080/00913367.2022.2098545.

Gray, A. (2022). Advertising agencies ask "where are all the people?' in battle for talent. *FT*. Retrieved from: https://www.ft.com/content/d378ccad-d614-4dae-8c8f-753b2285c442.

Hennessey, B.A., & Amabile, T.M. (1998). Reality, intrinsic motivation, and creativity. *American Psychologist*, 53 (6), 674–675. https://doi.org/10.1037/0003-066X.53.6.674.

Henry, S. (2011). Creative briefing: The creative perspective. In: Butterfield, L. (Ed.) *Excellence in advertising: the IPA guide to best practice*. New York: Routledge, pp. 161–176 (first published in 1999).

Kimbell, L. (2011) Rethinking design thinking: Part I, *Design and Culture*, 3 (3), 285–306, doi:10.2752/175470811X13071166525216.

Kohn, N.W., Paulus, P.B., & Korde, R.M. (2011) Conceptual combinations and subsequent creativity, *Creativity Research Journal*, 23 (3), 203–210, DOI: doi:10.1080/10400419.2011.595659.

Koslow, S. (2015). I love creative advertising: What it is, when to call for it, and how to achieve it, *Journal of Advertising Research*, 55(1), 5–8. https://doi-org.acg.idm.oclc.org/10.2501/JAR-55-1-005-008.

Kover, A.J. (2016) Advertising creativity: Some open questions. *Journal of Advertising Research*, 56 (3), 235–239. doi:10.2501/JAR-2016-033..

Koppman, S., Bechky, B.A., & Cohen, A.C. (2022). Overcoming conflict between symmetric occupations: How "Creatives" and "suits" use gender ordering in advertising. *AMJ*, 65, 1623–1651, https://doi.org/10.5465/amj.2020.0806.

Leroy, S., Schmidt, A.M., & Madjar, N. (2020). Interruptions and task transitions: understanding their characteristics, processes, and consequences. *ANNALS*, 14, 661–694, https://doi.org/10.5465/annals.2017.0146.

Lu, J., Akinola, M. & Mason, M. (2017). "Switching on " creativity: Task switching can increase creativity by reducing cognitive fixation, *Organizational Behavior and Human Decision Processes*, 139, 63–75. doi:10.1016/j.obhdp.2017.01.005..

Luecke, R., 2003. *Managing creativity and innovation*, Boston: Harvard Business Review Press.

Mallia, K. (2009). Rare birds: Why so few women become ad agency creative directors. *Advertising & Society Review*, 10 (3). https://doi.org/10.1353/asr.0.0032.

Mallia, K.L., Windels, K., & Broyles, S.J. (2013). The fire starter and the brand steward: An examination of successful leadership traits for the advertising-agency creative director, *Journal of Advertising Research*, 53 (3), 3 339–353, https://doi.org/10.2501/JAR-53-3-339-353.

Mauzy, J.H. (2006). Managing personal creativity. *Design Management Review*, 17(3).

McLeod, C., O'Donohoe, S. & Townley, B. (2009). The elephant in the room? Class and creative careers in British advertising agencies, *Human Relations*, 62 (7), 1011–1039. doi:10.1177/0018726709335551.

McPolin, E. (2018). The fundamentals of creativity. *Design Management Review*, 29 (2), 4–9. https://doi.org/10.1111/drev.12121.

Miliopoulou, G.-Z., & Kapareliotis, I. (2021). The toll of success: female leaders in the "women-friendly" Greek advertising agencies. *Gender, Work & Organization*, 28(5), 1741–1765. https://doi.org/10.1111/gwao.12636.

Mumford, M.D. (2000) Managing creative people: Strategies and tactics for innovation. *Human Resource Management Review*, 10 (3), 313–351.

Noller, R.B., Parnes, S.J., & Biondi, A.M. (1976). *Creative action book*. New York: Scribners.

Osborn, A.F. (1963). *Applied imagination: Principles and procedures of creative problem-solving* (3rd rev.). Scribner.

Ostwal, V. (2020). What's a creative brief, really? *Medium*. Available at: https://visha lostwal.medium.com/whats-a-creative-brief-really-6751c37182aa.

Parnes, S.J. (1985). Creative problem solving In: Costa, A. (Ed.), *Developing minds: A resource book for teaching thinking*, pp. 230–232.

Pickton, D. & Broderick, A. (2005) *Integrated marketing communications*. Harlow: Prentice Hall.

Pickton, D. & Hartley, B. (1998) Measuring integration: an assessment of the quality of IMC. *International Journal of Advertising*, 17 (4), 447–465.

Plattner, H. Meinel, C., & Leifer, L. (Eds.) (2010) *Design thinking: Understand – improve – apply*. Berlin: Springer.

Powell, S. (2008). The management and consumption of organisational creativity, *Journal of Consumer Marketing*, 25(3),158–166. https://doi.org/10.1108/07363760810870653.

Precourt, G. (2013) What we know about creativity. *Journal of Advertising Research*, 53 (3), 238–240. doi:10.2501/JAR-53-3-238-239..

Pueyo-Ayhan, N. (2010). Sex structure of occupations in the advertising industry: Where are the female ad practitioners? *Observatorio (OBS*) Journal*, 4(23), 243–267.

Razzouk R, Shute V. (2012). What is design thinking and why is it important? *Review of Educational Research*, 82 (3), 330–348. doi:10.3102/0034654312457429.

Reinartz, W. & Saffert, P. (2013). Creativity in advertising: When it works and when it doesn't. *Harvard Business Review online*. Available at: https://hbr.org/2013/06/crea tivity-in-advertising-when-it-works-and-when-it-doesnt.

Ren, F. & Zhang, J. (2015). Job stressors, organizational innovation climate, and employees' innovative behavior, *Creativity Research Journal*, 27 (1), 16–23, doi:10.1080/10400419.2015.992659.

Rhodes, M. (1961). An analysis of creativity. *The Phi Delta Kappan*, 42 (7), 305–310.

Robbs, B., & Lloyd, C. (2016). Account management and the changing advertising landscape. *Journal of Advertising Education*, 20(1–2),144–151. https://doi.org/10.1177/10980482160201-217.

Roca, D., Tena, D., Lazaro, P., & Gonzalez, A. (2016). Is there gender bias when creative directors judge advertising? Name cue effect in ad evaluation. *International Journal of Advertising*, 35 (6), 1008–1023.

Rossiter J.R. & Lilien G. L. (1994). New "brainstorming" principles. *Australian Journal of Management*, 19 (1), 61–72. doi:10.1177/031289629401900104.

Rowley, J., Sambrook, S. & Baregheh, A. (2011). Towards an innovation: Type mapping tool, *Management Decision*, 49 (1), 73–86.

Sadler-Smith, E. (2015) Wallas' four-stage model of the creative process: More than meets the eye? *Creativity Research Journal*, 27 (4), 342–352, doi:10.1080/10400419.2015.1087277..

Sasser, S.L., Koslow, S., & Kilgour, M. (2013) Matching creative agencies with results-driven marketers: Do clients really need highly creative advertising? *Journal of Advertising Research*, 53 (3), 297–313.

Scanlon, J. (2013). "A dozen ideas to the minute": Advertising women, advertising to women. *Journal of Historical Research in Marketing*, 5 (3), 273–290. https://doi.org/10.1108/JHRM-01-2013-0002.

Schütmaat, S., Kopka, J.F., Ang, L. & Langner, T. (2022) Take a break, but make it different! Moderating effects of incubation task specificity on advertising idea generation, *Journal of Advertising*, doi:10.1080/00913367.2022.2087200..

Simmons, J. (2006) Guinness and the role of strategic storytelling, *Journal of Strategic Marketing*, 14(1), 11–18, DOI: doi:10.1080/09652540500369068.

Simonton, D.K. (1998). Donald Campbell's model of the creative process: Creativity as blind variation and selective retention. *Journal of Creative Behavior*, 32, 153–158.

Simonton, D.K. (2006). Creativity around the world in 80 days… but with one destination. In: Kaufman, J.C. & Sternberg, R.J. (eds) *The International Handbook of Creativity*. Cambridge University Press, pp. 490–496.

Simonton D.K. (2015). On praising convergent thinking: creativity as blind variation and selective retention. *Creativity Research Journal*, 27 (3), 262–270.

Smith, R.E., & Yang, X. (2004). Toward a general theory of creativity in advertising: examining the role of divergence. *Marketing Theory*, 4(1–2),31–58.

Sternberg, R.J. (Ed.). (1988). *The nature of creativity: Contemporary psychological perspectives*. Cambridge University Press.

Stuhlfaut, M.W. & Windels, K. (2019) Altered states: The effects of media and technology on the creative process in advertising agencies, *Journal of Marketing Communications*, 25 (1), 1–27, doi:10.1080/13527266.2017.1380069.

Thompson-Whiteside, H. & Turnbull, S. (2021). #Metoovertising: The institutional work of creative women who are looking to change the rules of the advertising game, *Journal of Marketing Management*, 37(1–2),117–143.

Turnbull, S. & Wheeler, C. (2017) The advertising creative process: A study of U.K. agencies. *Journal of Marketing Communications* 23, 2, 176–194.

Vanden Bergh, B.G., Smith, S.J., & Wicks, J.L. (1986) Internal agency relationships: Account services and creative personnel, *Journal of Advertising*, 15 (2), 55–60, doi:10.1080/00913367.1986.10673006.

Venkataramani Johar, G., Holbrook, M.B. & Stern, B.B. (2001) The role of myth in creative advertising design: Theory, process and outcome, *Journal of Advertising*, 30(2), 1–25, doi:10.1080/00913367.2001.10673634.

Wallas, G. (2014 [1926]). *The art of thought*. Tunbridge Wells: Solis Press.

Wang, Yi-jing & Qiao, Yu-meng & Yu, Qin-ye & Wang, Li-feng & Zhao, Kang-yan. (2017). *Research on the impacts of time – Anticipatory stress on creativity*. DEStech Transactions on Social Science, Education and Human Science. 10.12783/dtssehs/icssm2017/10343.

Windels, K., & Lee, W. (2012). The construction of gender and creativity in advertising creative departments. *Gender in Management*, 27 (8), 502–519. https://doi.org/10.1108/17542411211279706.

Windels K., Mallia K.L., & Broyles S.J. (2013). Soft Skills: The difference between leading and leaving the advertising industry? *Journal of Advertising Education*, 17 (2), 17–27. doi:10.1177/109804821301700204..

Windels, K., & Mallia, K. (2015). How being female impacts learning and career growth in advertising creative departments. *Employee Relations*, 37 (1), 122–140. https://doi.org/10.1108/ER-02-2014-0011.

5 Text and image combinations: Print, outdoor, post, meme

1 Introduction

This chapter is dedicated to multimodal advertising that is advertising that creatively combines texts and images to deliver a message to the consumer. For the purposes of this book, multimodal advertising is juxtaposed to multimedia advertising which includes video and audio, and which will be discussed in the next chapter. Before delving into the making of multimodal advertising, let us examine in which touchpoints we may trace such ads.

Print advertisements, the oldest form of paid advertising, appears in newspapers and magazines. Before the web, print advertisements were the only way for an advertiser to demonstrate the product and inform about its attributes and benefits, therefore print advertising combined an informative and persuasive role, aiming to lead the customer to the point of sales. Print ads would typically consist of the following elements, usually in the order that reads the eye: a headline and visual; a body copy, i.e., a text that usually explains the headline, provides product information, and ends with a call-to-action; and the logo with or without an end line (also defined as slogan or tagline). Additional elements could include: more images, free samples, discount coupons, "scratch and sniff" stripes, etc.

The body copy once played a significant role in print advertising. Even though the assumption was that few people read it, the body copy addressed potentially interested readers who needed more information, thus increasing the possibility their curiosity would be triggered so they try the product or seek more information about it at the point of sales. In the era of the web and social media, the print ad serves less as means for information and more as means for awareness, brand image and loyalty. Today the body copy is considered less needed and content marketing activities or native advertising articles are more likely to provide information for products and services. Thus, today, print ads tend to resemble outdoor advertising and include links or QR codes rather than extensive body copies.

Despite a decline facing print media, print advertising is all but obsolete. Testing an idea on print is essential, to discover its robustness. A lot of young creatives focus too much on stories and video ads and then try to deliver such stories in print format. This is difficult. Working the other way round could be more helpful. Creating a script out of a print ad is much easier than creating a print ad out of a script.

DOI: 10.4324/9781003330721-5

Always start by creating print ads for your ideas.

Outdoor advertising, also defined as Out Of Home advertising (OOH) is meant to be placed in public spaces. To attract passers-by, outdoor ads must be single-minded and very clear, containing a very strong visual, the logo, and perhaps a message. The larger their size, the more single-minded their content should be, so that it is understood at a glance. With the advent of social media, outdoor has gained new power, as one may photograph and share creative posters or ambient installations. The poster NIKE created to celebrate the 30th anniversary of "Just do it", with the face of Colin Kaepernick, was seen not only by New Yorkers but also by millions of people on their newsfeeds. More broadly, interactive outdoor installations provide new possibilities for creatives to engage passers-by (indicatively: McCarthy, 2022).

Social media posts also frequently appear to combine visuals with some sort of text, whether that be a caption or a headline or a hashtag or a price tag or a link or a mix of the above. Thus, posts resemble print and outdoor advertising in the sense that their stopping power and memorability rely to a significant extent on image-text creative combinations. Therefore, the tools provided in this chapter also foster creativity for social media posts and multimodal branded content in general.

Display advertising which includes web-banners, skins, or pop-ups among many other display formats, may also benefit from text-image combinations, despite spatial limitations. Search engine advertising on the other hand mostly relies on text to attract attention, having to comply to a lot of limitations imposed by algorithms and space constraints. Text-based ads are more demanding in terms of eloquence and flexibility as the copywriter must constantly examine solutions the algorithm favours and adjust their work accordingly, relying on keyword usage, often at the expense of creativity.

Memes & gifs, whether branded or not, rely on image-text creative combinations as well (Miliopoulou, 2022). The term "meme" was introduced by Dawkins (1976), a biologist who explained how life evolves from simpler to more complex forms, while mutating to face environmental threats. In the last chapter of his book: "The selfish gene", Dawkins introduced an interesting analogy, claiming that culture evolves the same way life does: through sharing, clustering, and mutation (see also: Atran, 2001). In accordance with genes, the basic units of life, Dawkins introduced memes, the basic units of culture which, he argued, spread with imitation (mimesis). Examples of memes are tunes, ideas, catch-phrases, clothes fashions, even scientific ideas spreading in classrooms and conferences (Dawkins, 1976; 2006). A connection between memes and advertising had been noted long before the internet memes emerged (Gelb, 1997). With the proliferation of social media the term "meme" resurfaced. Memes can be studied as chunks of multimodal content spreading either by exact reproduction or through a game of Chinese whispers in which the combined parts mutate while shared, to become reusable or adapt to context (Wu & Ardley, 2007). Simply put, the same image may circulate combined with different captions or headlines; and the same text may circulate combined with different images. This is also the case with gifs. Users express their feelings or mood through memes and gifs (Miltner & Highfield, 2017), while brands use them to tap on popular culture and trends. Therefore, memes and gifs call for creative combinations of texts and images and have great potential if used in marketing communications (Murray et al., 2013).

This chapter focuses on how creative combinations of words or words with images can lead to successful advertising for all the above types of creative execution. The tools that are introduced, are borrowed from semiotics and rhetoric. Chapter 3 examined the process by which people "read" ads, introducing some basic key constructs from semiotics: the sign, denotation & connotation, the metaphor, and encoding & decoding. Using this construct, the chapter presented tools to analyse ads, to understand the process of signification as a meaning making process from advertisers to consumers. In this chapter, we will build on the knowledge and analytic skills that emerged from Chapter 3, we will introduce more semiotic tools, and we will delve in the making of ads. To put it simply, Chapter 3 examined decoding while Chapter 5 examines encoding: the making of signs through creative combinations; the making of multimodal content.

Multimodality is defined as the interplay between different modes of representation. Words and images are such ways to represent (Korhonen, 2009, p. 214) and the way these are combined affects both the encoding and decoding of meaning.

This book proposes learning by imitation, encouraging the reader to delve in discovering figurative language and then use it on three levels: first on the level of wordplay; second on the level of text-image combinations; and third, as a tool to conceive and express broader creative combinations which may pave the way for great ideas. By improving flexibility in the use of language, we can also improve flexibility in our way of thinking, thus combinations that start with words do not need to be confined to the verbal level. Combinational creativity has been studied extensively since the first attempts to define creativity as a skill (Boden, 2003) and it appears in its purest form in print advertising. This chapter, then, uses theoretic constructs that have been deployed to analyse cultural texts, as tools to synthesise, compose, and combine. Anchoring is the first step.

2 Anchoring

The term was introduced by Roland Barthes (1977 [1964]) who observed that text is often used next to images (his focus was on photographs) to confine meaning. Of all possible denoted or connoted interpretations an image could elicit, text would point the viewer towards a desired, specific direction. In advertising, as Barthes argues, the symbolic message does not guide identification but interpretation. The viewer is not asked to recognise what they see but to understand why they see it and what it means to them. By combining images with text, advertising produces symbolic meaning that is accurate and specific on the one hand, richer on the other, thus adding depth and eliminating breadth of rational and emotional interpretations. The headline or tagline of an ad direct the reader through the intended signifieds of the image, so that the reader avoids some and receives others. It "remote-controls" the reader towards a meaning chosen in advance (Barthes, 1977 [1964], pp. 155–157).

To follow the cliché, a picture is a thousand words, but a print ad often wants to narrow it down. Text guides our interpretation of a visual toward a specific direction. A puppy can make us think a million different things, but a puppy next to a headline that reads: "This one will die in the streets" and with an end line that calls us to: "Adopt a stray pet" guides our reading toward the intended meaning and desired action. The image is not left floating in an endless pool of possible meaning. Instead, it is anchored to mean something specific: the need to protect stray animals. Anchoring manages the degree of ambiguity and comprehension (Lagerwerf et al., 2012; Barthes, 1977 [1964]) thus affecting the type and degree of effort required for decoding and interpretation.

In most print ads, it's the text closest to the visual that serves as an anchor; or the only text that appears, even if it is tiny and downplayed somewhere at the bottom. If the text is completely missing, the logo of the brand usually serves as an anchor to help decode the visual(s) and guide the meaning-making process. Anchoring is also observed in television (and thus also video) advertising, where creators use either verbal or visual anchors to guide meaning, ensure comprehension and increase appreciation (van Enschot & Hoeken, 2015). Research has documented that explanatory headlines which completely give away the message of the ad increase comprehension but decrease liking because they deprive consumers from the gratification of interpreting the message (Phillips, 2000).

Art directors pay a lot of attention on the sequence of the elements that appear on a print ad or poster, following how the eye reads. In the western world, people read from top to bottom and from left to right. Therefore, the headline, key visual, body copy, and logo are usually placed for the eye to read in the desired order. Even the oldest ads would have the body copy below the visual because readers are first captured by the visual and then guided to read more. The end line appears at the bottom, often close to the logo.

Copywriters need to provide anchors, especially to complex or abstract visuals. As experience builds up, they should know when to select a very simple headline so as to stream the interpretation of a complex visual, or when to create skilful headlines that carry the weight of an insight combined with a simpler or more ordinary visual. Or when a headline is not needed at all. They should always focus on the need for intrigue and clarity at the same time.

The anchor is the element that holds the ad together. Without it, meaning is easy to miss. Even if one gets what the advertised product is and the call to action, the idea will likely remain elusive. With the anchoring, every other element on the ad contributes to this meaning.

Time to practise!

To trace the anchor, try hiding different elements on any ad, especially textual elements, and see whose absence obscures meaning and the creative idea, leaving the other elements seeming disconnected. Try this on some of the print ads discussed in this chapter or select print ads of your preference. Start with older and more complex ads.

3 Rhetorical figures

Rhetorical figures are among the many devices rhetors use aiming to persuade. A rhetorical figure can be defined as an artful deviation in the form taken by a statement (McQuarrie & Mick, 1996). This deviation is systematic and purposeful. Simply put, figurative language combines words in non-ordinary ways, so that their meaning is larger or more memorable than the sum of its parts. A rhetorical figure can impact its audience in two ways: by how it sounds or reads; and by what it denotes and connotes (McQuarrie & Mick, 1996).

Rhetorical figures can be divided to schemes and tropes. Schemes constitute an artful deviation from the ordinary arrangement of words, while tropes constitute an artful deviation from the principal signification of words (a distinction going at least as far back as De Mille, 1878). Many rhetorical figures have been examined in advertising and taxonomies have been proposed to classify these figures (Scott, 1994; McQuarrie & Mick, 1996; 1999; Phillips & McQuarrie, 2004; Jeong, 2008; Musté et al., 2015; Peterson, 2019). To understand the difference between schemes and tropes, compare two old end lines from two oil companies. The first one is: "Go well, go Shell" and the other one is: "ESSO. Put a tiger in your tank". The first one denotes the qualities of Shell, arranging words eloquently, using repetition and rhyme. The second one transfers the power of a tiger in a car's engine, connoting endurance, and speed, thus connecting to the properties of a less relevant object. Only the second uses a conceptual metaphor, transferring an idea from nature to civilisation.

Advertising is a linguistic and semiotic exchange between producers and consumers (Musté et al., 2015) in which a copywriter plays a key role and must work on two levels. First, they should be able to deliver a message in the most eloquent, unexpected, and memorable way; second, they should be able to conceive and express creative connotations which add value to the brand. When applying divergent thinking, copywriters should explore ideas and figurative language on the connotative, tropical level, experimenting with brand associations. When applying convergent thinking, copywriters should focus on expression and eloquence, engaging in meticulous and relentless editing.

Rhetorical figures are creative enablers, then. A copywriter should be able to identify and use as many as possible, working to maximise eloquence and inspiration. A systematic attempt to create great print advertising, should follow the steps proposed in Chapter 4:

- starting with a thorough study of the brief
- proceeding with free ideation
- taking breaks for incubation; and then
- using rhetorical figures to explore new ideas and to strive for the best possible expression of both denotative and connotative meaning.

3.1 Rhetorical schemes

Table 5.1. presents and defines rhetorical schemes traced in advertising. Though the list is not thorough, it paves the way for countless possibilities to think forward and increase eloquence.

Table 5.1 Rhetorical schemes in advertising

Level	Term	Definition	Example
Phonemes	Alliteration	Repeating the first letter of words in the same sentence (Abrams, 1999)	Dollar Shave Club. Shave time. Shave money.
	Assonance	Repeating the same stressed vowel in adjacent words (Abrams, 1999)	Bounty. The quicker picker upper.
	Consonance	Repeating two or more consonants in adjacent words (Abrams, 1999)	Car brand X. Bolder and wilder.
	Rhyme	Repeating the final syllable of two adjacent words; or the final stressed vowel and all the letters that follow (Abrams, 1999)	Go well, go shell
	Onomatopoeia	Creating words that imitate sounds (Abrams, 1999)	Kellogg's Rice Krispies. Snap! Crackle! Pop
Words	Anaphora	The repetition of a word or phrase at the beginning of successive clauses.	Go well, go shell
	Epistrophe	The repetition of a word or phrase at the end of successive clauses.	The Mail on Sunday. A news paper, not a snooze paper
	Palilogia	Repetition of adjacent word(s)	Energizer. It keeps going and going and going
	Anastrophe	Inversion of adjacent words	Adidas. Impossible is nothing
Clauses	Parallelism	Similar word-order and structure in adjacent clauses (Abrams, 1999)	Harley Davidson. American by birth, rebel by choice
	Antimetabole / Chiasmus	Words repeated in reverse order, in adjacent clauses (Abrams, 1999; Kara-Yakoubian et al., 2022)	Harley Davidson. All for freedom and freedom for all.
	Antithesis (contrast)	Words that have an opposite meaning are used in the same sentence or clause, or in parallelism (Abrams, 1999; McQuarrie & Mick, 1996; Roque, 2017, p. 42).	PlayStation. Live in your world. Play in ours.

There are two reasons why rhetorical schemes are important in advertising. First, messages involving wordplay are more memorable, thus achieving more resonance with less media exposure. Second, if a sentence is perfect and reads seamlessly, then its meaning appears more credible or truthful. McQuarrie & Mick (1996) have argued that: "… a manner in which a statement is expressed may be more important than its propositional content" (p. 424). Kara-Yakoubian et al. (2022) provide a good overview of the established connection between eloquence and aesthetics on the one hand, and truth or credibility on the other hand. Creatively expressed messages appear more believable. What sounds right, feels right.

Often, however, rhetorical schemes are language specific. They do not translate well. "Maybe it's Maybelline" would not work in French or Italian where the word "Maybe" sounds completely different. This is very challenging when adapting global campaigns in local markets where eloquence, and to some extent credibility, might be lost in an effort to preserve meaning (see also: Smith, 2006).

The key question for aspiring copywriters is: can one take a plain statement and keep editing or rephrasing, to bring it to its best possible form? A statement that remains clear and yet sounds unanticipated? A statement that creates words like the "picker-upper" and "the snooze-paper", or gets rid of overused words like "quality" or "new" or "experience" or "taste" … A lot of copywriters might think that once they come up with a good insight or a good idea, then editing is less of a priority and more of a burden. Others may think that instead of finding a great idea, they might as well settle for fancy wordplay. Neither is enough. In advertising, form is as important as content.

Time to practise!

- Find at least 3 print ads or posters for every one of the rhetorical schemes presented above.
- Find at least 3 rhetorical schemes not presented on the above list and create headlines based on these schemes for any brand of your choice.
- Find at least 3 print ads containing rhetorical schemes that you cannot identify using the classification of this chapter. Discuss your views.
- Use a meme generator app, pick a visual, and create a series of memes about exam periods, using at least half of the schemes discussed above.

3.2 Rhetorical tropes

Rhetorical tropes function on the level of connotation rather than denotation, enriching meaning. Rhetorical schemes discussed above, create a sense of regularity, while rhetorical tropes presented below create a sense of irregularity or a sense of upsetting, curiosity, and disorder (McQuarrie & Mick, 1996) thus calling for more effort to decode, more mental and emotional engagement with the ad.

SCAMPER, discussed in Chapter 4, appears to be a way to create rhetorical figures. SCAMPER is a tool that transfers figurative thinking to figurative language. "S", "A", and "P" lead to metaphors, similes, personifications, metonymies. "M" and "E" relate closely to hyperbole and ellipsis, respectively. "R" leads to ironies, contrasts, and paradoxes. SCAMPER though is meant to be not language specific.

Creative thinking paths and patterns might seem finite but lead to countless outcomes and apply in many different contexts, like using a finite number of stencils on different surfaces, with different colours, to create countless designs and combinations. Language is the terrain where these processes come into play.

Theoretic viewpoints: The metaphor

Metaphors have been excessively studied in advertising, to enlighten consumer understandings, educational approaches, as well as strategic requirements. This is because metaphors closely relate to analogic thinking that helps the human mind conceive and convey the tacit and the intangible.

We use metaphors in everyday life to discuss everything from our "tsunami of feelings" to the "filter bubble" we live in. Metaphor is the most widely studied trope, not only in literary studies but also in communication (Berger, 2006, 2010) and in the broader realm of the humanities and social sciences.

Metaphors occur not only on the linguistic and semiotic level but also on the cognitive and psychological operations that involve meaning making in the social sciences (Ricoeur, 1977). The works of Lacan (as discussed in Kelen, 2007, for example) or Foucault or even McLuhan rely on metaphor and analogy to convey abstract constructs. Bricolage is a metaphor that resonates in postmodern contexts (Kelen, 2007). Sociolinguists like Lakoff & Johnson (1980) have connected metaphors to broader cognitive processes, explaining how one idea, or conceptual domain, can be approached using examples or analogies from another idea or conceptual domain, moving from concrete to abstract thinking through analogy.

Truth be told, metaphors mean something quite different to literary scholars, linguists, philosophers, cognitive or social scientists, and communicators and every definition which makes sense in one context could be found lacking in another.

Many tropes are often defined as metaphors in a synecdochic manner (Phillips & McQuarrie, 2004; Kelen, 2007), especially metonymy and synecdoche (Chandler, 2000) but a close analysis of most tropes reveals the

Table 5.2 Rhetorical tropes in advertising

	Term	Definition	Example
Resem-blance	Metaphor	A word or expression that in literal usage denotes one kind of thing is applied to a distinctly different kind of thing, without asserting a comparison (Abrams, 1999). "The essence of metaphor is understanding and experiencing one kind of thing in terms of another" (Lakoff and Johnson, 1980, p. 5).	United Airlines. Fly the friendly skies.
	Simile	A comparison between two different things, clearly indicated by the word "like" or "as" (Abrams, 1999). Simile displays explicitly what a metaphor suggests implicitly (Ricoeur, 1977, p. 30).	Like a good neighbour, State Farm is there.
	Personifica-tion	Giving human attributes or feelings to an inanimate object or an abstract concept (Abrams, 1999; Ricoeur, 1977).	Yellow Pages. Let your fingers do the walking.
	Metonymy	(Greek for "a change of name") One thing is applied to another because experience indicates the two are related (Abrams, 1999; see also: Ricoeur, 1977; Chandler, 2002; Berger, 2010). Metonymy builds on perceived similarity, thus "condenses and gives access to a complex chain of connections" (Rocci et al., 2018).	Orange juice X. Drink fruit Where's the beef? Wendys
	Synecdoche	A part of something is used to signify the whole, or vice versa (Abrams, 1999; Chandler, 2002).	Lubricant X. Let your wheels roll.
	Hyperbole	Bold overstatement or exaggeration (Abrams, 1999) to be used with caution. Overstating product benefits may be deceptive and misleading or lead to unmet expectations (Toncar & Fetscherin, 2012). Hyperbole can make a strong impression, become memorable and liked, when consumers can identify it as such. But it may also be considered puffery or even false if taken at face value (Callister, 2007). Literacy plays a critical role in identifying hyperbole but also in discerning between hyperbolic and misleading advertising.	FedEx. When there's no tomorrow
	Meiosis	Understating; representing something as very much less in magnitude or importance (Abrams, 1999).	Volkswagen. Think small.
	Ellipsis (elimination)	Omitting a word whose meaning or effect is supplied by context (Kelen, 2007, p. 34; Wilson, 2000, p. 18).	Schhh...You-Know-Who. Schweppes
	Pun	A play on words that are identical or similar in sound but diverse in meaning (Abrams, 1999; see also: Myers, 1954; Tanaka, 1994; Goddard, 1998). Pun is language specific, thus hard to translate.	Cats like Felix like Felix.

	Term	Definition	Example
Differ-ence or juxtapo-sition	Irony	The writer expresses a statement which implies a sharply different meaning (Abrams, 1999). A sentence that means the opposite of what it says that may refer to feelings, thoughts or even facts and is always perceived in context (Bredin, 1998; Chandler, 2002). Postmodern advertising uses irony more frequently. Irony requires skill and effort to decode (Andersen, 2003).	No one grows ketchup like Heinz
	Oxymoron	Two words placed together, which are considered contrary in ordinary usage (Abrams, 1999). Usually, an adjective precedes a seemingly opposite word (Shen, 1987).	Ready meals X. Expectedly surprising. Earphones X. Hi fidelity silence.
	Paradox	A statement which seems absurd or contradictory yet may be interpreted in a way that makes sense (Kennedy, 1983; Bredin, 1998; Abrams, 1999), within a specific context.	Samsung. Do what you can't.
	Antithesis	A contrast or opposition in the meanings of contiguous phrases or clauses (Abrams, 1999)	X investors. Because big ideas start small.
	Rhetorical Question	A question that is not meant to be answered but to achieve more expressive force than a direct assertion (Abrams, 1999), often also encountered in competitive advertising (Tellis, 2003, p. 142).	Where do you want to go today? Microsoft

different ways of conceptualising through language thus enabling copywriters to develop more flexibility when exploring different ways to articulate their message.

Thinking through tropical use of language and analogy goes beyond the scope of this book but it is important to acknowledge the interplay of linguistic and cognitive processes in creative advertising. Advertising discourse is becoming more complex as its audiences become savvier and as parity products seek differentiation through claims, messages, taglines, and storytelling.

At the same time, creativity is bound to overcome any proposed taxonomy. Complying to the pre-conceived is all but the aim, and as de Man (1978, p. 29) observes, trying to confine the rhetorical structure of texts in the name of uncritically preconceived text models will always be futile. However, creative copywriting needs enablers to help the mind take different directions.

Metaphors allow for conceptual thinking and emotional expressions thus helping ideas come to life in all realms of life.

Figurative language offers eloquence and adds meaning, thus building brand-consumer connections. Some successful taglines often involve both a scheme and a trope and there is no unanimous approach in defining the dominant figure of speech. Often, the solution lies in the mind of the linguist. However, as one learns to identify figures of speech, they also learn to create them, forcing their writing in different directions that would otherwise not be evident.

Time to practise!

- Find at least 3 print ads or posters for every one of the rhetorical tropes presented above.
- Find at least 3 print ads containing rhetorical tropes that you cannot identify using the classification of this chapter. Discuss your views.
- Trace the key rhetorical figure in the following taglines:

  o BMW. The ultimate driving machine
  o Nike. Just do it
  o Red Bull gives you wings
  o California Milk Processors. Got milk?
  o ADIDAS. Impossible is nothing
  o Avis. We are number two, but we try harder
  o Victoria's Secret: A Body for Every Body.
  o Audi. Truth in Engineering
  o Castlemaine XXXX. Australians wouldn't give a XXXX for anything else.
  o KFC. Finger licking good.
  o Pacific Bell. Phone out of service? Give us a call.
  o Our Most Important Package is Yours. FedEx
  o Avis. We are number two, but we try harder

- Create at least two alternatives for each of the following taglines, using tropes:

  o Go well, go shell
  o Energizer. It keeps going and going and going
  o PlayStation. Live in your world. Play in ours.

- Rewrite the following taglines, keeping their meaning but changing their schemes or tropes:

  o Disneyland. The happiest place on earth
  o Toyota. Let's go places
  o United Airlines. Fly the friendly skies
  o Sprite. Obey your thirst

- Read the article by E. Brant on BBC (Oct. 9, 2014) titled: So Red Bull doesn't actually "give you wings (https://www.bbc.com/news/newsbeat-29550003). Discuss the implications of metaphor and/or hyperbole in this campaign.

The next section examines how rhetorical tropes can lead to combinational creativity in multimodal texts which include both words and images. Such tropes might be easier to adapt in different languages if there is cultural relevance.

4 Visual rhetoric and combinational creativity

Visual objects are rhetorical objects which can be used to influence and persuade people as effectively as rhetorical oratory (Danesi, 2017). Visual signs shape cultural understanding on a global level, even though there are cultural differences in the way visual cues are interpreted (Bulmer & Buchanan-Oliver, 2006). Visuals interact with their cultural context through symbolism and representation, shaping the way individuals understand the world, and have profound effects in building brands or changing brand image (Combe et al., 2003). There is no media literacy without visual literacy.

From a copywriter's point of view, language often stands alone to convey powerful messages (like a tagline on a company's branded truck); or language can stand next to visuals, providing an anchor while enriching their meaning. Imagine a photo of a group of homeless people under a bridge and a headline that reads: "Who does not love hanging out with friends every night?" The contrast between what the headline claims and what the picture shows, makes the reader part of the problem of homelessness: while each of us, the readers, are having fun, some people are suffering. Making the reader part of the problem might also mean they will consider becoming part of the solution, contributing to the NGO that airs such a print ad. In this case, the contrasting combination between words and images creates all the impact of the ad. The headline alone would be an empty statement while the visual alone would be sad but, more likely, less engaging.

Text-image synergy is fundamental in creative advertising. In traditional marketing studies, the term synergy is used to define the fruitful interplay of integrated marketing activities, which produces greater outcomes compared to isolated initiatives (Belch & Belch, 2017; Naik & Raman, 2003). In visual rhetoric, however, synergy defines visual-verbal combinations whose total is larger than the sum of its parts. This type of synergy is discussed in the context of visual rhetoric and visual studies (indicatively: Scott, 1994; Martinec & Salway, 2005); is relevant to combinational creativity and helps create unique print advertising.

Table 5.3. presents rhetorical tropes deployed in multimodal advertising texts, where the trope needs both text and visual, to be complete.

Typologies of visual rhetoric in advertising have mostly been studied from a consumer perspective, focusing on the processes of decoding and on consumer appreciation (Scott, 1994; McQuarrie & Mick, 1996; 1999; Phillips & McQuarrie, 2004; Jeong, 2008; Peterson, 2019). Using these to create multimodal advertising content can help creatives – both copywriters and art directors – expand their thinking. Visual tropes can be more persuasive when presenting a significant argument that adds to consumers' understanding of the product's function and meaning; or by delivering a message in ways that are more eloquent and therefore more

Table 5.3 Rhetorical tropes combining words and images

	Term	Example
Resemblance – enhanced or clarified meaning	Metaphor	Surfrider Foundation Headline: What goes in the ocean, goes in you. Visual: two pieces of sushi wrapped in plastic instead of seaweed.
	Personification	M&Ms Headline: "I know people undress me in their minds. Chocolate… Peanut… That's what they see" Visual: The blue M&M character, lying in a sea of M&Ms.
	Metonymy	Absolut Headline: Absolut security. Visual: The Absolut bottle tied up with a chain and a locker.
	Hyperbole	WWF Headline: Don't buy exotic animal souvenirs Visual: A woman dragging her suitcase inside an empty airport. The suitcase is leaving a huge trail of blood
	Ellipsis	WWF Double page spread. On the left side, a shark's fin in open sea. Headline: Horrifying. On the right side, open sea, no fin. Headline: More horrifying.
Difference or juxtaposition – enriched or contradictory meaning	Irony	WWF Headline: Fashion Claims More Victims than you think Visual: A leopard and their cub in a jungle, each with a size tag. XL for the leopard and S for the cub.
	Paradox	AXE Headline: The Cleaner You are, The Dirtier You Get Visual: two side-by side images of the same person, through the same perspective, in the shower. On one image the person is applying soap, on the other image the person is applying whip cream.
	Antithesis	Volkswagen EOS Headline: The Eos. The coupé-cabriolet by Volkswagen. Open. Closed. Visual: Two umbrellas on a neutral background. One is open and one is closed.

memorable and convincing (Scott, 1994; Jeong, 2008). Visual rhetoric can also bring to life consumer insights.

In advertising, combinational creativity can also be traced in ads which present a composition of visuals – even without any text. In such cases, a copywriter must carefully study the synthesis and experiment with different types of messages. Sometimes all that is needed is a discrete anchor with no excessive wordplay. In other cases, the copywriter and art director may decide that no message is needed because all conceivable interpretations of the visual point toward desired directions. In general, the more complex a visual, the more essential the use of a clear and simple anchor to ensure the message is clear and single minded. And, on the other hand, most times, the more elaborate or complex a headline is, the simpler the visual one should aim for.

Combinational creativity (Boden, 2003; 2010) involving tropes can also be of great use when designing creative outdoor or ambient installations as well. Just imagine any rhetoric trope whose first part is space where an ad could be placed, and the other part is the message, verbal, visual, or both. Here are some examples:

- Life is too short for the wrong job: https://www.designboom.com/design/jobsintown-campaign-life-is-too-short-for-the-wrong-job/
- Kit Kat Breaker Benches: https://www.adforum.com/creative-work/ad/player/34530937/breaker-benches/kit-kat
- Movie poster for Bram Stoker's Dracula: https://www.adweek.com/creativity/this-bloody-clever-dracula-ad-gets-creepier-as-the-sun-goes-down/

By exploring and re-imagining space, creative combinations can emerge through the transferring of unexpected elements from the site to the ad and vice versa; or through the transformation of existing elements on site. The right message will anchor the intervention and make it appear purposeful and meaningful, provided it is created with respect to the site and the people.

Time to practise!

- Try to come up with at least 5 visuals for a print ad promoting recycling, whose headline is: "Give them a second life" signed by the London Rubbish Collection.
- Try to write at least 5 headlines for a print ad promoting the adoption of stray pets, whose main visual is a rubber toy.
- Choosing different angles and insights, find at least 10 headlines promoting inclusion of disabled people, for a print ad with an illustration of the steadfast tin soldier. Read the fairy-tale.
- Find at least 10 unexpected places where you could promote a mobile provider's 5G offering. Consider designing an installation or modifying an area, not just adding a visual and a tagline. Create at least 2 different messages for each one of your ideas.
- Create 10 memes that convey a message against animal abuse.
- In the first five, select a visual and then write headlines leading to multimodal tropes.
- In the next five, create intriguing messages and look for visuals leading to multimodal tropes.

5 Copywriters and art directors in tandem: working in a creative ad agency

Putting words and images together and creating a total that is larger than the sum of its parts is the epitome of creative advertising. Such combinations, however, often benefit from two brains rather than just one.

In the traditional creative agency, copywriters usually work with art directors, either in steady, long-lasting pairs serving one or more clients, or in ad hoc pairings for specific tasks. For every word that appears, or not, on a print ad the copywriter bears responsibility; and for every visual or design element, responsibility falls on the art director. In this context, one would expect the copywriter to come up with headlines and taglines, and the art director to come up with visuals and design elements. Quite often, however, a copywriter could think of an interesting visual, or an art director could come up with a headline. The way two creative skillsets work together is defined in terms of responsibility toward the brief, not in terms of allocating tasks in a confining and restrictive way.

A steady pair of a copywriter and an art director goes through the four stages of group development (Tuckman, 1965). During the stage of forming, they explore each other's personality and style, as well as their views on creative work, the agency, clients, etc. During the stage of storming, they try to not only create ideas and respond to briefs but also to explore each other's thinking patterns and explicit or implicit usage of creative techniques, aesthetic preferences and more. During the stage of norming, they discuss each work thoroughly, implicitly determining their standards and ways of collaboration. Finally, during the stage of performing, they start delivering work to the best of their potential. This is indeed exciting and fulfilling as they end up communicating in more ways than just talking or sketching or writing. They share common connotations, developing a feeling of profound tacit understanding, and complementing one another. This is what the pair and their surroundings might experience as magic. However, a steady pair might have a more turbulent relationship in which power play inhibits one of the two, criticism prevents openness, or group think makes both members become more defensive and less receptive to outside feedback. This depends on personalities, thinking styles, seniority, even on the life stage of each professional. Without trying, however, nobody can know which pair will deliver. Experimental pairing is essential especially during the first stages of a creative professional's career in advertising. Even more so, a great pair might experience fatigue at some point. Therefore, steady pairs and ad hoc pairings are both needed within an agency.

When copywriters start thinking by browsing images or art directors seek the perfect anchor for their visual; when a pair first comes together and explore ways to collaborate; when pressure escalates or when personalities collide, maintaining an efficient and productive working relationship is very important. But it takes two to tango. Regardless of seniority, experience, or any other skillset, the one who manages to foster such a relationship ends up having a leading role. To succeed, one must re-visit the essentials of interpersonal communication: great listening skills, empathy, openness, and acceptance as well as a strong focus on results and on the professional aspects of the relationship. Creative ideas and their critical assessment will not emerge in any other way. Last but not least, within a pair, both members need to combine individual thinking with team storming. Each should have their time alone to browse, explore, ideate, study, form some initial ideas and then get together to share, expand, contribute and combine; or they could work the other way round: start with a discussion or a storming session and then process individually the raw material that emerged. Either way, this back-and-forth is necessary for both, to make the most of their potential.

To this date pairs are the most frequent arrangement within creative departments. However, the advent of new media has brought new opportunities. Some digital agencies have added a developer (defined here as a professional who writes code) creating teams of three, usually ad hoc, to develop websites, applications, or other digital projects. Furthermore, as copywriters learn to use design software and cultivate their visual skills; and as designers explore their visual literacy and multimodal capabilities, the traditional pairing is often questioned even if still prevailing (Kay, 2021; Watson, 2020).

Copywriters are now needed in many more areas and activities. For example, search engine advertising requires the skills of a copywriter who often works individually, using a multitude of data about the product, the offering, the intended target group, as well as data about previous responses to key words or phrasings, trends regarding the use of tags or hashtags or metadata etc. This type of copywriting strengthens eloquence and flexibility. One must learn to construct successful headlines and calls to action tailored to specific campaign requirements and to specific algorithmic imperatives. However, concept, idea generation, and storytelling are somewhat left behind.

New options for copywriters also appear in the areas of content marketing. Copywriters are asked to develop content for websites or social media accounts. Such content has a broad range, from long-form articles and native advertising all the way to social media posts and offers. This line of work often matches traditional advertising skills with broader editorial activity, thus helping professionals acquire eloquence and a lot of knowledge in many different types of content.

In many markets, entry level jobs requesting or cultivating copywriting skills often revolve around web and social media. Thus, a young professional might work as a content manager or community manager for some time and then explore two options. One option is to stay and progress in this line of work, another could be to join a creative team.

References

Abrams, M.H. (1999). *A glossary of literary terms*. Heinle & Heinle, Thomson Learning.

Andersen, L.P. (2003). Ironic branding? The concept of ironic selling propositions in Danish TV-ADS. *European Advances in Consumer Research*, 6, 121–126.

Atran, S. (2001). The trouble with memes: inference versus imitation in cultural creation. *Human Nature: An Interdisciplinary Biosocial Perspective*, 12 (4), 351–381. https://doi.org/10.1007/s12110-001-1003-0.

Barthes, R. (1977) *Image, music, text.* London: Fontana Press.

Belch, G.E., & Belch, M.A. (2017). *Advertising and promotion: Integrated marketing communications perspective* (11th). New York: McGraw-Hill Education.

Berger, A.A. (2006). *50 Ways to understand communication: A guided tour of key ideas and theorists in communication, media, and culture.* Rowman & Littlefield.

Berger, A.A. (2010). *The objects of affection: Semiotics and consumer culture* (1st ed., Ser. Semiotics and popular culture). Palgrave Macmillan

Boden, M. (2003). *The creative mind: Myths and mechanisms.* 2ndLondon: Routledge.

Boden, M. (2010). *Creativity and art: Three roads to surprise.* Oxford University Press.

Bredin, H. (1998). Ironies and paradoxes. *The Paideia Archive: Twentieth World Congress of Philosophy*, 21, 1–5. https://doi.org/10.5840/wcp20-paideia199821376.

Bulmer, S. & Buchanan-Oliver, M. (2006). Visual rhetoric and global advertising imagery. *Journal of Marketing Communications*, 12 (1), 49–61.

Callister, M.A. & Stern, L.A. (2007). The role of visual hyperbole in advertising effectiveness, *Journal of Current Issues & Research in Advertising*, 29 (2), 1–14, doi:10.1080/10641734.2007.10505212.

Chandler, D. (2000) *Semiotics for beginners.* University of Wales, Aberystwyth, Wales.

Chandler, D. (2002) *Semiotics: The basics* (1st edn). London: Routledge.

Combe, I., Crowther, D., & Greenland, S. (2003). The semiology of changing brand image. *Journal of Research in Marketing and Entrepreneurship*, 5(1), 1–24. https://doi.org/10.1108/14715200380001277.

Costello, F.J. & Keane, M.T. (2000). Efficient creativity: Constraint-guided conceptual combination, *Cognitive Science*, 24 (2), 299–349.

Danesi, M. (2017). Visual rhetoric and semiotic. *Oxford Research Encyclopedia of Communication.* Retrieved 1 Feb. 2022, from https://oxfordre.com/communication/view/10.1093/acrefore/9780190228613.001.0001/acrefore-9780190228613-e-43.

Dawkins, R. (1976). *The selfish gene.* Oxford University Press.

Dawkins, R. (2006). Richard Dawkins on meme, YouTube video available at: https://www.youtube.com/watch?v=TRggkkAIC5A.

de Man, P. (1978). The epistemology of metaphor. *Critical Inquiry*, 5 (1), 13–30.

De Mille, J. (2018). The elements of rhetoric. Harper. Retrieved December 16, 2022, from http://online.canadiana.ca/view/oocihm.06019.

Gelb, B.D. (1997). Creating "memes" while creating advertising. *Journal of Advertising Research*, 37 (6), 57–59.

Goddard, A. (1998). *The language of advertising.* Routledge.

Jeong, S.H. (2008) Visual metaphor in advertising: Is the persuasive effect attributable to visual argumentation or metaphorical rhetoric?, *Journal of Marketing Communications*, 14:1, 59–73, doi:10.1080/14697010701717488.

Kara-Yakoubian, M., Walker, A.C., Sharpinskyi, K., Assadourian, G., Fugelsang, J.A., & Harris, R.A. (2022). Beauty and truth, truth and beauty: chiastic structure increases the subjective accuracy of statements. *Canadian Journal of Experimental Psychology/Revue Canadienne De Psychologie Expérimentale*, 76 (2), 144–155.

Kay, B. (2021, 29/11). Art director vs copywriter? The ad industry has long paired two creatives in the roles of art director and copywriter, but how do the positions divide up in the modern industry? *Creative Review.* Available at: https://www.creativereview.co.uk/art-director-vs-copywriter-advertising-creatives/.

Kelen, C. (2007). *An introduction to rhetorical terms* (Ser. Humanities insights). Humanities-Ebooks LLC.

Kennedy, X.J. (1983). *Literature: An Introduction to Fiction, Poetry and Drama*. New York: Longman Publishers.

Kohn, N.W., Paulus, P.B. & Korde, R.M. (2011) Conceptual combinations and subsequent creativity, *Creativity Research Journal*, 23 (3), 203–210. doi:10.1080/10400419.2011.595659.

Korhonen, V. (2009) Dialogic literacy: A sociocultural literacy learning approach. In: Lloyd, A., Talja, S., & Charles Sturt (Eds.) *Practising information literacy: bringing theories of learning, practice and information literacy together*. Centre for Information Studies, Charles Sturt University, pp. 211–226.

Lakoff, G. and Johnson, M. (1980). *Metaphors we live by*. University of Chicago Press.

Lagerwerf, L.L., van Hooijdonk, C.M.J., & Korenberg, A. (2012). Processing visual rhetoric in advertisements: Interpretations determined by verbal anchoring and visual structure, *Journal of Pragmatics*, 44 (13), 1836–1852.

Martinec, R., & Salway, A. (2005). A system for image-text relations in new (and old) media. *Visual Communication*, 4 (3), 337–371.

McCarthy, J. (2022, December 13). 6 clever OOH campaigns that embraced extrasensory ideas. *The Drum*. Available at: https://www.thedrum.com/news/2022/12/13/6-clever-ooh-campaigns-embraced-extrasensory-ideas.

McQuarrie, E.F. & Mick, D.G. (1996) Figures of rhetoric in advertising language, *Journal of Consumer Research*, 22 (4), 424–438, https://doi.org/10.1086/209459.

McQuarrie, E.F. & Mick, D.G. (1999). Visual Rhetoric in Advertising: Text-interpretive, experimental, and reader-response analyses, *Journal of Consumer Research*, 26 (1), 37–54, https://doi.org/10.1086/209549.

McQuarrie, E.F. & Phillips, B.J. (2008) *Go figure! New directions in advertising rhetoric*. Armonk, NY: Sharpe.

Miliopoulou, G. Z. (2022). *Memes in class? Using multimodal texts to feed open-ended creativity. 100 Ideas for Active Learning*.

Miltner, K. M. & Highfield, T. (2017). Never gonna gif you up: Analyzing the cultural significance of the animated gif. *Social media and Society*, 3 (3). https://doi.org/10.1177/2056305117725223.

Murray, N., Manrai, A., & Manrai, L. (2013). Memes, memetics and marketing: A state-of-the-art review and a lifecycle model of meme management in advertising. In Moutinho, L., Bigné, E., & Manrai, A.K. (Eds.) *The Routledge companion to the future of marketing* (1st ed.). Routledge. https://doi.org/10.4324/9780203103036.

Musté, Paloma, Stuart, K., & Botella, A. (2015). Linguistic choice in a corpus of brand slogans: repetition or variation, *Procedia – Social and Behavioral Sciences*, 198, 350–358. https://doi.org/10.1016/j.sbspro.2015.07.454.

Myers, G. (1994). *Words in ads* (Ser. Routledge, Chapman and Hall). E. Arnold.

Naik, P. A., & Raman, K. (2003). Understanding the impact of synergy in multimedia communications. *Journal of Marketing Research*, 40 (4), 375–388.

Peterson, M.O. (2019) Aspects of visual metaphor: an operational typology of visual rhetoric for research in advertising, *International Journal of Advertising*, 38:1, 67–96, doi:10.1080/02650487.2018.1447760.

Phillips, B. J. (2000). The impact of verbal anchoring on consumer response to image ads, *Journal of Advertising*, 29 (1), 15–24, doi:10.1080/00913367.2000.10673600.

Phillips, B.J., & McQuarrie, E.F. (2004). Beyond visual metaphor: a new typology of visual rhetoric in advertising. *Marketing Theory*, 4(1–2), 113–136. https://doi.org/10.1177/1470593104044089.

Ricoeur, P. (1977 [1975]). *The Rule of Metaphor: The creation of meaning in language.* University of Toronto Press

Rocci, A., Mazzali-Lurati, S., & Pollaroli, C. (2018). The argumentative and rhetorical function of multimodal metonymy. *Semiotica*, (220), 123–153. https://doi.org/10.1515/sem-2015-0152.

Roque, G. (2017). In Tseronis, A. and Forceville, C. *Multimodal argumentation and rhetoric in media genres.* John Benjamin's Publishing Company, pp. 25–50.

Scott, L. M. (1994). Images in advertising: the need for a theory of visual rhetoric. *Journal of Consumer Research*, 21 (2), 252–273.

Shen, Y. (1987). On the structure and understanding of poetic oxymoron. *poetics today*, 8 (1), 105–122. https://doi.org/10.2307/1773004.

Smith, K. (2006). Rhetorical figures and the translation of advertising headlines. *Language and Literature*, 15 (2),159–182. doi:10.1177/0963947006063745.

Sternberg, R.J. (ed.) (1988), *The nature of creativity: Contemporary psychological perspectives.* Cambridge: Cambridge University Press.

Sternberg, R.J. (ed.) (1999), *Handbook of creativity.* Cambridge: Cambridge University Press.

Tanaka, L.K. (1994). *Advertising language: A pragmatic approach to advertisements in Britain and Japan. Routledge.*

Tellis, G.J. (2003) *Effective advertising: Understanding when, how, and why advertising works.* Sage.

Toncar, M., & Fetscherin, M. (2012). A study of visual puffery in fragrance advertising. *European Journal of Marketing*, 46(1–2),52–72. https://doi.org/10.1108/03090561211189239/.

Tuckman, B.W. (1965). Developmental sequence in small groups. *Psychological Bulletin*, 63 (6), 384–399.

van Enschot, R. & Hoeken, H. (2015) The occurrence and effects of verbal and visual anchoring of tropes on the perceived comprehensibility and liking of tv commercials, *Journal of Advertising*, 44 (1), 25–36, doi:10.1080/00913367.2014.933688..

Watson, I. (2020/30/11). Just the two of us: how creative duos are surviving remote working. *The Drum.* Available at: https://www.thedrum.com/news/2020/11/30/just-the-two-us-how-creative-duos-are-surviving-remote-working.

Wilson, P. (2000). *Mind the gap: ellipsis and stylistic variation in spoken and written English* (Ser. Textual explorations). Longman.

Wu, Y. & Ardley, B. (2007). Brand strategy and brand evolution: Welcome to the world of the meme. *The Marketing Review*, 7 (3), 301–310. DOI: https://doi.org/10.1362/146934707X230112.

6 Storytelling: Creating TV, radio, and video ads

1 Introduction

Approaching storytelling as creative manipulation of narrative elements and patterns, this chapter discusses what theory reveals and how such knowledge can inform the practice of advertising storytelling that viewers will see on TV or online or will listen to on the radio.

Once upon a time, TV held immense and immersive power by combining what Roberts (2005) defined as SiSoMo (Sight, Sound, Motion). Creativity combined with great production values has given us advertising stories that remain popular after decades. Radio advertising, on the other hand, creates stories using sound and has proven to be quite influential, especially in localised contexts, building brands, promoting offers, and helping top-of-mind awareness.

TV and radio advertising are disseminated differently in each country. Media landscapes change by the hour both globally and locally. Consumers often watch more than one screen at the same time, and get exposed to advertising content from multiple sources, which is one more reason why advertising should be creative, resonant, and captivating thus overcoming content overload and the unpleasant feelings of interruption and repetition that consumers often experience.

Even more so, in the context of integrated communications and interactive new media, storytelling should be easy to adapt for different media requirements. One story could appear edited in different ways; with different durations; be disseminated on different platforms; be fractured in multiple chapters; enable the creation of similar other stories; transform for video or audio executions; or call for interactive responses and user generated content.

Storytelling remains the most powerful way to draw users in a world where they not only enjoy experiences and identification but also participate, create, and share stories. This helps both sales and building brand image. Storytelling helps align human experience of events, human values, and the understanding of facts, holding immense persuasive power.

DOI: 10.4324/9781003330721-6

2 Narrative theory: a brief overview

The purpose of this section is to provide some basic works of narrative theory used in the study of advertising before delving in specific tools that have been selected to assist with the making of advertising stories.

A narrative can be broadly defined as a "representation of an event or a series of events" (Abbott, 2002, p. 13). By creating, consuming, and sharing narratives, by placing facts in some sequence, individuals make sense of events, combine, connect, seek cause-effect relations, and interpret their experiences, including brand-related ones (Escalas, 2004). Narratives shape and convey the way one sees the world (Abbott, 2002). Narrative is less about the events and more about how the narrator selected or omitted, arranged, and connected these events in a way that "makes sense" to their audience. Through stories individuals share meanings and align feelings.

In a series of academic exchanges and fruitful influences, narrative theory was shaped when Russian formalism met French structuralism (indicatively: Degeorge, 1977). Meticulous analyses of narrative forms, patterns, archetypes, and contexts led to important contributions regarding the functions and roles of narrative. Aristotle's Poetics was the starting point.

Formalism shed light on the structure of narratives, the perspectives of different narrators and the meaning making processes in which narrators and narratees engage. How plots are crafted, how patterns emerge (Herman et et al., 2005, p. ix), how archetypes are shaped (Herman et al., 2005, p. 26–27; Frye, 1957), and how the narrator shapes the perspective of their narratee were key interests of the modern narratologists.

Yet, it took a few more decades to combine narrative theory with popular culture; to move beyond art and literature and touch upon film, comics, news, or advertising. Following the broader trend of using literary tools to analyse advertising, scholars have applied narrative constructs to explore the structure and effects of advertising at large (indicatively: Vestergaard and Schrøder 1985; Stern, 1988, 1991, 1993; Berger, 2015; 1997; Goldman and Papson 2000; 1994; Goldman 1994; 1992). Since then, narrative theory has been used to study brand storytelling and its connection with consumers (Elliott & Wattanasuwan, 1998; Escalas, 2004, Jensen, 2007; Rossiter, 2008; Brown & Patterson, 2010; Fog et al., 2010; Herskovitz & Crystal, 2010; Chiu et al., 2012; Dion & Mazzalovo, 2016). Advertising storytelling remains prominent in brand communication (Joo et al., 2016; Fossen & Schweidel, 2016; Pauwels et al., 2016; Liaukonyte et al., 2015; Lim et al., 2015). Even within the postmodern setting of bricolage and fluidity, structuralism provides tools that help us understand and make stories. However, narrative theory has not sufficiently been used to help conceive and develop advertising stories which are both creative and strategically appropriate. The next section presents tools that can help copywriters develop their skills in advertising storytelling.

To this end, stories are approached as backbones or skeletons, on which visual, textual, or audio elaboration will add quality and aesthetic value which will be achieved during the development of the script and then during the production stage. When thinking of stories and writing scripts, what matters are the narrative elements that hold the entire narrative together:

- The key conflict of the story
- The roles around this key conflict
- The plot that emerges as the roles are played and create events
- The arrangement and sequence of events in time
- The storyteller's point of view and potential involvement in the story.

These elements are discussed in the next section. The left side presents theoretic guidance while the right side connects with creative strategy thus guiding the making of new stories.

3 Narrative tools

Table 6.1 Narrative theory in advertising practice

Narrative theory elements	Instructions for advertising stories
1 Conflict	
Every story emerges from conflict. Conflict lies at the heart of every narrative. A narrative starts from an equilibrium, entails disequilibrium, and concludes with a re-established equilibrium (Porter Abbott, 2020, pp. 61–72; Todorov, 1968; Propp, 1971 [1928]). According to Brooks & Warren (1959, p. 172, also cited in Herman et al., 2005, p. 83), conflict is the element that links characters with the plot. Advertising stories always touch upon conflict. For example, in "problem-solution" advertising or in "slice-of-life" advertising (Drewniany & Jewler, 2014, p. 190) discussed later in this chapter, the consumer faces a problem that the product solves, offering a benefit such as convenience or popularity. But there are also narratives touching upon social conflict like the Nike 'Equality' advert which need not even have a linear plot or appear as a series of events.	At the heart of the creative brief lies the key proposition or main message (Altstiel et al., 2023). For creative ideas to be strategically appropriate, the key proposition should become the conflict of an ad story. Converting the main message to express conflict; expressing the main message as a metaphor or analogy; reconceptualising the main message so it can be conceived as a conflict; or connecting the message with broader cultural, personal, or social conflict (Holt, 2004) should be the start of creative thinking and help assess first ideas in terms of strategic appropriateness. Ensuring that the conflict of the story reflects the main message of the creative brief is of primary importance because this is the only way to create a story that will be strategically appropriate to achieve communication objectives, even if it appears to deviate from anticipated typologies. This exploration may include figurative thinking as discussed in the previous chapter. The savvier audiences become, the more implicit and tacit the advertising message, then; the more the demand for cultural reference; and the more intense the need to borrow from context in a figurative way.

2   Roles

Building on the work of Propp (1971 [1928]), Greimas (2002 [1966]) introduced the actantial model. Greimas suggested that there are six roles in total, that anything or anyone can play in a narrative, thus advancing the plot.

1   The hero is the one whose task is to solve the conflict.

2   The trophy awaits the hero if s/he succeeds.

3   The helper supports the hero's actions.

4   The adversary obstructs the hero.

5   The benefactor is the one who creates the conflict thus benefitting the narratee by offering the narrative.

6   The beneficiary benefits from the hero's actions (Greimas, 2002 [1966]).

A narrative may contain less than six roles but never more. Whoever or whatever advances the plot, plays one of these six roles.

In storytelling, roles should be considered before the plot because different characters will respond to the same event in different ways, thus taking the plot to different directions (Herman et al., 2005, p. 25).

Fog et al. (2010) have explained how this model may apply in various aspects of brand storytelling. They align the actantial model with different types of brand narratives, involving the brand as well as stakeholders or consumers. Combined with personas, the study and exploration of roles might help the creative team bring the target group to life (Herskovitz & Crystal, 2010).

Even more so, thinking of roles helps creatives go beyond plots and plot twists to conceive more abstract and symbolic, less linear narratives.

Although the actantial model relies only on six roles, there are infinite ways to engage the brand and the consumer, or their symbolic representations, around a conflict. So, once there is a conflict, it is the roles that will bring it to life, including everyday people, celebrities, objects, or symbols.

Literally or figuratively; realistically or symbolically, these roles should include a representation of the target group's traits and insights, to create resonance and identification.

In traditional advertising, there are well-traced pairs of roles involving products and consumers. Frequently, the hero is the consumer, and the brand is the helper, for example. However, there is a multitude of examples of different role distributions. In the Perrier 1991 ad titled: "Le Lion"[1], the consumer is the hero, and the product is the trophy. In the Spike Jonze IKEA 2002 lamp commercial, the hero is an old lamp thrown in the street; the consumer and her home are the trophy; and the new IKEA lamp is the adversary.

The brand or branded offering might not play a role at all. This could be the copywriter's choice, but one should consider different parameters beyond the creative idea, including the product category, the product life cycle, and the intensity of the competition. The interplay between potential roles, realistic or symbolic, involving the product or not, is a source of endless inspiration.

3   Plot & timing

The narrative plot has been discussed through many theoretic frameworks (indicatively: Booker, 2006; Brown & Patterson, 2010). A flexible way to define and create plots is chosen here, which goes back to Aristotle and has been developed by Freytag (2008 [1900]). According to this approach, every narrative starts with the exposition: an introductory stage in which the narratee discovers the setting and some roles. At this stage, the conflict emerges.

Defining the most appropriate plot may seem easy. Most stories emerge as a rough plot during thinking or brainstorming. However, and despite limits in the overall duration of a video ad, the creative team should not be confined to simple and linear plots.

The most effective way to begin defining a plot is not to follow events but to start by deciding which event will constitute the climax. This is where the hero's conflict reaches its peak, hence it may be the right place for the product to appear, like in slice-of-life commercials; or for the value to manifest itself, like in the Apple 1984 commercial[2]; or for the twist to emerge, like in the tabasco 1997 mosquito commercial.

During the second stage, the rising action, events caused by the conflict build up, escalating, creating tension, and preparing for the next stage.

Climax, the third stage, is the turning point, one in which the conflict reaches a peak and the hero's challenge reaches the maximum, thus changing fate. It becomes clear that the previous order will never be restored, and a major change is required to re-establish an equilibrium.

During the fourth stage, falling action, this change occurs, often appearing as a solution or as a "Deus ex machina". The conflict is resolved, the tension gradually eases, and the outcome becomes clearer.

Denouement, the fifth stage, is when a new sense of order is re-established. Things return to a new normal whether this is a 'happy end' as with popular fiction or a 'katharsis' in the case of ancient drama (Hall, 2017).

Such a plot scheme usually assumes that events are presented in a linear, chronological order. However, the storyteller can manipulate time (Genette, 1966; 1972; 1987) to maximise tension.

Narrative time is defined by three elements: order, duration, and frequency (Genette, 1972; 1966; see also: Chatman, 1974).

- A narrator may change the order of events for various purposes, among which the manipulation of the narratee's emotions. Analepse is the narration of an event that has happened in the past. Prolepse is the narration of an event which will happen in the future.

- Duration focuses on the proportional difference between the time an event lasted and the time it lasts within a specific narrative. A narrator may dedicate little time to long lasting events and vice versa.

- Frequency suggests that a narrator may refer to the same event more than once, or to many events just once (Genette, 1972). The narrator chooses the sequence and order of events, to manipulate the narratee's emotions and maximize the effects of narration.

After defining the climax, the best way to proceed is to determine the rising action and the falling action. Then, proceed by considering the exposition and the denouement.

Once a linear plot is clear, it's time to experiment on the narrative sequence, thus managing time. Could we start in medias res like the Pepsi 'Uncle Drew' video ads[3] who reveal that the old man thriving among teens in a New Jersey court is in fact a well-known NBA celebrity? Should we have a story within the story, like a product demo? Which choice will give a better twist?

Then comes duration: the creative team may choose a slow rising action and a rapid falling action as is the case of IKEA lamp, or vice versa.

If a commercial does not revolve around a storyline but includes multiple stories or moments, then their sequence and duration should also be considered. Watch the Coca-Cola 2016 'Under Pressure' commercial in which moments of failure and tension are presented in the rising action, a bottle opens in the climax and then, in the falling action, the same stories re-appear this time converted to moments of success or resolution. In this case, there is a balance between the rising and falling action.

Even when an ad appears as an abstract bricolage of images, the five stages should be considered. Not all video advertising is a linear story, but every video ad is a narrative. Maintaining the stages of the plot helps maximise tension and engagement.

An example of how a simple narrative incorporates the five stages of the plot is the Southern Comfort 'Whatever's comfortable' advertisement in which filming helps viewers understand that the climax is the point where the hero turns and leaves the screen, and the solution comes when he re-enters the frame holding a glass, doing what he considers 'comfortable'. Music and camera angles can help convey the rising action, the climax and falling action, for ads that do not rely on plot.

In advertising the denouement is always the last scene in which the brand signs and manifests its presence. This is often called a pack-shot, even when the "pack" is not actually there. Considering the last shot as denouement comes with theoretic implications, as denouement re-establishes the new order of things, in which the brand finds its place. At this stage, one should consider whether the denouement could be separate from the falling action, a distinct shot, or appear while action continues, on the background.

4 The storyteller

The distinction between the story as content and the narration as an act brings to light the role of the narrator. The narrator is a medium conveying a story to their audience (Genette, 1972, p. 256; Chatman, 1978; Onega and Landa, 1996). Narrators could tell their own story (autodiegesis); or the story of someone else, in which they played a role (homodiegesis); or even a story they took no part in (heterodiegesis). A story might have more than one narrator or even incorporate smaller narratives that shed light to events (Genette, 1972).

A narrative may undergo significant transformation if conveyed by different narrators who may aim to inform or persuade thus altering significant aspects or events, adding or omitting or rearranging facts (Berendsen, 1984). Such changes may occur because of subjectivity in viewpoints or because of intention. Either way, the narrator is a manipulator of stories and audiences. Studying advertising, Stern (1991) describes three approaches in delivering a brand story.

Direct drama

The roles of the story reveal themselves and perform their actions without any intervening storyteller. Direct drama allows for empathy and involvement as the viewer is drawn into the story.

First person narration

A presenter tells their own story revealing personal details which appear hard to question and create a sense of intimacy. Often like a testimony, a confession or eavesdropping,

Deciding who will tell the story is the last step. Keeping an open mind and not sticking to the original idea is important. Considering alternatives can help improve a script both in terms of creative originality and in terms of strategic appropriateness. While considering the type of delivery, a copywriter should also consider the product category and the competitors, the degree of consumer investment and involvement, as well as the product's lifecycle. Having brands simply tell their own story seems easy and straightforward but could also appear dull and self-centered. Having brands play a role in a story narrated by a voice of authority or a consumer can increase credibility, if well done. Having brands sign an ad in which they play no role can either prove to be extremely impactful or miss the mark completely if consumers remember a great ad but not the brand that aired it.

If the creator opts for direct drama, and the viewer is exposed to the unraveling of the story, then they can identify with one of the roles in the plot without any perceived mediator. Thus, if a story is powerful enough and clear to interpret, the recipient might become involved and empathise. Ads involving a linear plot usually come in the form of direct drama.

Using a first-person story will help create a more personal, intimate connection between the consumer and the brand. This might seem like a frequent option for personal care products that often use consumer testimonies but has also been used for large service providers or low involvement products. First-person storytelling can elicit a feeling of trust and approachability.

the first-person perspective is about values or feelings, calling for identification. A brand using first-person narratives may seem more human or humane, more genuine. However, if the testimony is too product oriented, this approach may become self-centered or monotonous.

Third person narration

A third person tells stories about other people and has a full view of their thoughts and the events that occurred, even if (or because) the storyteller does not participate. This storyteller selects what to present and emphasise, hence standing in a position of authority. Advertising often involves an omniscient storyteller who presents facts and product information, educating consumers on changes and innovations. However, a third-person narrator might also appear fictitious, less approachable and imposing, often leading to dis-trust.

Testimonials are an easy example but not the only example. And first-person narration need not be product oriented. Consider the "No excuses[4]" ad by Nike.

Third-person storytelling might help the viewer interpret a story in the desired way, convey authority and confidence. An omniscient third-person storyteller might also help integrate multiple stories that often appear in lifestyle advertising or in bricolage advertising – types which are discussed below. Using a voice over or announcing the tagline, this narrator can create a unified narrative out of different consumer moments or abstract images. New brands wishing to establish authority or convince about innovations might benefit from this approach.

It is important to consider the different voices that can convey a story to the audience and creatively use these voices to give each story a unique perspective.

Time to practise!

- After studying the narrative tools, select your favourite three stories. Trace the key conflict facing the hero. Consider how this conflict might reflect broader human values or challenges.

- Select three global TV ads from the '80s and the '90s. Trace the conflict that instigates their narrative. Connect this conflict with brand attributes and benefits. Connect this conflict with consumer values and ideals. Try to contemplate on which strategic message or insight strategists wanted to build on.

- Select five movies of different genres. Trace all the roles in each.

- Select at least three TV or video ads. Trace all the roles in each. Then examine the following:

  o Does the product or brand play a role? Which role is this?
  o Is the consumer represented by one of the roles? Which one?

- Re-imagine the story in each of the ads you examined, by:

  o adding or replacing a role that reflects the consumer
  o adding or removing the product

Examine how the above changes would affect the plot.

- Select ten different TV or video ads whose narrative seems minimal, vague, or complicated. Try to locate all the stages of the plot. After you do, look for:

  o Changes in camera angles or movement as the story unfolds

- The escalation of music or sound effects.

- Continue working on three of those ads and explore how:

  - You could change the climax
  - You could provide a solution with a twist or change the twist
  - You could re-arrange the sequence of events
  - You could incorporate a story within the main narrative.

- Find at least three movies or books where the trophy is different from the beneficiary
- Find at least three movies or books where denouement is not a happy end
- Watch the "CIF-Prison" ad. Trace the conflict. Use it to describe the insight strategists may have had in mind. Can you guess how did the creative(s) worked toward the script that finally aired?
- Trace who plays which role in the "Hellmann's-Mayo" 2021 Superbowl ad[5]. Start by identifying the conflict. Then find the hero who must solve this conflict.
- Trace the stages of the plot in the: "Southern Comfort-Whatever's comfortable" ad.
- Find at least 5 ads in which the product is the helper.
- Find at least 5 ads in which the product is the hero.
- Find at least 5 ads in which the product is the trophy.
- Rewrite the Perrier-Lion ad by changing or adding at least one role. Revise the plot accordingly.
- Rewrite a script for the "VW Passat – Darth Vader" ad by changing the timeline of events.

4 Writing the TV script

Once the creative team has come up with a story, putting it down on paper appears easier than it is, and requires focused, convergent thinking. A script needs a lot of study and attention to detail and cannot be written sequentially, from the beginning to the end. As the script reflects the plot, the best way to begin writing is by determining the climax. Then, you should work with the rising action and falling action, deciding whether the events should appear in chronological order. If the script is well written, then the roles will emerge. Even when the idea is abstract and there is no concrete plot, the viewers need a sense of rising and falling action, in which case the type of visuals and music that can be used to build up tension.

In the introduction but also throughout, descriptions must be accurate yet concise. Details are only used to highlight what is essential for the idea to work, for the brand to be presented correctly and for the consumer to be profiled appropriately. "Woman in her 30s" might suffice for a passer-by, but not for the hero of the story. She could be more like: "Woman in her 30s, athletic, overweight"; or: "Woman in her 30s, office attire, glasses and ponytail"; or: "Woman in her 30s, in heavy make-up and an impressive evening dress". Keep the details which are of strategic importance.

Duration is also important to consider. In most countries, the unit for media planning is 30" both for radio and for TV ads but in others, 60" versions are also quite frequent, mainly for big budget integrated campaigns. Some campaigns start by airing a minute long version before releasing their standard 30" one. Many, then include cut versions that could be as short as 15" long, serving as reminders.

Aside from the media aspect, another factor which affects the duration of an ad is the number of words needed, to convey product information or for the story to deploy. Telling a story in just 30" is not easy and some ideas are too complicated to work. Normally, the English language allows for 3 words per second, but, especially on TV, 90 words can create a very confusing and unpleasant result. And even if there is an option to first air a 60" version, one must be sure that the idea will also work if cut down to 30". Reading the audio out loud while timing ensures that the script is not too text heavy. Inserting too much product information in a script might create gaps in the video.

Scripts often contain terms one should be familiar with. Overusing such terms though is not always appropriate. The purpose of the initial script is to convey the idea, not to specify what the final video will be like. Such terms should be used sparsely for clarity and without confining prematurely the contribution of the director and other experts.

Table 6.2 Basic terms for video advertising scripts

Sound	
M.V.ON	Male voice on camera
F.V.ON	Female voice on camera
C.V.ON	Child voice on camera
M.V.OVER	Male
F.V.OVER	Female
C.V.OVER	Child voice over (not on camera)
M.ANNCR	Main announcer (usually at the end, repeating consistently the tagline in every TVC)
SFX	Sound effects
Description	
SUPERS	Letters imposed on the screen
PACK SHOT	The product pack – last shot (often with some action on the background or with logo & supers)
Camera movement	
Zoom in / out	The camera lens makes the object look bigger or smaller.
Track in / out	Camera approaches (or goes back at a distance) from an object, making it look bigger or smaller
CU	Close up: a close shot focusing on detail (i.e. face or flower)
Full frame	The object occupies the entire shot / screen
Freeze frame	Motion stops. Image is still.
Pan	From: panoramic. Camera films on top of the object providing a broad view of its surroundings.
LS / TS	Long (Distant) Shot / Tight Shot

Traveling	Camera moves horizontally leftwards or rightwards, remaining at the same hight.
Slow / fast motion	Movement appears slower or accelerated.
P.O.V.	(Point Of View): camera films imitating the human eye perspective

Basic editing	
Cut	The simpler way to put two shots one next to the other: one stops, the other appears.
Dissolve	One shot fades out while the other fades in. For a few frames one can see both. Some special effects make the dissolving effect last longer thus blurring the two shots.

A script can be written using the single-column or the two-column format. The former is more useful when a story contains little or no audio. The latter helps align video with audio per scene and when duration is of essence.

Table 6.3 Single column script – example

Client: Cretan Farmers' Association
Product: Cretan Honey
Working title: "Making of"
Duration: 20"

SFX: Loud, intense bee buzz throughout, sounding like a fighter aircraft
Panoramic view of a spring landscape, grass, and bushes full of flowers, light blue sky and sunshine. A bee buzzes in the frame and starts flying straight forward.

The camera follows the bee that moves in a fast, determined way, doing spectacular manoeuvres as if it were a fighter aircraft (Reference: Top Gun). The bee lands on numerous flowers, sipping, and then flies off again to the next target.
Supers: You are watching the making of

The bee arrives in its hive and mingles with its peers.
Supers: Cretan Honey.
Supers: Organic. 100% natural. No preservatives.

We see the honey jar with its label. A bee flies on the cap and then takes off spectacularly vanishing in the horizon.
Supers: Cretan Honey by the Cretan Farmers' Association
Supers: Logo; Nature's all star. Coming soon to a market near you.

Table 6.4 Double column script – example

Client: Cretan Farmers' Association **Product:** Cretan Honey	**Working title:** "Making of" **Duration:** 20"
Video	**Audio**
Panoramic view of a spring landscape, grass, and bushes full of flowers, light blue sky and sunshine. A bee buzzes in the frame and starts flying straight forward.	SFX: Bee buzz throughout, sounding like a fighter aircraft, creating tension
The camera follows the bee that moves in a fast, determined way, doing spectacular manoeuvres as if it were a fighter aircraft. The bee lands on numerous flowers, sipping, and then flies off again to the next target.	MVO (heavy, imposing, as if announcing an action movie trailer): Power. Passion. Thrill. Determination.

The bee lands on a spectacular flower. Close up.	You are watching the making of …
The bee takes off abruptly and lands in its hive. Supers: "organic", and "no preservatives".	Organic, natural, Greek honey.
Packshot & supers	Cretan Honey. Nature's all star. Coming soon to a market near you

Here are some examples of scripts written ad hoc to show what a famous ad might have looked like on paper, before being filmed. This is a very interesting exercise to try: re-write the script for existing ads! The left column indicating the stages of the plot is optional and can be ignored.

Table 6.5 IKEA lamp ad – attempt to retrospectively write a script

Brand: IKEA
Title: Lamp
Duration: 1:00
Link: https://www.youtube.com/watch?v=jU-cori12KU

	Video	Audio
Exposition	Open on a cosy home. A woman takes an old lamp out of the plug and takes it out with the garbage.	Emotional music
Rising action	The lamp stands outside next to the garbage, alone. It is windy and rainy. The lamp is turned as if facing the window of the house where we see the woman placing a new lamp where the old one used to be and sitting next to it.	
Climax	The lamp is still out in the cold and the rain. From the window we can see the woman getting up and turning the lights off.	
Falling action	A passer-by stops and speaks on camera.	MVON: Many of you feel bad for this lamp. That is because you are crazy. It has no feelings and the new one is much better.
Denouement	Logo IKEA. Supers: unböring	

Table 6.6 NIKE Equality ad – attempt to retrospectively write a script

Brand: Nike
Title: Equality
Duration: 1:31
Link: https://www.youtube.com/watch?v=DWsUrMfDaG4

	Video	Audio
Exposition	View of an open basketball court. The image is grey and only the white lines stand out.	Music background MVO: Is this the land history promised?

Rising action	We see young people playing basketball. Among them stands Lebron James who turns and looks on camera.	Here, within these lines, on this concrete court, this patch of turf.
	We see open tennis courts. In one of the courts stands Serena Williams looking on camera. We see a football (soccer) court. Megan Rapinoe is there, looking on camera. Two children are playing basketball outside a church. Intercuts of Dalilah Muhammad, Kevin Durant, Gabby Douglas, and Victor Cruiz, looking at the camera.	Here, you're defined by your actions, not your looks or beliefs. Equality should have no boundaries.
Climax	A hand is shaking a spray with white paint and starts painting the court's white line. This white line expands beyond the court. All the athletes are seen painting the streets, cars, or house stairs, until the entire city is crossed by a white line that keeps spreading and becoming more intense.	The bonds we find here should run past these lines. Opportunity should not discriminate. The ball should bounce the same for everyone. Worth should outshine color
Falling action	This white line has also painted the entire court of justice. Outside we can see people seating peacefully but looking straight on camera without smiling. Intercuts of the athletes already seen. Lebron James speaks on camera	Lebron James VO: If we can be equals here, we can be equals everywhere.
Denouement	Panoramic city view. Supers: Equality has no boundaries	

Table 6.7 Tabasco Mosquito ad – attempt to retrospectively write a script

Brand: Tabasco
Title: Mosquito
Duration: 30"
Link: https://superbowl-ads.com/1997-tabasco-mosquito/

	Video	Audio
Exposition	A young, chubby man in his early 20s sits alone at his porch on a very hot and humid night, eating pizza.	Natural SFX
Rising action	The man pours Tabasco on every slice. A lot of empty bottles of Tabasco can be seen next to him.	
Rising action	The man turns his eyes looking around but does not seem particularly annoyed or distracted	SFX: mosquito sound approaching
Climax	Close up on the man's thigh as the mosquito bites him	
Falling action	The man keeps eating pizza and staring into the night sky. The mosquito flies away and explodes.	SFX: mosquito flying away SFX: bomb explosion.
Denouement	Logo appears while we see the man on the background.	

Table 6.8 Southern Comfort "Whatever's comfortable" ad – attempt to retrospectively write a script

Brand: Southern Comfort Title: Whatever's comfortable Duration: 1'45" Link: https://www.youtube.com/watch?v=Uq-9QBUmELA	
Expo-sition	Light summer music throughout Close up on man walking along the beach. He is middle aged, wears thick glasses, his haircut is sloppy, He appears cheerful.
Rising action	As the man keeps walking, we see he is wearing an old fashion tight swimsuit that is unflattering and a pair of shoes that are barely suitable for the beach. The man appears carefree and relaxed. He passes by other people who enjoy the beach, appears blissful and not particularly interested on what he encounters along the way. A dog starts following him, but the man barely reacts. His walk appears long.
Climax	The man suddenly takes a sharp turn and vanishes from the screen. We can see the beach behind him. Nothing has changed.
Falling action	The man walks back in the frame holding a glass of whisky and starts walking again. We see a general shot of the entire beach.
Denouement	Pack-shot: on his glass we see the logo of Southern Comfort and supers: "Whatever's comfortable".

Table 6.9 Coca-Cola "Under Pressure" ad – attempt to retrospectively write a script

Brand: Coca Cola Title: Under pressure Duration: 1' Link: https://www.youtube.com/watch?v=Gilt7lGU-5g	
Exposition	Under pressure by D. Bowie & the Queen Close up on an alarm that starts lighting and ringing. It's 7:00.
Rising action	Intercuts of people during their everyday activities. A student is taking a test and appears anxious and nervous. A girl holding a violin looks anxiously behind the scenes at the audience. Boys are playing football. One of them gets expelled by the game in disappointment. Another boy is working at a restaurant kitchen, while a woman yells at him. A boy is about to take a high dive but loses his balance and falls in the pool. A ballet dancer sprains her ankle. A mother and a daughter are arguing inside a car. The girl slams the door and leaves frustrated.
Climax	Close up on a Coca Cola bottle opening, releasing the bubbles and the drink as if exploding.
Falling action	The boy in the pool makes the perfect dive. The violin girl enters the stage. The football team cheers. The mother and daughter hug and make amends. The boy taking the test now smiles confidently. Intercuts of the characters drinking Coca Cola, looking happy, smiling, and relaxed.
Denouement	Logo & supers: Taste the feeling

Time to practise!

- Watch the "Lucky Dog" LOTTO TV advert carefully. Then write the script.
- Watch the "Kenzo World' video ad by Caroll Lim & Humberto Leon. Can you trace the climax and the solution? Study how a simple plot is built up to create a sense of escalating tension delivered through choreography. How would you describe this in a draft script that would help the team align around the idea without delving in too much detail?
- Watch 3 Doritos ads and write the script profiling the roles concisely but accurately.

5 Types of TV advertising

Existing literature on TV advertising often discerns between types of TV adverts though there is no universally accepted typology. In some cases, the criteria permeating these typologies are not always clear, thus there is overlapping, and categories proposed are not mutually exclusive, but this is what creativity is about, after all. Creative ideas can combine more than one type. The question is: can the copywriter explore different types to tell the same (or similar) story, thus developing an idea in different ways? Could consideration of each type help a copywriter create new ideas which can then develop toward different directions?

The list below compiles types encountered in many sources (indicatively: Altstiel et al., 2023; Drewniany & Jewler, 2014; Belch & Belch, 2012; Felton, 2006; Pricken, 2008) focusing on their narrative elements and on their use in specific product categories.

Typologies are made for creatives to overcome rather than blindly follow. But one must know the norm in order to be able to deviate.

- **Testimonies and endorsements**: Coming from consumers, expert users, or professionals, testimonies may add credibility or desirability combining product information with the user's positive experience (Karpinska-Krakowiak & Eisend, 2020). TV ads involving testimonies are frequent in personal care or house cleaning products. Testimonies might go beyond the product though, to bring to life consumer insights. Two examples from Nike are the 1988 "Just do it" advert[6] and the Warhawk Matt Scott "No Excuses" advert. What makes testimonials stand out is first-person narrative and the fact that the person offering testimony usually represents the targeted or ideal consumer. Compared to the past, today's testimonies are less overt, more subtle, featuring imperfect consumers or not so glorified celebrity moments. Celebrities participating in advertising stories do not necessarily offer first-person testimony, even if their endorsement is implied.
- **Celebrity stories**: Superbowl thrives recently on spectacular productions involving celebrities who play a role just like in a short film, even when their calls to action are direct. The Nespresso-Clooney ads or Ed Sheeran's Heinz

Ketchup[7] feature celebrities in less conventional ways. Experience has shown that celebrity endorsement can work for any product in any market, allowing for all kinds of plots beyond simple endorsement. Sometimes though, celebrities are the easier way to attract attention, substituting for the lack of a great idea. Before using a celebrity, one should answer three questions:

- would the story be equally compelling without the celebrity?
- is the script written around a specific celebrity or could any famous person find its way in the story?
- does the celebrity overshadow the product, meaning that people might forget the brand the ad was created for?

- **Create a character**: The Pillsbury Dough Boy, Unilever's Snuggle (also branded as Cajoline or Coccolino in some markets), the Michelin Man are examples of brands who created a character representing their qualities and eliciting emotions. Personifying the brand is a way to create multiple stories and a coherent identity especially in highly competitive or low involvement product categories. In such stories, the character is usually the hero or the helper.
- **Problem solution**: An advert which demonstrates how a product solves a problem; what the problem looks like and / or what the solution feels like. The plot might focus more on the former or the latter. Usually, there is a "before / after" comparison, shown or implied. Taken too literally, this type might appear a bit obsolete or too overt. However, the problem or the solution or both could be expressed using symbols, metaphors, or analogies, as in the case of the "CIF-Prison" advert. Examples are easy to find as this type of ad has been used to advertise all kinds of products, from cars to insurance. The type of figurative thinking one could use to create problem-solution ads relates to Chapters 4 & 5 whose instructions can be used as a source of inspiration. Usually in problem-solution advertising the product is the helper addressing the consumer's problem more effectively than other alternatives. Again, this is one norm that can be broken.
- **Demo**: The product benefit is visualised, literally or figuratively, often in an exaggerated manner or by creating a story-within-a story. Comparing clean shirts; or expressions of taste; showing a red rose petal instead of dripping blood; showing animated magic bubbles removing stains; these are examples of demo(nstration) in advertising. Comparisons and direct presentations also fall under this category in which the product turns from helper to hero whose trophy is a satisfied consumer. There will always be more than one way to go beyond the obvious and demonstrate the product's uniqueness. Watch how the "Tabasco-Mosquito" ad demonstrates the product benefit.
- **Slice of life**: everyday products, especially FMCGs, find their way in specific moments of our everyday life by isolating and addressing a specific moment's need or desire: a tasty snack, fast and easy cleaning, a low-calorie breakfast and more. Then, they develop a plot around this moment, thus introducing the "role" of the product in narrative and in reality. An example could be OXO, featuring the stories of Kate, a housewife[8]. This is one of the oldest and therefore most overused types of advertising but can still pave the way for

compelling scripts like the VW Passat – Darth Vader one, which elaborates on the moment dad comes home from work[9]. The type alone is never an indication of how creative a script will be.

- **Create a place**: an imaginary place where the brand rules or where consumers live happily helped by the brand. An old Fairy ad presented two imaginary neighbouring towns, Villabajo & Villarriba, competing over cooking the largest paella. Only one of the towns used Fairy to clean easily and then party all night, while the inhabitants of the competing town would spend the rest of the night cleaning. A land or place may serve as a platform for multiple stories. Creating places can also take more abstract turns. The Nike Equality ad imagines a city where the courts' white lines paint every street and building to remind viewers that in life, people should be equal as in sport. This is also an analogy – a type discussed below. Remember, types of TV ads are not mutually exclusive, and creativity is supposed to blend boundaries.

- **Analogy or loan**: a story which borrows from another story which was developed in a different context. In the case of loan, one could keep some roles and parts of the plot, inserting the consumer or the product, like in the Mercedes "Rabbit & Tortoise" ad. In the case of analogy, a familiar narrative transfers to a new era or place; or the plot is carried out with different roles. Usually, analogies help put a consumer and a product in a story, establishing a specific connection between them. By borrowing a familiar story, brands might speak of values and timelessness, as in the case of the Apple 1984 advert; or brands benefit from the popularity of trending stories as in the Channel 5 2004 advert where Nicole Kidman carries on with her role in Moulin Rouge (Brook, 2004). Analogy is connected to metaphors which have been extensively discussed in previous chapters.

- **Parody**: Advertising often makes fun of itself by changing anticipated stories or deconstructing predictable types like the ones described here. From the Dos Equis "Most Interesting Man in the World" to the Australian tourism advertising "There is nothing like Australia", parodies make fun of the familiar thus becoming entertaining and memorable.

- **Multi-narrative, no narrative or anti-narrative**: Though almost every TV advert can be analysed using narrative terms, not all ads rely on storytelling with a specific conflict or plot. Some TV adverts are like vignettes, comprising short stories or moments under a common theme, like the 2012 P&G "Moms" ad or the 2017 Coca Cola "Under Pressure" ad. Others present a bricolage of abstract images playing with free association, conveying descriptions rather than narrations as in the case of fragrance advertising like "Gabrielle" by Chanel, or Gucci Bloom. Many such ads resemble video clips. Even when a storyline is not evident, these bricolages rely a lot on rising and falling action, with imagery and music (Hung, 2001) contributing to creating tension and maximising emotional impact, thus the basics of plot should be considered meticulously.

The above types or styles are not mutually exclusive. Their narrative patterns frequently seem familiar or obsolete, reasonably so. As the dialogue between consumers and brands evolves; as new media allow for larger durations or more complex stories; and as advertising takes different directions toward the postmodern, these types often blur or mix. The Superbowl Tide Ad discussed in Chapter 4 shows how TV viewers become accustomed to associating specific imagery or story patterns with specific types of products or with specific brands. Brand patterns help awareness and synergy, but clichés often lead to boring, mundane advertising.

To break patterns and norms, one must first know patterns and norms. None of the above types has to lead to predictable creative outcomes. Experimentation with types and with all the narrative elements can always lead to the unpredictable.

Time to practise!

- Find at least 5 ads that belong to more than one of the types listed above.
- Watch the Coca Cola "Under Pressure" ad. Convert it to a slice of life ad by developing one of the stories into a script. Now, re-write it and convert it to a different type of ad (testimonial, celebrity endorsement, storyline, it's up to you). Trace the advantages and disadvantages of your script compared to the initial ad. Consider twists in timing or plotting to make your script less predictable or anticipated.
- Take the 2016 "Doritos – Ultrasound" ad and convert it to a first-person narration. Whose narration would be more interesting?
- Watch the 2017 Superbowl ad "Audi – Daughter" and consider using a celebrity. Which role would be more appropriate to replace?
- On a more abstract level, you could twist your brain to apply narrative elements on all the types discussed in section 6.5: can you trace similar plot elements, especially around climax and falling action? Can you trace pairs of roles? For example, which of the above types is more likely to follow the "consumer-as-hero and product-as-helper" pattern?

---

6 Writing for the radio or for podcasts

Children grow up listening to stories and creating their own images for these stories. Radio advertising can be a great storytelling medium. However, radio advertising is not easy. Using sound to tell stories is a great challenge, especially to the less experienced copywriter who must stretch both their imagination and their auditory observation skills to make such stories happen. The process is always the same:

- immersing in the brief
- spontaneous thinking, storming, and noting
- meticulous effort to turn ideas into stories using narrative tools
- meticulous effort to turn stories into scripts using music, sound, and voice.

Creative work is done in layers.

Radio commercials can also be classified into different types. For example:

- The announcer or straight-line radio spot, often with a creative twist
- The jingle or song
- The stitching of soundbites
- The narrative radio spot that may include:
  - One narrator only
  - Dialogue
  - More than one voices interacting and building a plot.

These can help a copywriter start developing first ideas but should not confine thinking. One can always mix and match, blend, twist or break the established patterns.

Radio ideas can be fuelled by constant observation of how people talk or how things sound. Foreign accents; airport announcements; vox pops; adults talking to pets or babies; nagging babies; quarrelling neighbours heard from afar; bad singing in the shower... all these may lead to unbearable clichés or great ideas and the difference is up to the copywriter and their mental repository of interesting sounds.

Distinctive sounds have an impact on the radio increasing memorability, only if they are easy to recognise. The sound effect of a "plastic bottle thrown out the window" is impossible to identify, while the sound of two glasses cheering, the cling, might be more distinctive, especially if the text appears relevant. Finally, the rule of 3 words or less per second, or an equivalent for each language, is always important to remember.

Again, one can use the single- or double-column format. The former appears, so far, to be more useful for podcasts while the latter is more helpful when duration is important and when one needs to plan for the interaction between voice, sound, and music more carefully and accurately. Here is an example:

Table 6.10 Radio script - example

Client: Cretan Farmers Association Product: Cretan Honey	Working title: Movie Trailer Duration: 30"
Instructions	Audio
SFX: Bee buzz throughout, sounding like a fighter aircraft, creating tension	
Announcer (pompous, imposing, as if covering air races):	Power. Passion. The thrill of fulfilling your destiny. This is the journey of Betty the Bee. Watch the famous fighter from Crete, as she sits on the marvellous poppy! And here she flies again over the daisies and thyme bushes. Wow, what a show!
Bee buzz sounds loud but then fades out.	
Announcer (low key, friendly)	Cretan Honey. The natural blockbuster. Coming soon to a market near you

> **Time to practise!**
>
> - Listen to at least five radio commercials and analyse them considering: the narrative elements; their type; whether and how they integrate sound and music in the story.
> - Take any simple radio announcer commercial you came across and turn it into a story. How will you allocate the roles in this story? What will the climax be? How can sound and music help? Write this story in indirect speech – using first person narration. Rewrite this story using direct drama.

7 Transmedia storytelling and advergames

Narratives change in the digital environment, becoming more fluid, abstract, interactive, fragmented. When it comes to advertising, there is still plenty of room for creative ideas that blend narratives with consumers and touchpoints achieving transformational creativity that changes the advertising landscape for good.

However, the key challenge is to create some sort of core or thread that holds narratives together around a brand so that initiatives can be measured and capitalized. The "Dumb Ways to Die" campaign examined in Chapter 3, achieved this by presenting countless roles / heroes around a limited plot, using a distinctive animated look & feel. When fragmented narratives become viral, a lot of people might interact not knowing where the story started or what its aims are, as in the case of Dumb Ways to Die app. This is the price of going viral.

Brands explore digital narratives in many ways.

First, brands use new touchpoints to disseminate their stories creating longer versions of their TV adverts and promo videos or even branded series like the Lenovo Extreme I.T. series[10].

A second approach is to create a story and break it down to chapters or mini spin-offs which are then placed in different media. Users fall into one of the rabbit holes, so they start following a trail, chasing the narrative, and connecting the dots. This type of engagement is not easy to achieve. The Blair Witch Project (Stewart, 2016) and the AI movie (Transmedia Marketing, N.D.) promotions were such cases.

A third frequent use of transmedia storytelling is when brands ask consumers to contribute to brand narratives by playing a role, by acting as narrators changing the plot, or by participating in the production by proposing the cast, soundtrack or even filming locations. Lacta, a Mondelez confectionary brand in Greece, crowdsourced an entire film which aired in movie theatres in 2016, titled: "Love in the end". The film narrated three stories of unfulfilled love, among the many which consumers shared with the brand, and re-made them in one film giving each a happy end[11].

According to the Interactive Advertising Bureau (IAB) advergames "are custom-made games specifically designed around a brand and, act as de-facto longer format ads, cleverly blending brand messaging with a fun, interactive gaming experience to achieve campaign objectives"[12]. Such games can be engaging, connecting the consumer to the brand much more effectively compared to non-interactive advertising. Advergames have also been accused of promoting unhealthy habits, especially to children[13], even though they could also be used to educate.

Jenkins (2007) argues that digital narratives are not linear, concrete and finite. On the contrary, they seem to create entire worlds open to possibility. Narrative theory can help design such possibility for advertising purposes. Porter Abbott (2005, p. 530) explains how conflict can constitute the epicentre of a multitude of narratives, especially in the digital environment.

One way to engage with complex narratives, then, would be to create a very specific plot but provide an ample choice of roles who can explore the story from different points of focalisation (Genette, 1972), just like in League of Legends or in an online football game where one may spend hours forming the perfect team just to play a game for a few minutes. Dumb ways to die also created a multitude of characters around one single plot theme: dumb dying. To exercise the brain, each of us could think of at least a dozen new dumb ways to die.

There is one more option: provide a limited set of roles but an ample choice of possible plots and outcomes, as is the case in online games like the Assassin's Creed, where a finite number of roles can engage in endless, different types of battles. The 2023 Mayo Superbowl ad could be such an example if, in the future, Mayo kept interfering in unpredictable instances of food waste.

Advergames and interactive narratives have created a lot of buzz and have led to successful campaigns. At this stage it is hard to tell if these are part of a new tech fad or the next big thing in the world of advertising, though indeed they have the power to transform this landscape. Such ideas pose significant managerial challenges and complexities. Developing scripts for advergames requires a lot of programming, meticulous touchpoint planning, and a significant investment of human and financial resources. Interactive narratives often go out of control for brands who wish to maintain a unified image, an appropriate look & feel and a consistent tone of voice. All these alternatives involve significant risk as brands end up competing with digital pop culture and content overload. And, beyond the initial idea or planning, the creative team will need a lot of expert support to be able to complete and launch.

Once there is an idea, concept-testing and mapping simple versions will be needed to present even an early version. Truth be told, for those who love storytelling, creating an interactive narrative or an advergame might prove to be even more fun than playing it…

Notes

1 https://www.youtube.com/watch?v=YYDV1I6yYOc
2 https://superbowl-ads.com/things-you-probably-didnt-know-about-apples-famous-1984-super-bowl-ad-that-almost-didnt-air/
3 https://www.youtube.com/watch?v=axxDaV2d0LM
4 https://www.uww.edu/news/archive/2008-01-matt-scott-nike
5 https://www.youtube.com/watch?v=1L3h-PqISso
6 https://www.youtube.com/watch?v=GzUvMXPuvVI

7 https://www.youtube.com/watch?v=keOaQm6RpBg
8 https://www.hatads.org.uk/catalogue/record/e6490752-a5cd-4c0d-98f6-831f70bd03a0
9 https://www.youtube.com/watch?v=1n6hf3adNqk
10 https://shortyawards.com/11th/extreme-it-series
11 https://creativecriminals.com/ambient/lacta/love-in-the-end
12 https://www.iab.com/wp-content/uploads/2015/10/IAB_Games_Ad_Eco_Guide.pdf
13 https://theconversation.com/advergames-play-with-nutrition-by-making-fast-food-rewarding-20816

References

Abbott, H.P. (2002). *The cambridge introduction to narrative*. Cambridge, UK: Cambridge University Press.

Altstiel, T., & Grow, J. (2006). *Advertising strategy: Creative tactics from the outside/in*. Sage Publications.

Altstiel, T., Grow, J., Augustine, D., & Jennings, M. (2023). *Advertising creative: Strategy, copy, and design* (Sixth). SAGE Publishing.

Barthes, R. (1977). *Image, music, text*. New York: Hill and Wang.

Belch, G.E., & Belch, M.A. (2012). *Advertising and promotion: An integrated marketing communications perspective* (9th ed., global, Ser. Mcgraw-hill series in marketing). McGraw-Hill Irwin.

Berendsen, M. (1984). The teller and the observer: Narration and focalization in narrative texts. *Style*, 18 (2), 140–158.

Berger, A.A. (2015). *Ads, fads, and consumer culture: Advertising's impact on American character and society*. London: Rowman & Littlefield.

Berger, A.A. (1997). *Narratives in popular culture, media and everyday life*. California: Sage.

Booker, C. (2006). *The seven basic plots: Why we tell stories*. Continuum.

Brechman, J.M. & Purvis, S.C. (2015) Narrative, transportation and advertising, *International Journal of Advertising*, 34 (2), 366–381, DOI:1doi:0.1080/02650487.2014.994803.

Brook, S. (2004). Kidman reprises Moulin Rouge role for Chanel. *The Guardian*. Retrieved from: https://www.theguardian.com/media/2004/oct/15/advertising.uknews.

Brooks, C. & Warren, R.P. (1959 [1943]). *Understanding fiction*. New York: Appleton Century-Crofts.

Brown, S., & Patterson, A. (2010). Selling stories: Harry Potter and the marketing plot. *Psychology and Marketing*, 27 (6), 541–556.

Campbell, J. (2014 [1949]) The hero with a thousand faces. In: Campbell, J. (au), Cousineau (Ed.) *The hero's journey: Joseph Campbell on his life and work (the collected works of joseph campbell)*. New World Library.

Catmull, E., & Wallace, A. (2014). *Creativity, Inc: Overcoming the unseen forces that stand in the way of true inspiration*. London: Bantam Press.

Cavazza, M., & Pizzi, D. (2006). Narratology for Interactive Storytelling: A critical introduction. In: Göbel, S. and Malkewitz, R. (Eds.) *Technologies for Interactive digital storytelling and entertainment*. Third International Conference, TIDSE 2006, Darmstadt, Germany, December 4–6, 2006. Proceedings. Berlin: Springer, pp. 72–83.

Chatman, S. (1978), *Story and discourse: Narrative structure in fiction and film*. Ithaca: Cornell University Press.

Chatman, S. (1974). *Genette's analysis of narrative time relations new critical practices*, II (Structuralism, Narratology, "Tel Quel, Change"), *14(4)*: 353–368.

Chiu, H.-C., Hsieh, Y.-C., & Kuo, Y.-C. (2012). How to align your brand stories with your products. *Journal of Retailing*, 88 (2), 262–275.

Cohen, A.C., & Dromi, S.M. (2018). Advertising morality: Maintaining moral worth in a stigmatized profession. *Theory & Society* 47, 175–206. https://doi.org/10.1007/s11186-018-9309-7.

de Waal Malefyt, T. & Morais, R.J. (2010). Creativity, brands, and the ritual process: Confrontation and resolution in advertising agencies. *Culture and Organization*, 16 (4), 333–347.

Degeorge, F.M. (1977) From Russian formalism to French structuralism, *Comparative Literature Studies* 14 (1), 20–29. http://www.jstor.org/stable/40245981.

Dion, D. & Mazzalovo, G. (2016). Reviving sleeping beauty brands by rearticulating brand heritage, *Journal of Business Research*, 69 (12), 5894–5900.

Drake, M. (1984) The basics of creative development research, *International Journal of Advertising*, 3 (1), 43–49, doi:10.1080/02650487.1984.11104998.

Drewniany, B.L., & Jewler, A.J. (2014). *Creative strategy in advertising*. Boston MA: Cengage Learning.

Elliott, R., & Wattanasuwan, K. (1998). Brands as symbolic resources for the construction of identity, *International Journal of Advertising*, 17:2, 131–144.

Elliott, S. (2002, September 16). The media business advertising; Ikea challenges the attachment to old stuff, in favor of brighter, new stuff. *New York Times*, Section C, p. 6. Retrieved December 2019 from: https://www.nytimes.com/2002/09/16/business/media-business-advertising-ikea-challenges-attachment-old-stuff-favor-brighter.html.

Eng, L.L. & Tat Keh, H. (2007). The effects of advertising and brand value on future operating and market performance, *Journal of Advertising*, 36 (4), 91–100, doi:10.2753/JOA0091-3367360407.

Escalas, J.E. (2004). Narrative processing: Building consumer connections to brands. *Journal of Consumer Psychology*, 14 (1), 168–180.

Felton, G. (2006). *Advertising: concept and copy* (2nd ed.). W.W. Norton.

Feng, Y., Chen, H. & Kong, Q. (2021) An expert with whom I can identify: The role of narratives in influencer marketing, *International Journal of Advertising*, 40 (7), 972–993, doi:10.1080/02650487.2020.1824751.

Ferri, G. (2013) Satire, propaganda, play, storytelling. Notes on critical interactive digital narratives. In: Koenitz H., Sezen T.I., Ferri G., Haahr M., Sezen D., Çatak G. (eds) *Interactive storytelling*. ICIDS 2013. Lecture Notes in Computer Science, vol 8230. Berlin: Springer, Cham. https://doi.org/10.1007/978-3-319-02756-2_21.

Fischbach, S., & Guerrero, V. (2020). Brand stories: Transformative learning through digital brand storytelling (DBS). *Journal of Advertising Education*, 24 (2), 133–149. https://doi.org/10.1177/1098048220948515.

Fletcher, W. (1990) The management of creativity, *International Journal of Advertising*, 9 (1), 1–37, doi:10.1080/02650487.1990.11107129.

Fog, K., Budtz, C., & Yakagoylu, B. (2005). *Storytelling: Branding in practice*. Berlin: Springer.

Fossen, B.L., & Schweidel, D.A. (2016). Television advertising and online word-of-mouth: An empirical investigation of social TV activity. *Marketing Science*, 36 (1). https://doi.org/10.1287/mksc.2016.1002.

Freytag, G. (2008) *Freytag's technique of the drama: An exposition of dramatic composition and art*. Translated by Elias J. MacEwan. Charleston, South Carolina: Bibliobazaar

Frye, Northrop (1957). *Anatomy of criticism: Four essays*. Princeton: Princeton University Press.

Gavilanes, J.M., Flatten, T.C. & Brettel, M. (2018) Content strategies for digital consumer engagement in social networks: Why advertising is an antecedent of engagement, *Journal of Advertising*, 47 (1), 4–23, doi:10.1080/00913367.2017.1405751.

Genette, G. (1966). *Figures I*. Paris: Éditions du Seuil.

Genette, G. (1972). *Figures III*. Paris: Éditions du Seuil.

Genette G. (1980). *Narrative discourse: An essay in method*. Cornell University Press.

Genette, G., L. Marin και, M. Mathieu-Colas (1987). *The limits of narration*. Athens: Kardamitsas.

Gensler, S., Völcknerb, F., Liu-Thompkins, Y., & Wiertz, C. (2013). Managing brands in the social media environment. *Journal of Interactive Marketing*, 27 (4): 242–256. https://doi.org/10.1016/j.intmar.2013.09.004.

Goldman, R. & Papson, S. (2000) *Nike culture: The sign of the swoosh*. London: Sage (First published in 1998).

Goldman, R. & Papson, S.. (1994) Advertising in the age of hypersignification, *Theory, Culture & Society*, 11 (3), pp.23–53.

Goldman, R. (1994). Contradictions in a political economy of sign value, *Current Perspectives in Social Theory*, 14, 183–211.

Goldman, R. (1992). *Reading ads socially*. London: Routledge.

Greimas, A.J. (2002 [1966]). *Sémantique structural*. Paris: Presses Universitaires de France PUF.

Gurrieri, L., Tuncay Zayer, L. & Coleman, C.A. (2022) Transformative advertising research: Reimagining the future of advertising, *Journal of Advertising*, 51 (5), 539–556, doi:10.1080/00913367.2022.2098545.

Hall, E. (2017). Aristotle's theory of katharsis in its historical and social contexts. In: Fischer-Lichte, E. & Wihstutz, B. (Eds.) *Transformative aesthetics*. London: Routledge, pp. 26–47.

Henry, S. (2011). Creative briefing: The creative perspective. In: Butterfield, L. (Ed.) *Excellence in advertising: the IPA guide to best practice*. New York: Routledge, pp. 161–176 (first published in 1999).

Herman, D., Jahn, M., & Ryan, M. L. (Eds.) (2005). *Routledge Encyclopedia of Narrative Theory*. New York: Routledge.

Herskovitz, S., & Crystal, M. (2010). The essential brand persona: storytelling and branding, *Journal of Business Strategy*, 31 (3), 21–28.

Hill, R. & Johnson, L.W. (2004) Understanding creative service: a qualitative study of the advertising problem delineation, communication and response (APDCR) process, *International Journal of Advertising*, 23 (3), 285–307, doi:10.1080/02650487.2004.11072886.

Holt, D.B. (2016). Branding in the age of social media. *Harvard Business Review*, 3, 3–11. Retrieved December 2019 from: https://hbr.org/2016/03/branding-in-the-age-of-social-media.

Holt, D.B. (2004). *How brands become icons: The principles of cultural branding*. Harvard Business Review Press

Hooton, C. (2017, April 5). Pepsi ad review: A scene by scene dissection of possibly the worst commercial of all time. *The Independent*. Retrieved December 2019 from: https://www.independent.co.uk/arts-entertainment/tv/reviews/pepsi-ad-advert-commercial-kendall-jenner-police-protest-black-lives-matter-review-a7667486.html.

Hung, K. (2001). Framing meaning perceptions with music: The case of teaser Ads. *Journal of Advertising*, 3 (3), 39–49.

Jenkins, F. (2007) *Transmedia storytelling* 101. Retrieved from: http://henryjenkins.org/2007/03/transmedia_storytelling_101.html.

Jensen, O.B. (2007). Culture stories: Understanding cultural urban branding. *Planning Theory*, 6 (3), 211–236.

Joo, M., Wilbur, K.C., & Zhu, Y. (2016). Effects of TV advertising on keyword search, *International Journal of Research in Marketing*, 33 (3), 508–523. https://doi.org/10.1016/j.ijresmar.2014.12.005.

Karpinska-Krakowiak, M., & Eisend, M. (2020). Mini-film advertising and digital brand engagement: The moderating effects of drama and lecture. *International Journal of Advertising: The Review of Marketing Communications*, 39(3), 387–409. https://doi.org/10.1080/02650487.2019.1633841.

Keel, A., & Nataraajan, R. (2012). Celebrity endorsements and beyond: New avenues for celebrity branding. *Psychology & Marketing*, 29 (9), 690–703. https://doi.org/10.1002/mar.20555.

Knoll, J. & Matthes, J. (2017). The effectiveness of celebrity endorsements: a meta-analysis. *Journal of the Academy of Marketing Science*, 45 (1), 55–75. https://doi.org/10.1007/s11747-016-0503-8.

Kubicek, T. (2009). Focalization, the subject and the art of shaping perspective. In: Huhn, P., Schmid, W. and Schonert, J. (Eds.) *Point of view, perspective and focalization: modeling mediation in narrative*. Berlin: Walter de Gruyter, pp. 183–200.

Liaukonyte, J., Teixeira, T., & Wilbur, K.C. (2015). Television Advertising and Online Shopping, *Marketing Science*, 34 (3). https://doi.org/10.1287/mksc.2014.0899.

Lim, J.S., Ri, S.Y., Egan, B.D., & Biocca, F.A. (2015). The cross-platform synergies of digital video advertising: Implications for cross-media campaigns in television, Internet and mobile TV. *Computers in Human Behavior*, 48, 463–472. https://doi.org/10.1016/j.chb.2015.02.001.

MacInnis, D.J. (2011). "A Framework for conceptual contributions in marketing", *Journal of Marketing*, Vol. 75 No. 4, pp. 136–154.

McCormick, K. (2016). Celebrity endorsements: Influence of a product-endorser match on Millennials attitudes and purchase intentions, *Journal of Retailing and Consumer Services*, 32, 39–45. https://doi.org/10.1016/j.jretconser.2016.05.012.

Meenaghan, T. (1995). The role of advertising in brand image development. *Journal of Product & Brand Management*, 4 (4), 23–34. https://doi.org/10.1108/10610429510097672.

Mikos L. (2017). Transmedia storytelling and mega-narration: Audiovisual production in converged media environments. In: Sparviero, S., Peil, C., Balbi, G. (Eds.) *Media convergence and deconvergence: Global transformations in media and communication research* – A Palgrave and IAMCR Series. Palgrave Macmillan, Cham.

Miller, J.H. (2005). Henry James and "focalization", or why James loves GYP. In: Phelan, J. & Rabinowitz, P. J. (Eds.) *A companion to narrative theory*. Blackwell Publishing, pp. 124–135.

Miller, C.H. (2014). *Digital storytelling: A creator's guide to interactive entertainment* (3rd). Focal Press.

Moran, G., Muzellec, L. & Nolan, E. (2014). Consumer moments of truth in the digital context, *Journal of Advertising Research*, 54 (2), 200–204, doi:10.2501/JAR-54-2-200-204.

Nandan, S. (2005). An exploration of the brand identity–brand image linkage: A communications perspective, *Journal of Brand Management*, 12 (4), 264–278.

Nowlin, E.L., & Germelmann, C.C. (2018). The Values of Storytelling: From tactics to transformative action: An abstract. In: Krey, N., Rossi, P. (eds) *Back to the future: Using marketing basics to provide customer value*. AMSAC 2017. Developments in Marketing Science: Proceedings of the Academy of Marketing Science. Springer, Cham. https://doi.org/10.1007/978-3-319-66023-3_132.

Onega, S., & García Landa, J.A. (1996). *Narratology: An introduction*. Edited and introduced by Susana Onega and José Angel García Landa. Longman.

Pauwels, K., Aksehirli, Z., & Lackman, A. (2016). Like the ad or the brand? Marketing stimulates different electronic word-of-mouth content to drive online and offline performance, *International Journal of Research in Marketing*, 33 (3), 639–655. https://doi.org/10.1016/j.ijresmar.2016.01.005.

Porter Abbott, H. (2020). *The Cambridge introduction to narrative.* Cambridge University Press. https://doi.org/10.1017/9781108913928.

Porter Abbott, H. (2005) The future of all narrative futures. In: Phelan, J., & Rabinowitz, P. J. (Eds.) *A companion to narrative theory.* Maden MA: Blackwell Publishing, pp. 529–541.

Pricken, M. (2008). *Creative advertising: ideas and techniques from the world's best campaigns.* Thames & Hudson.

Propp, V. (1971 [1928]) *Morphology of the folktale,* trans. Laurence Scott, revised by Louis A. Wagner, Austin: University of Texas Press.

Richards, K. (2017, August 10). Is Ikea's "Lamp" ad by Spike Jonze the best rug-pull in advertising history? John Matejczyk picks his three favorite ads. *Adweek.* Retrieved December 2019 from: https://www.adweek.com/creativity/is-ikeas-lamp-ad-by-spike-jonze-the-best-rug-pull-in-advertising-history/.

Roberts, K. (2005). *Sisomo: The future on screen.* PowerHouse books.

Rodgers, S. & Thorson, E. (2018) Special issue introduction: Digital engagement with advertising, *Journal of Advertising,* 47 (1), 1–3, doi:10.1080/00913367.2017.1414003.

Rossiter, J.R. (2008). Defining the necessary components of creative, effective ads. *Journal of Advertising,* 37 (4), 139–144.

Sellas, T., & Solà, S. (2019). Podium podcast and the freedom of podcasting: Beyond the limits of radio programming and production constraints. *Radio Journal: International Studies in Broadcast & Audio Media,* 17 (1), 63–81. DOI: https://doi.org/10.1386/rjao.17.1.63_1.

Sheehan, K.B. & Morrison, D.K. (2009) The creativity challenge, *Journal of Interactive Advertising,* 9 (2), 40–43, doi:10.1080/15252019.2009.10722154.

Simmons, J. (2006). Guinness and the role of strategic storytelling. *Journal of Strategic Marketing,* 14 (1), 11–18, doi:10.1080/09652540500369068..

Stackelberg, P.V. (2011). *Creating digital narratives: The structure and design of stories told across multiple media.* Thesis submitted to State University of New York Institute of Technology. Available at: http://hdl.handle.net/20.500.12648/1008.

Stern, B.B. (1988). Medieval allegory: Roots of advertising strategy for the mass market. *Journal of Marketing,* 52 (3), 84–94. https://doi-org.acg.idm.oclc.org/10.1177/002224298805200308.

Stern, B.B. (1991). Who talks advertising? Literary theory and narrative "point of view". *Journal of Advertising,* 20 (3), 9–22.

Stern, B.B. (1993). The Firm, the Author, and the Persona: A Literacy model of the source of advertising. *Journal of Current Issues & Research in Advertising* (CTC Press), 15(2), 15. https://doi-org.acg.idm.oclc.org/10.1080/10641734.1993.10505001.

Stewart, R. (2016). How the original Blair Witch Project ushered in a new era of viral movie marketing. *The Drum.* Retrieved from: https://www.thedrum.com/news/2016/09/23/how-the-original-blair-witch-project-ushered-new-era-viral-movie-marketing.

The Editors of Creativity (2006, March 20). The Creative 50. *Adage.* Retrieved December 2019 from: https://adage.com/article/creativity-50/creativity-50/107767.

Todorov, T. (1968). La Grammaire du recit, *Languages,* 12, 94–102.

Transmedia Marketing (N.D.) *From film and TV to games and digital media: Major case studies.* Retrieved from: https://routledgetextbooks.com/textbooks/9780415716116/casestudies.php.

Vestergaard, T. & Schrøder, K. (1985). *The language of advertising.* Oxford: Basil Blackwell.

Youssef, L.B., Leicht. T., & Marongiu, L. (2019). Storytelling in the context of destination marketing: An analysis of conceptualisations and impact measurement, *Journal of Strategic Marketing,* 27 (8), 696–713, doi:10.1080/0965254X.2018.1464498.

7   What creatives need to know about media planning

1 Introduction

This chapter discusses media focusing less on the media planning process per se and more on its connection to creative work. Characteristics of different media have been discussed in previous chapters, so here the emphasis is on media strategy and the interplay with creative work. Emphasis is less on the particularities of each country of market and on variables or terms used during media planning; and more on what creatives need to understand, to ideate, filter, and develop their ideas accordingly.

Media take up the lion's share of any advertising budget. Before the advent of the web, the 80–20 rule of thumb suggested that up to 80% of the advertising budget would go to the media, to air the ads, and approximately 20% would go to production, to make the ads. Even if this was never an actual rule, creatives should always remember that media absorb a significant amount of money and resources. There is no point in creating unique advertising that cannot reach consumers.

Creatives should be able to understand the basic principles underlying media selection and the basic steps involved in media planning. First, because they acquire a better sense of the overall advertising strategy, ensuring their ideas are not just original but also appropriate and applicable across the media mix. Second, because creatives become more realistic when it comes to budget allocation and production demands, thus understanding scalability of their ideas in a more efficient way. Third, they learn to gradually adjust their work and tailor their ideas to specific requirements. Finally, creatives along with media planners can provide input for creative use of media increasing impact, memorability, and returns of an advertising campaign.

Media planning is about finding the right moment and the right context to convey the right message to the right person. This is a complex process requiring combined use of data from multiple sources. In the mass media era things were somewhat simpler: comparing the demographics of media consumption (who watches, reads, or listens to what and when) with demographics and psychographics relevant to product consumption (who consumes the specific product, when and why; and how they decide to buy it) would guide toward an appropriate media mix (Moriarty et al., 2015; Bruce et al., 2012).

DOI: 10.4324/9781003330721-7

In the new media landscape, we can know more about each consumer, based on the information they share, and the information gathered from cookies, thus we are able to deliver a customised message. Microtargeting can have detrimental consequences when it comes to privacy, politics and the need for accurate information but has served advertisers who wish to promote tailored offers. Striking the right balance between customization and deception poses significant ethical questions. However, overall, algorithmic approaches to advertising seem to allow marketers to optimise Return on Investment (ROI).

Media planning is a demanding process albeit one that differs significantly from one country or market to another depending on market size, saturation, and number of media outlets, on product category, life cycle, competitors, and more. Established practices change by the hour due to changes new media bring to the overall media consumption patterns and to the ways a brand can advertise. Keeping up with trends, globally and in each market, is a major challenge for practitioners and educators alike (Kim & Patel, 2012). Small or local brands seek immediate and less labour-intensive results, while larger ones invest in experimentation to advance knowhow in an everchanging environment, torn between risking with innovative options or going along the well-worn path; between building the brand and achieving instant return on investment.

From big satellite news providers to tiny forums and nano-influencers, there is still a lot of creative potential to not just select but also create media, establishing unique points of contact with consumers. Though the term media remains widely used, the term touchpoints gradually proliferates in the new media era. This is a more inclusive term which considers alternative ways to reaching consumers, like the urban environment where ambient advertising could thrive, the subway, hotel lobbies or even restrooms, online forums, old-fashioned postcards, influencers, product placement, etc.

Although this chapter uses the term "media" in a synecdochical manner, we must also acknowledge the significant differences between traditional media and new media. In both cases there is a mediating function between audiences and messages. However, there are also significant differences. Mass media bear responsibility for the content they produce and disseminate, while social media platforms try to denounce responsibility for content which their users post. Mass media operate within each country's national laws while social media are mostly accountable to the laws applying in their chosen headquarters. Mass media boast selection and quality while social media proclaim pluralism, diversity, and customization. Social media offer the feeling of community, proximity, immediacy, as well as engagement, interactivity, and a sense of peer interaction. And this is just to scratch the tip of the iceberg, because we should not overelaborate on media theories. We should focus on the perspective of media usage for creative advertising.

Why is it important that creatives understand the basics of mass media planning? First because an overview of all advertising processes leads to empathy and understanding across different functions, alignment and, of course, an overview needed for professional progression. Second, because media planning affects creative choices to some extent. Knowing how budget is allocated to cover media costs and production costs allows creatives to put their ideas within a feasibility framework. A tiny budget will not leave much for extreme production demands. A big media budget will probably require a significant number of adaptations and cut versions which means that production costs will also increase. Even the initial duration and dimension of creative executions might be defined based on media requirements. Plus, media selection might help creatives stream their ideas on creative media usage.

Media are not just suitable for placement. Media also provide context which can make an ad appear more relevant, congruent, credible, thus convincing. However, there is always a tension between the needs for an integrated, ROI based media plan; and the need for a perfect fit between a creative execution and its context (Dahlén, 2005). Usually, campaigns rely on the first, thus developing creative ideas on a context-free basis but try to find at least some opportunity for tailored, creative, unexpected placement as will be discussed below.

2 Paid, owned, earned media

There are three broad categories of media that a brand can choose to disseminate its message. First come **paid** media, the media whose revenue comes from brands paying to buy time or space, interrupting consumers with advertising messages and content. Mass media are paid media. Then come **owned** media: a brand's website or forum, for example, or even a brand's call center. These belong to the brand and consumers access them voluntarily or "arrive" there after clicking on a message received, for example, via email or seen on a banner ad. Finally, **earned** media – the most desirable – is a term indicating that a campaign attracted attention so that consumers talk about it; or share it on their social media accounts; so that news media or content sites post news stories or feature stories about this campaign. The value of earned media becomes measurable online through the number of views, shares, comments, and reactions (for a more thorough review from an advertising standpoint: Moriarty et al., 2015).

In the past, some would argue that Public Relations traditionally aimed at earned media, while advertising used paid media to get the message across. New media initially blurred such boundaries: a post or video could appear for free on a brand's page and yet could also be boosted or promoted.

Initially, brands invested their hopes on organic content, that is content uploaded online but not promoted. The argument was that if the content is good, then users will interact with it willingly and even share it, thus the brand would achieve engagement with little or no media spending (Dahlén & Rosengren, 2016; an interesting set of comments followed this publication). Today, this is no longer realistic: too much content and platform monetisation push brands toward spending for visibility, again, just like in the traditional media. Thus, the role of media remains important, and a large proportion of the advertising budget goes back to dissemination, even though organic reach and shared media are still largely desired.

Yes, hopefully, some campaigns, even when running on a tight media budget, might gain significant exposure and reputation because users choose to share them. But this has always been a wished-for effect of creativity: that an ad becomes a point of reference, a topic or catchphrase popping up in our daily thoughts and interactions. There is still no recipe to ensure that a campaign will become shared, even when using best practice toward this direction. Paid media is what we focus on in this chapter, while content marketing is covered in Chapter 8.

3 Media planning in traditional media – key terms

Media planning has always been data driven. For decades now, planners have been using complex calculating models to determine the most effective media mix for a given budget and set of objectives. Online advertising provides more information about consumers, thus enabling the targeting process to become more accurate as discussed in Chapter 2 and will be elaborated below.

There are two significant terms media planners consider when planning and when assessing a campaign outcome. These are:

- Campaign **reach**: How many people from the target group got exposed to the campaign? If we reach too many people who are not part of the target group, we waste money. If we reach too few, creative efforts go astray.
- Campaign **frequency**: How many times people from the target group got exposed to the campaign? Too little exposure does not create awareness and memorability and, thus, is a wase of money. Too much exposure is over-spending. For an ad to work, some repetition is required. The more the clutter or the more intense the competition, the larger the frequency required for the targeted consumer to remember the ad. Today's prevailing term is "the rule of seven", suggesting that the optimal number is seven exposures to an ad. Rules change. Two decades ago, this would have been five; a decade from now, nobody knows. However, it is widely accepted that the more creative a message is, the lower the frequency needed for consumers to remember or to act on this message. Thus, creativity pays off.

Another important aspect is the **flow** of the campaign which depends on budget, seasonality, and objectives. A brand might choose to allocate its budget evenly across 12 months of the year; or it may choose to increase advertising during a specific time like, let's say, Christmas. Brands often work in bursts, meaning that they create an annual plan with picks and valleys in spending. Some months may be silent while other months may be very intense in advertising spending. Ice cream brands might not advertise during the winter; educational institutions may spend more around the time preceding each registration period; retailers often advertise intensely when they have discounts (Belch & Belch, 2003, pp.300–347).

4 Media planning in traditional media – selecting the appropriate mix

Media selection is a complex process that deploys in layers.

First, on the macro-level in each market, a planner chooses which medium to use. Should a brand appear on national TV? On local radio stations? On bus stop posters? And the list goes on. This choice depends on factors including:

- Budget: some media are more expensive than others. Usually, a radio commercial is much cheaper to produce and air, compared to a TV commercial, for example. However, in larger markets where TV has high viewership the absolute cost per consumer exposure might end up being quite low.
- Locality: a local business might invest in local media, like radio or Out Of Home (OOH) advertising, while a national business might need to advertise on national TV and national news outlets.
- Competitors: where do they advertise? Should the brand "stand next to them" our build distinctive touchpoints?

These are not "tick-the-box" choices. Each decision entails risk and must be well informed. A routine or "business-as-usual" approach will not yield results.

At the second stage, the meso-level, the planner will select particular media vehicles, that is the specific media brands to be used. Will it be BBC? Fox? The Discovery Channel? Eurosport? And so forth. This choice primarily depends on one factor: what does the target group watch? Each TV station usually provides both free and restricted information around viewership and the profile of its viewers, so that advertisers can make the best choice. Pricing is also important, especially when choosing among two TV stations with similar audience profiles.

Finally, the planner must delve in the micro-level and select the specific sub-section of each medium. Will it be the 8 o'clock news? The Saturday night movie? The kids' zone? If that were a newspaper or magazine, the planner should choose a specific section and page. Will it be page 3, the first one to see when opening the newspaper? The sports section the cultural section or the foreign affairs section? (For a more extensive reading on the levels of media planning: Katz, 2016; Rossiter & Danaher, 2014; Danaher, 2008; Kelly et al., 2012; Keller, 2001).

After all these decisions have been made, a huge, detailed spreadsheet or Gant chart emerges, demonstrating each exposure, i.e., each and every ad that will air for the entire duration of the campaign.

In traditional media planning, despite everyday monitoring of media popularity, viewership etc., data can become consolidated and meaningful after a campaign ends. To estimate campaign outcomes, planners and marketers together must combine total exposure (reach and frequency) with marketing results like sales or store visits, and consumer research results, as discussed in Chapter 3, even though in today's media landscape response to advertising can also be assessed to some extent by the amount of social media reactions an ad creates during airing (Fossen & Schweidel, 2016).

5 Display ads on the web and social media

Display advertising includes paid messages appearing on websites, search engine results, and social media feeds, though in social media the term might vary: boosted posts or page promotion are terms used frequently to express paying for a broader display of a brand's content or page or offering. Display ads may also appear on smartphones via web browsers or in the apps we use.

Paying to promote distinguishes between content marketing and advertising. Content marketing, covered more extensively in the next chapter, started with the premise that brands need not intrude. Instead, by creating and posting good quality content, brands might engage in discussions, empower their customers, and have users interact with the brand because they want to, not because they were interrupted. As discussed, this assumption has deflated with brand promotion being, so far, the dominant source of revenue for search engines and social media platforms whose algorithms tend to prioritise paid over organic content, often on the premise that users want to interact with each other rather than with brands.

Display advertising resembles its mass media predecessors: the advertiser pays a fee to place an advertising message in the desired online environment, trying to grasp the attention of a target group that will click to find out more or to buy or to donate, subscribe, etc. Display advertising is interruptive in nature. Square or rectangular, full screen, or in pop-up windows, ads may appear on the homepage or in any specific sub-section of a website.

Display ads are priced and measured mostly in two ways:

a   Cost Per Thousand Impressions (Cost per Mille – CPM): how many times an ad appeared when a webpage loaded on a user's screen.
b   Cost Per Click (CPC): how many times a user clicked on a display ad and stayed on the landing page for at least a few seconds. When users immediately click the "back" button or close the new tab, their click is exempted. This is defined as bounce rate.

Note that CPC was originally considered revolutionary, as it proved real time that the ad worked: if the user clicked, then the ad was effective. This is what differentiated web advertising initially, from its mass media counterparts. CPM reminds more of traditional media effectiveness: results are indirectly assessed, and a more accurate picture is available after the campaign stops running.

An option, usually for small scale advertisers, is to collaborate directly with one or more websites and "book" a place for their ad. Usually, however, display advertising is planned and executed by media agency planners with the support of algorithms, as will be discussed below.

Another option is to collaborate with a search engine like Google. In this case, although there are alternatives, a brand usually selects key-terms that users in the target group would likely type when searching. These terms might be simple, like "hotels" or composite, like "pet friendly hotels in Perth". The advertiser will write the ad copy and select a target group based on Google's available options. Then,

Google will place it in the relevant search results. How high and on which page this ad will appear depends on the cost. The brand might wish to pay, let's say, for one million impressions, first result, first page which would be a very expensive choice; or the brand might say something like: I can pay a thousand euros, what do I get? So, this is more like a bidding process for a search term, whose price depends on seasonality and popularity though algorithms often make this pricing process appear a bit obscure.

Google also has its own "display network" that is a vast number of websites across the world, which lease "space" to Google. Then Google subleases this space to brands wishing to advertise on the web, offering relevance which is based on content keywords, geolocation, and target group preferences. Such ads may contain images or video and may be a good fit for companies which either want to reach a global audience or want to target a very specific consumer segment.

Media shops have recently developed their own tools to provide display advertising for their clients. They use their own algorithms and big data management systems to provide effective and efficient solutions with real-time targeting, bidding, and optimisation. This is usually defined as programmatic advertising.

6 A few words on programmatic advertising

Programmatic advertising is media buying preformed automatically using algorithms to reach a suitable web user within a suitable context, thus increasing the possibility to click. Programmatic advertising allows for customisation and personalisation of each advertising message. Instead of serving the same execution to a vast audience, the copywriter can tailor their message, visual, even the offering to different segments. Tailoring the offering, however, is a contested practice as some users may receive better discounts or lower prices than others, based on what we know about their profile.

With programmatic advertising, a media shop uses algorithmic and AI tools to optimise every exposure real-time, without pre-planning which message will appear to whom and when. As soon as an opportunity appears, let's say, someone is typing the words "energy, crisis, winter" on a search engine or on a news website, an algorithm finds the opportunity to serve an ad for heating devices, also considering who that someone is, based on the IP address, location, or other information that cookies may provide (for a thorough review: Boerman et al., 2017). Programmatic advertising faces criticism around the lack of transparency and equal treatment of all consumer segments, as well as around the abuse of personal data (Aiolfi et al., 2021; Eaca, 2022). Programmatic advertising also has a long way to go when it comes to perceiving relevance of context.

Contextual advertising is about matching ads within media content thus making these ads contextually relevant. This is what Google tries to do with its display network. Tags and keywords help establish such relevance, hence the emphasis on Search Engine Optimisation (SEO). The effort websites invest in, benefits not only their retrievability but also the engine itself that can target more accurately.

Behavioural targeting relies on evidence of prior user behaviour: what the user did, where they clicked, what they searched for. Such evidence indicates this user should be (re)targeted. Advertising makes use of personal data that can be automatically processed so that an ad is served to a potentially interested consumer who belongs in the desired target group. Thus, both contextual and behavioural and contextual targeting both rely on prior evidence.

As with most CPC or CPM campaigns, response or proof of exposure to an ad is the key criterion of success so it is sometimes argued that programmatic advertising follows a behaviouristic approach: if the campaign is efficient, the consumer will click, which reminds of the Pavlov's dogs. While being direct and to-the-point, programmatic advertising may also appear shallow or blunt and sometimes repetitive, tiring, or even manipulative, invasive, and controlling (Nadler & McGuigan, 2018). But there is evidence it works, at least for some products in some markets, while its creative potential remains to be further explored.

As the case study in this chapter indicates, too much programmatic advertising might eventually harm a brand's image. Allocation of the advertising budget should ensure a balance between sales and brand building or, in other words, between short-term and mid-term effects. Though these two are not contradictory by default, the new media often appear to favour either one over the other.

Programmatic advertising can keep improving results as algorithms are trained. A lot of split testing and real-time optimisation, powered by big data, is required to maximise efficiency. Such data includes web user information about browsing and shopping, retrieved from cookies, as well as data from a brand's Customer Relationship Management systems, and from mobile apps (Deloitte, 2017; Fulgoni, 2013). Consumer analytics are a gigantic source of value (Erevelles et al., 2016). All these, when combined, help create customer segments or clusters, based on consumption patterns around the advertised brand, in a way that is more accurate and detailed compared to traditional advertising. Beyond programmatic advertising, big data is useful in consumer research (Hofacker et al., 2016) and in advertising account planning where data may help reveal creative insights (Malthouse & Li, 2017). According to a white paper by Deloitte (2017, p. 6), whoever owns the data owns the customer relationship.

Done well, programmatic advertising leads to less wasted effort, more relevance for consumers, higher click through rates, more sales and better user experience. This approach is rapidly spreading beyond websites to reach TV audiences through streaming platforms, customising the advertising message based on user profile and content relevance (Malthouse et al., 2018).

Customer journeys are mostly fed by big data, enabling brands to learn more about consumers (Ammerman, 2019; Strong, 2015), critical moments of choice and word of mouth around their brands (Moran et al., 2014). Privacy and data ownership issues arise, however, along with practical challenges that are still to be dealt with (Walker & Moran, 2019).

Gradually, Integrated Data Driven Marketing (iDDM) expands in areas of marketing that go beyond consumer research and programmatic advertising, from product development to distribution and to pricing (Bibby et al., 2021), provided data sources are combined across different ranks and functions (Carey, 2017).

How does programmatic affect the work of creatives? A copywriter working for programmatic advertising must be a master in flexibility and eloquence; able to articulate the same simple sentence in several different ways, select the one that delivers the best results and keep incorporating the findings of message and key-word split testing throughout the duration of a campaign, because the type of proposition and type of argument used to persuade consumers seem to differ depending on whether an ad prioritises clicks over conversions or vice versa (Haans et al., 2013).

Accordingly, a web designer must be able to adapt similar visuals across different formats at a great speed or adjust visuals for the purposes of split testing to finally select the one that performs best. Compared to the conceptual work in more traditional creative agencies, this process may appear less inspiring and simulating, more repetitive and tiring. Concepts developed for programmatic advertising also present particularities and demands for application in broader contexts, leveraging the benefits of integration that will be discussed below (Meyers & Muche, 2016; Weisbrich & Owens, 2016). However, a professional who has had some experience in this line of work may find themselves gaining significant advantage when it comes to flexibility. Editing and optimising an advertising message under time constraints is a very useful skill that can sometimes make or break a creative idea.

Some argue that the use of big data and Artificial Intelligence (AI) might also come to serve as support, or even as substitute, to creative work, especially since the advent of ChatGPT and other AI tools, which may also provide visual and design services. Currently, some greet the power of algorithms and artificial intelligence evangelising more promising campaign planning and ideas, while others show resistance and hold the flag of talent higher than ever. Truth is usually somewhere in the middle.

Case study: ADIDAS goes programmatic and back

At some point around the mid-2010s, Adidas decided to invest heavily in digital advertising, aiming at greater results in terms of sales. They shifted a significant part of the budget toward digital advertising but then noticed that although sales went well, there was a decline in brand image.

Adidas had focused on efficiency rather than effectiveness; on decreasing advertising cost rather than increasing brand equity. Furthermore, too many offerings or special discounts in digital marketing – which are often needed to create a sense of urgency and encourage instant action – created price sensitive consumers.

Thus, the brand did not see where results were really coming from: "... while Adidas thought only performance drove ecommerce sales, in fact it was brand activity driving 65% of sales across wholesale, retail and ecommerce" (Vizard, 2019). Having spent too much time focusing on sales, the brand used up its equity.

A spokesperson labeled this as "short-termism" and called these results vanity metrics, explaining that, from that point on, the brand would follow a new campaign approach combining programmatic advertising and sales promotions with emotional brand-driving campaigns.

Commenting on the issue, another spokesperson noted: "Building cultural attention means understanding people, communities, and culture, and adding value to those groups. It takes more than data to do this".

Lesson learnt: media is a mix. Trends are to experiment with but a balance in budget allocation and media choices is always needed. And there is no way to keep driving sales in the long run, without considering brand personality and cultural context.

Further reading

- https://www.marketingweek.com/adidas-marketing-effectiveness/.
- https://www.campaignlive.co.uk/article/stop-optimising-the-sht-marketing-says-adidas-brand-boss/1345296.
- https://digiday.com/media/adidas-tests-new-media-strategy-world-cup-campaign/.
- https://huntsman.usu.edu/learntwice/articles/adidas-we-over-invested-in-digital-advertising.

7 A few words on social media advertising

Social media also provide plenty of options for brands that wish to advertise, and this is where their revenue comes from. Significant knowhow is being invested to develop an entire ecosystem just for advertisers who plan, execute, and measure their campaigns. Social media platforms provide tailored interfaces, step-by-step options, multiple formats (stories, videos, carousels, etc.) and tips for brands to run campaigns. Constant training is required to keep up with changes in platform functions and the algorithmic processing of content. This is also a bidding process in which the advertiser determines spending. Transparency issues exist here as well (Eaca, 2022).

The emotional impact of social media is widely documented (Buffard & Papasava, 2020). To achieve campaign results, however, there is need for frequent, multi-platform promotion of branded content, offerings and activation, to maintain users' interest (Ashley & Tuten, 2014). This section describes the steps Meta proposes for campaign planning[1]:

Define objectives. Objectives are defined based on the metrics Meta provides, such as website traffic, conversion, sales promotion, reach, etc. Do note that using metrics as objectives is somewhat self-serving for the platform. Such metrics always need to align with broader communication objectives.

Define the target audience using demographic, psychographic, and lifestyle information that the platform can detect based on user profile and activity.

When social media advertising began, there was one significant difference: advertisers could profile their target group using tags that included lifestyle. One could choose to run a campaign targeting pet owners or sports fans or culture vultures, etc. This feature soon became abused and users were unethically targeted. An example was promoting conversion therapy to LGBTQ+ users (Picheta, 2020), which created a huge backlash. Gradually, platforms limit such lifestyle options to the basics, to avoid outing sensitive lifestyle information[2] or appearing intrusive. From an ethical standpoint, microtargeting can have detrimental political and personal implications. From an advertising perspective, this type of abusive targeting deprived social media advertising of a potential advantage that would ensure accuracy and relevance. Thus, social media advertising gradually resembles traditional advertising reaching out to many, hoping to catch the few.

Select the platform. Meta allows an advertiser to deliver ads on Facebook or Instagram, on Messenger, on the Facebook market and so forth.

Decide on the budget for a given time frame. Meta proposes a suitable budget and duration based on the above, but the advertiser can increase or decrease.

Decide on the format of the ad. Meta offers a list of alternatives: promoted posts, carousels, collection ads, video ads, stories etc. – these are constantly updated. Within these formats, the advertiser creates the desired message and visual.

Then, the advertiser orders the campaign and measures the results. The platform suggests posts that may be worth promoting, as well as the right timing, and notifies when budget has been used up. All platforms use similar steps. Do notice the similarity with overall advertising campaign planning as described in Chapter 1, and then developed throughout this book. Gradually, all forms of digital advertising become to some degree part of every brand's media mix.

8 Conversions and connections

Digital marketing uses a plethora of digital touchpoints, paid or not, to convey a message and then relies on click-through and conversion (Seiler & Yao, 2017; Chaffey and Smith, 2012). To achieve high conversion rates, we need first a compelling message, short, specific, appealing, with a promise and call to action, with a single-minded image where applicable. Then, we need a landing page. Simply put, creating a landing page is like creating a shortcut and opening a new door to the website, which allows a visitor to follow their clicking course rather than go to the home page and start searching from scratch. Each campaign comes with at least one landing page which connects the promotional message with the desired online activity, shortening the number of clicks. A landing page must contain relevant items of information, such as extensive descriptions, more images, as well as "learn more", "request a demo" or "buy now" calls to action. A/B (aka split) testing (Gallo, 2017) is often used to optimise user experience, examining positions, colours, sizes, proportions, types of visuals, etc. both for ads and for landing pages.

Conversion marketing is useful for offerings that can be purchased, used, or experienced online, from downloading apps to donating, to customising an insurance contract or even a car. But what about the products that cannot be bought online? Fast moving consumer goods, for example, have had little to benefit from conversions. Seeking good practices, such products paved the way for a significant yet somewhat neglected alternative: connection planning.

Connection planning, coined by Coca-Cola (i-com, 2016; Manjur, 2015; Zmuda, 2013; Sellers, 2012), is "the discipline of deploying your resources across owned, earned, shared and paid media in such a way that it delivers business results" (Zmuda, 2013). This approach focuses on offering experiences to the user, rather than on optimising user experience. A connection campaign uses multiple touchpoints and multiple types of content, aiming to create synergies between these different executions. Keeping the consumer in the loop for as long as possible and avoiding dead-ends, that is touchpoints which do not allow the user to continue engaging with the brand, are the two basic challenges of a connection campaign that usually also includes tailored activations. Instead of having all touchpoints lead to one landing page, connection planning is about media and touchpoints connected one to the other, enabling prolonged consumer engagement and interaction. Even mass media advertising can be effectively used to guide users to online touchpoints (Joo et al., 2016; Liaukonyte et al., 2015) where they can create, post, share, and comment.

For connection planning to succeed, the brand needs one strong, single-minded idea and campaign theme, based on unique insights. This idea breeds executions in all possible touchpoints. Mass media allow for dissemination while social media allow for interactivity and user generated content. Tailored activities also help bring virality and earned media. While engaging with the campaign in one platform, the user is encouraged to view more content or create and post content on another platform: upload your photo; share with a friend; play and win; and more. Examples include the "Dumb ways to die" campaign discussed in Chapter 3, the "Share a Coke" campaign (Neal, 2014), and "Better for it" by Nike (O'Reilly, 2015), among many.

Top-of-mind awareness, engagement, loyalty, and maintenance of a positive image are the objectives connection planning can achieve, especially for products that are not usually bought and consumed online. Successful connection campaigns frequently leave a long tail and are remembered long after airing. To get a good understanding of connection planning, just jump on board the next online campaign for a product you cannot buy online and trace the opportunities for engagement across media.

Connection planning can be challenging for creatives. They need a strong idea which applies in as many touchpoints as possible while generating potential for user generated content and creative use of media. Unique visuals and memorable messages are also needed, to break through the clutter and boost consumer engagement. Connection planning requires creative storytelling where stories are developed around the main theme but executed differently to fit different touchpoints: video ads, podcasts, gifs, infographics, long-form articles, comic strips, etc. A significant degree of integration is necessary so that users can connect the dots and associate each media execution with the main campaign theme.

9 Integrated and omnichannel campaigns

Integrated marketing is a planning process which combines all marketing and communication activities to provide a unified and consistent product and message experience (Schultz & Schultz, 1998), incorporating the online environment (Kerr & Patti, 2015). Beyond advertising, an integrated marketing approach would include public relations, sales promotion, in-store experience and the entirety of brand-customer contacts (Smith & Zook, 2019) hence integration often begins in the client's office, not in the agency's (Ots & Nyilasy, 2017). Even more so, integration is about seeking one voice, one sound, and one story that are seamlessly conveyed across all touchpoints, while studies also advocate cocreation of this unified narrative with consumers (Johansen & Andersen, 2012). Integration challenges compartmentalisation and offers an opportunity to brands to explore their identity and personality more deeply, calling for the brand's organisational alignment on a multitude of functions that go beyond campaigning and promotion (Ots & Nyilasy, 2017).

Accordingly, from a creative's perspective, integrated campaigns are not just about combined and synergistic media planning and deployment. They revolve around a strong, single-minded idea, visual, and message. This idea should be profoundly connected with brand identity and delivered with a unified, consistent tone of voice. An integrated campaign requires multiple creative executions, so that the consumer gets exposed to the same message through stories, images, and sounds, in different media. The strongest advantage of an integrated campaign is its cumulative effect, where the total is larger than the sum of its parts and each media exposure reminds of all previous ones without becoming repetitive or monotonous. Integration is a major challenge for creatives. There is no better indication for an idea's robustness than the ability to keep generating consistent, synergistic executions for different media.

As discussed in Chapter 4, from a creative's perspective, an integrated campaign should achieve the **4Cs**: Consistency, Coherence, Continuity, and Complementary (Pickton & Broderick, 2004; see also: Pickton & Hartley, 1998; for a slightly different approach with a more strategic orientation: Keller, 2016).

Integrated campaigns, then, require robust and flexible creative ideas, solid enough to bring uniqueness, yet broad enough to allow for interactivity and engagement across touchpoints – just like with connection planning. Common approaches to the need for integration require strong, well targeted consumer insights and common creative elements: the same tagline, the same look and feel, analogous story patterns, similar iconography, similar shapes, proportions, and positions, creating unique characters, using celebrities exclusively, selecting distinctive music, and so forth. Integration, however, moves beyond media synergies to cover broader organisational functions and longer term brand strategy, beyond the scope of an advertising campaign.

The benefits and advantages of integrated communication are well established (Patti et al., 2017; Keller, 2016; Kerr & Patti, 2015). It is important for Integrated Marketing Communications (IMC) to constantly adapt to changing media landscapes; to follow consumer trends; to break organisational silos, and to align with the brand identity and the organisational vision. IMC permeates an entire organisation, hence beyond acknowledging its importance, establishing efficient and effective collaboration between stakeholders on a large scale and maintaining alignment is essential (Ots & Nyilasy, 2017; Kerr & Patti, 2015).

However, from a creative's perspective, one should always keep in mind that too much integration for too long, might create fixed mindsets among professionals, leading to less flexibility, less spontaneity, less adaptability to market changes and less room for tactic creative ideas that may help create buzz or invigorate the brand. And, of course, in new media environments where more diverse professional skillsets than ever before need to be aligned to deliver a unified outcome, challenges involving collaboration, coordination and logistics are also significant. Integration requires alignment among different teams with different priorities and KPIs which, in turn, need to be carefully allocated and tailored (see also: Ots & Nyilasy, 2015).

In the new media environment, a term that has proliferated is "omnichannel campaigns" which also promises an intuitive, effortless customer experience between different media and points of contact. The term is usually juxtaposed with "multichannel marketing". Whereas a multichannel approach focuses on optimizing campaigns on each separate touchpoint, an omnichannel approach would focus on alignment between all touchpoints, from first exposure all the way to repeat buying. Such alignment yields better results compared to separate attempts of optimising (de Haan et al., 2016). There are significant similarities on the mindset, steps, and principles guiding omnichannel and integrated campaigns (Berman & Thelen, 2018; Payne et al., 2017): consumer-centrism, cumulative effects, unified design, single-minded messages. The effort to align, integrate, coordinate, and combine remains the same, albeit under more complex circumstances.

The challenge for seamless integration and omnichannel approaches is about to rise to a different level in the near future. The distinction between display ads, search engine ads, and content gradually fades away. Currently, younger users seem to start their searches on visual platforms like TikTok rather than Google; ChatGPT is also used for consumption related suggestions; streaming TV is part of a programmatic media mix. All these trends will keep instigating changes. Text-based search is now being replaced by search in platforms supporting a visual experience and the use of Artificial Intelligence (AI) (WARC, 2023).

10 Local, global, glocal – in the context of new media

The juxtaposition of large-scale, global campaigns and smaller-scale, national or local activities had been a prominent topic in advertising. On the one hand, global campaigns have the benefit of wide reach, consistent brand image and economies of scale. On the other hand, local campaigns can be tailored more appropriately to each local market, language, culture, competition, and trends. In-between are approaches like "Think global, act local" or "go glocal" (indicatively: Wind et al., 2013; see also: Zandpour et al., 1994; Kanso, 1992). According to these approaches, global strategies or ideas should be implemented and complemented within each specific local context.

A few years into digital marketing and the discussion re-opened (indicatively: Jacobs et al., 2016). From big satellite news providers to tiny forums for people with similar interests, brands have countless options to create their own media and tailor content to each specific market. Such possibilities are not yet fully explored. For example, global campaigns could be complemented by local activations, local brand communities (Bagozzi and Dholakia, 2006; Cova and Pace, 2006), and tailored local content which could help interactivity and engagement in a way that is consistent and synergistic for the brand.

However, such approaches sometimes appear labour intensive or too complex and resources are not often allocated toward this direction, especially in smaller markets. Furthermore, a lot of global brands fear the loss of control over local content, often engaging in gatekeeping (Miliopoulou, 2021), thus preferring a simple translation of unified content in different languages rather than actual local content. Treating new media like mass media seems to gradually become the norm, at the expense of interactivity and engagement. The alignment of global strategies with local needs, and the consequent customisation of branded content appears to be the best practice so far, keeping the old "glocal" discussion still open. There are a few ideas and values that can bring people on board on a global scale and a few brands who can afford the resources to implement them. There are sharp differences in cultural contexts, market needs, and consumer aspirations which pave the way for more specific, authentic, and relevant ideas, especially if one considers how advertising has entered the realm of identity politics (De Mooij, 2003). The degree of local freedom is always a challenge when it comes to global brands, but this is where true social media potential lies.

11 Creative use of media

During the last decades of the 20th century, the mass media became highly standardised, and creatives need to follow rules relating to dimensions, sizes, durations, use of colour, proportions, and more. The web at first seemed like a land of opportunity lacking rules, best practices, and limitations. Today, however, the online landscape is also highly standardised, complying with best practices for user experience, as well as with terms, conditions, policies, and ethical regulations, even if these are not always effectively imposed. However, there was, there is, and there will always be room for unconventional use of media. Great ideas can and should always explore possibilities for such use.

An interesting change the online environment has brought is the proliferation of opportunities for guerrilla marketing interventions in the urban environment. These often fall within the broader context of Out-Of-Home Advertising (OOH) or ambient advertising, that is, advertising appearing in the urban environment, in places where one would least expect it, from public restrooms to highways, to utility poles and so on (Hutter, 2015). Such interventions may also include installations like pop-up stores (Grant et al., 2015) or events like flash mobs and treasure hunts. These activities are not new per se. What is new is that these can be filmed and shared on social media by the brand or, even better, by the users. This type of sharing multiplies content reach and content lifecycle, harvesting the value of shared media and consumers' reactions. Every creatively potent local activity thus travels further and lasts longer than where and when it took place. The Contrexperience exercise event (Serdarevic, 2011), the Axe / Lynx angels falling from the sky (McCabe, 2011), or the panic button by TNT channel (Berkowitz, 2012) have been such examples.

However, the interesting aspect here is that any unconventional use of medium, if successful once, becomes mainstream afterwards and might gradually find its way in a more conventional media mix. Ten years ago, "skins" (static background branded images, often with a message or a call-to-action, which appeared on the sides of a website) would be considered unconventional; twenty years ago, a two-minute TV advert would be considered unconventional; a few years back, inter-active outdoor was a novelty; not anymore. Successful attempts gradually become mainstream. Now, what?

Unconventional use of media may fall under what is broadly defined as trans-formational creativity (Boden, 2003) – the type of creativity that thereafter chan-ges the advertising landscape, having paved the way for truly innovative ideas. Alternate Reality Games (ARGs) with online rabbit holes (indicatively: Hanas, 2006, Gray, 2019), campaigns like Oreo 365 (Elliott, 2012), advergames which are also briefly discussed in Chapter 6 are among the many examples of today's potential for creative use of media.

Creatives and media planners in tandem should keep exploring opportunities for unconventional use of media, where the medium can provide context to the adver-tising content and where unexpected combinations can benefit from the element of surprise which, in turn, increases credibility and brand favourability (Dahlén, 2005). There are two basic principles to follow: first, ensure that the creative medium insti-gates the appropriate associations, by keeping the positive ones and eliminating any negative ones; second, render obvious the connection between the brand and the medium (Dahlén, 2005). This could be achieved through the right message.

Creative options are always out there. It takes one who knows the rules to break the rules; one who knows established practices and standards, to be able to come up with an unexpected alternative. Media planners know the media landscape and together with creatives can consider unexplored alternatives; or creatives can come up with a novel idea and media planners could look for the appropriate placement. For creatives, media savviness, constant benchmarking, cultural capital, and some experience in advertising can help enrich the advertising media mix in unexpected ways. There is no blueprint for creative, unconventional use of media. One must stay alert and seek opportunities for creative combination, in every advertising campaign (see also Chapter 5).

***

No better way to end this chapter than by circling back to the beginning and to the 80–20 rule of thumb. Though this book is written for professionals in creative advertising, remembering that the largest proportion of a client's budget goes to the media is always significant, as this poses limitations to creative freedom and puts pressure on clients to ensure Return On Investment (ROI).

When digital and social media came along, there was this promise that the 80–20 rule would change; that brands could invest more in content, since it would be free to disseminate and, if worthy, it would be shared by users, instigate interaction, and maximise engagement without paid placement. Today, the vast amount of content is promoted and, in this respect, new media remind more and more of traditional media.

Circling back to where it all started emphasises the significance of studying the history of marketing and advertising, globally and in each country or market. History brings to light significant parallelisms in the development of mass media and new media: how the conceptualisation of consumers shifts from simplistic behaviourism to more contextual and socially oriented approaches; how media outlets tend to become more standardised; how consumers gradually become savvier, and harder to impress.

Analogies from the past may foster critical and creative thinking, among both practitioners and academics. Re-examining old advertising success stories, theories, and models; or re-applying past thoughts in new landscapes may lead to more or better insight. Theory and history lead to a deeper and better understanding of current experience.

Time to practise!

- Trace at least ten campaigns that make creative use of media. Try to write one sentence in which you explain the combination between the creative idea and the space it was placed. Then, try to adapt this idea for different brands and / or different media.
- Use two browsers in two different devices. Enable cookies in one browser; disable cookies, install ad blocks and use no personal profile in the other browser. See what happens after 15 days. Take detailed notes of your observations.
- Try to trace at least three large scale campaigns in your country and discover all the media these campaigns used.
- Think of an ARG to promote a local brand of carbonated soft drink to teenagers over 15 years old, in your city. Consider cultural context and what your desired target group will most likely engage with.
- Think of at least five unexpected places to place a poster promoting life insurance.
- Think of at least five unexpected places to make audio announcements on blood donation.
- Think of at least five unexpected places to promote gender equality.
- For all the above, compare notes with fellow students and check for overlaps or unique thoughts.

- Copy the text of an ad which you encountered in the Google Search Network and rewrite it in at least three different ways. Then, write three more messages to be used for retargeting.
- Select one ad that appeared as a static banner in one of the websites you visit. Click and observe the landing page. Rewrite the copy of the ad and the landing page, so these are in accordance; consider how the visual could change on both the banner and the landing page.

Notes

1 https://www.facebook.com/business/ads
2 https://www.facebook.com/business/news/removing-certain-ad-targeting-options-and-expanding-our-ad-controls

References

Aiolfi, S., Bellini, S. & Pellegrini, D. (2021), Data-driven digital advertising: benefits and risks of online behavioral advertising, *International Journal of Retail & Distribution Management*, 49 (7), 1089–1110. https://doi.org/10.1108/IJRDM-10-2020-0410.

Ammerman, W. (2019). *The Invisible Brand: Marketing in the age of automation, big data, and machine learning*. New York: McGraw Hill.

Ashley, C., & Tuten, T. (2014). Creative strategies in social media marketing: An exploratory study of branded social content and consumer engagement. *Psychology and Marketing*, 32 (1), 15–27. https://doi.org/10.1002/mar.20761.

Bagozzi, R.P. & Dholakia, U.M. (2006). Antecedents and purchase consequences of customer participation in small group brand communities, *International Journal of Research in Marketing*, 23 (1), 45–61, doi:10.1016/j.ijresmar.2006.01.005..

Belch, G.E., & Belch, M.A. (2003). *Advertising and promotion: an integrated marketing communications perspective*6th ed. The McGraw-Hill Companies.

Berman B, & Thelen S. (2018). Planning and implementing an effective omnichannel marketing program. *International journal of retail & distribution management*, 46 (7), 598–614. doi:10.1108/IJRDM-08-2016-0131.

Berkowitz, J. (2012, November 4). TNT pushes the drama button on unsuspecting Belgians. *Fast Company*. Available at: https://www.fastcompany.com/1680531/tnt-pushes-the-drama-button-on-unsuspecting-belgians.

Bibby, C., Gordon, J., Schuler, G., & Stein, E. (2021, March 25). Savvy marketers are rethinking their tech and data strategies to double down on precision marketing following COVID-19. *McKinsey*. Available at: https://www.mckinsey.com/business-functions/growth-marketing-and-sales/our-insights/the-big-reset-data-driven-marketing-in-the-next-normal.

Boden, M. (2003). *The creative mind: Myths and mechanisms*2nd. London: Routledge.

Boerman, S.C., Kruikemeier, S., & Zuiderveen Borgesius, F.J. (2017). Online behavioral advertising: A literature review and research agenda. *Journal of Advertising*, 46(3), 363–376.

Bruce, N.I., Peters, K., & Naik, P.A. (2012). Discovering how advertising grows sales and builds brands. *Journal of Marketing Research*, 49 (6), 793–806. https://doi.org/10.1509/jmr.11.0060.

Buffard, J., & Papasava, A. (2020). A quantitative study on the impact of emotion on social media engagement and conversion. *Journal of Digital & Social Media Marketing*, 7 (4), 355–375.

Carey, C. (2017, June). Better together: Why integrating data strategy, teams, and technology leads to marketing success. *Think with Google*. Available at: https://www.thinkwithgoogle.com/marketing-strategies/data-and-measurement/data-strategy-technology-marketing-analytics/.

Chaffey, D. & Smith, P.R. (2012) *E-marketing excellence: Planning and optimizing your digital marketing*. London: Routledge. https://doi.org/10.4324/9780203082812.

Cova, B. & Pace, S. (2006). Brand community of convenience products: new forms of customer empowerment – the case "my Nutella The Community", *European Journal of Marketing*, 40(9/10), S1087–1105. https://doi.org/10.1108/03090560610681023.

Dahlén, M. (2005). The medium as a contextual cue: effects of creative media choice. *Journal of Advertising*, 34(3), 89–98.

Dahlén, M., & Rosengren, S. (2016). If advertising won't die, what will it be? toward a working definition of advertising. *Journal of Advertising*, 45(3).

Danaher, P.J. (2008). Media planning. In G. J. Tellis, & T. Ambler, *The SAGE handbook of advertising*. Sage UK. Credo Reference: https://acg.idm.oclc.org/login?url=https://search.credoreference.com/content/entry/sageukadver/media_planning/0?institutionId=5970.

de Haan, E., Wiesel, T., & Pauwels, K. (2016). The effectiveness of different forms of online advertising for purchase conversion in a multiple-channel attribution framework. *International Journal of Research in Marketing*, 33 (3), 491–507. https://doi.org/10.1016/j.ijresmar.2015.12.001.

De Mooij, M. (2003). Convergence and divergence in consumer behaviour: implications for global advertising. *International Journal of Advertising*, 22 (2), 183–202. https://doi.org/10.1080/02650487.2003.11072848.

Deloitte Digital (2017). *Data driven marketing: How efficient and personalized customer dialog will work in future?* Available at: https://www2.deloitte.com/content/dam/Deloitte/de/Documents/technology/Data-Driven-Marketing-Whitepaper-Deloitte-Digital-2017-English.pdf.

Eaca (2022). *The digital marketers' act and its impact on communication agencies*. Available at: https://eaca.eu/wp-content/uploads/2022/07/The-DMA-Impact-on-agencies-EACA-.pdf.

Elliott, S. (2012, September 24). For Oreo campaign finale, a twist on collaboration. *The NY Times*. Available at: https://www.nytimes.com/2012/09/25/business/media/oreos-daily-twist-campaign-finale-enlists-consumers.html.

Erevelles, S., Fukawa, N., & Swayne, L. (2016). Big data consumer analytics and the transformation of marketing, *Journal of Business Research*, 69 (2), 897–904.

Fossen, B.L., & Schweidel, D.A. (2016). Television advertising and online word-of-mouth: An empirical investigation of social tv activity. *Marketing Science*, 36 (1). https://doi.org/10.1287/mksc.2016.1002.

Fulgoni, G. (2013). Big data: Friend or foe of digital advertising? *Journal of Advertising Research* 53 (4) 372–376; doi:10.2501/JAR-53-4-372-376..

Gallo, A. (2017). A refresher on A/B testing. *HBR*. Available at: https://hbr.org/2017/06/a-refresher-on-ab-testing.

Grant, P., Botha, E., & Kietzmann, J. (2015) Branded flash mobs: Moving toward a deeper understanding of consumers" responses to video advertising, *Journal of Interactive Advertising*, 15 (1), 28–42, DOI: doi:10.1080/15252019.2015.1013229.

Gray, T. (2019, Feb. 1). "Blair Witch project" Cast a marketing spell on audiences 20 years ago. *Variety.* Available at: https://variety.com/2019/vintage/features/blair-witch-project-1203123291/.

Haans, H., Raassens, Néomie, & van Hout, R. (2013). Search engine advertisements: the impact of advertising statements on click-through and conversion rates. *Marketing Letters,* 24 (2), 151–163.

Hanas, T. (2016, Jan. 1) Games people play. *AdAge.* Available at: https://adage.com/article/feature-%28from-print%29/games-people-play/106068.

Hofacker, C.F., Malthouse, E.C. & Sultan, F. (2016), Big Data and consumer behavior: imminent opportunities, *Journal of Consumer Marketing,* 33 (2), 89–97. https://doi.org/10.1108/JCM-04-2015-1399.

Hutter, K. (2015). Unusual location and unexpected execution in advertising: A content analysis and test of effectiveness in ambient advertisements, *Journal of Marketing Communications,* 21 (1), 33–47, DOI: doi:10.1080/13527266.2014.970823.

i-com news (2016, October 6). In US, Shubu Mitra of The Coca-Cola Company joins I-COM global board. *I-COM.* Available at: http://www.i-com.org/news-articles/in-us-shubu-mitra-of-the-coca-cola-company-joins-i-com-global-board.

Jacobs, K., Spierings, N., & Jacobs, Kristof. (2016). Social media, parties, and political inequalities. In *Social media go "glocal": The local and European arenas* (pp. 131–155). essay, New York: Palgrave Macmillan US: Palgrave Macmillan. https://doi.org/10.1057/9781137533906_6.

Johansen, T.S., & Andersen, S.E. (2012). Co-creating ONE: Rethinking integration within communication. *Corporate Communications: An International Journal,* 17(3), 272–288.

Joo, M., Wilbur, K.C., & Zhu, Y. (2016). Effects of TV advertising on keyword search. *International Journal of Research in Marketing,* 33(3), 508–523. https://doi.org/10.1016/j.ijresmar.2014.12.005.

Kanso, A. (1992). International advertising strategies: Global commitment to local vision. *Journal of Advertising Research,* 32 (1), 10–14.

Katz, H.E. (2016). *The media handbook: A complete guide to advertising media selection, planning, research, and buying* (2nd ed., Ser. Lea's communication series). Lawrence Erlbaum.

Keller, K.L. (2001) Mastering the marketing communications mix: Micro and macro perspectives on integrated marketing communication programs, *Journal of Marketing Management,* 17(7–8), 819–847, doi:10.1362/026725701323366836.

Keller, K.L. (2016). Unlocking the power of integrated marketing communications: how integrated is your IMC program? *Journal of Advertising,* 45(3), 286–301. https://doi.org/10.1080/00913367.2016.1204967.

Kelly, L.D., Jugenheimer, D.W. & Sheehan, K.B. (2012). *Advertising media planning: A brand management approach.* New York: Routledge. https://doi.org/10.4324/9781315706696.

Kerr, G., & Patti, C. (2015). Strategic IMC: From abstract concept to marketing management tool. *Journal of Marketing Communications,* 21(5), 317–339. https://doi.org/10.1080/13527266.2013.786748.

Kim, Y. & Patel, S. (2012). Teaching advertising media planning in a changing media landscape. *Journal of Advertising Education,* 16 (2),15–26. doi:10.1177/109804821201600203.

Liaukonyte, J., Teixeira, T., & Wilbur, K.C. (2015). Television advertising and online shopping. *Marketing Science,* 34(3). https://doi.org/10.1287/mksc.2014.0899.

Malthouse, E.C., Maslowska, E., & Franks, J.U. (2018). Understanding programmatic tv advertising. *International Journal of Advertising*, 37 (5), 769–784. https://doi.org/10.1080/02650487.2018.1461733.

Malthouse, E.C. & Li, H. (2017) Opportunities for and Pitfalls of Using Big Data in Advertising Research, *Journal of Advertising*, 46 (2), 227–235, doi:10.1080/00913367.2017.1299653.

Manjur, R. (2015, June 3), Is O&M pitching for Coca-Cola's media account the start of a new trend? *Marketing-Interactive*. Available at: http://www.marketing-interactive.com/om-pitch-coca-colas-media-account/.

McCabe, M. (2011, March 21). Lynx turns to outdoor augmented reality. *Campaign Live*. Available at: https://www.campaignlive.co.uk/article/lynx-turns-outdoor-augmented-reality/1061042.

Meyers, C., Muche, C. (2016). Unleashing the power of greater creatives for brands. In: Busch, O. (eds) *Programmatic advertising: Management for professionals*. Springer, Cham. https://doi.org/10.1007/978-3-319-25023-6_11.

Miliopoulou, G.-Z. (2021). Brand communities, fans or publics? How social media interests and brand management practices define the rules of engagement, *European Journal of Marketing*, 55 (12), 3129–3161. https://doi.org/10.1108/EJM-09-2019-0692.

Moran, G., Muzellec, L. & Nolan, E. (2014). Consumer moments of truth in the digital context, *Journal of Advertising Research*, 54 (2), 200–204, doi:10.2501/JAR-54-2-200-204.

Moriarty, S., Mitchell, N. & Wells, W. (2015) *Advertising & IMC: Principles and practice*. Pearson, Global Edition.

Nadler, A. & McGuigan, L. (2018) An impulse to exploit: the behavioral turn in data-driven marketing, *Critical Studies in Media Communication*, 35 (2), 151–165, doi:10.1080/15295036.2017.1387279.

Neal, C. (2014, August 28). Share a coke: it's all in a name; a case study on Coca-Cola's bold new interactive marketing campaign. *Medium*. Available at: https://medium.com/marketing-and-advertising/share-a-coke-its-all-in-a-name-8700a7e30df5.

O'Reilly, L. (2015, April 13). Nike is making its biggest ever women's push. *Business Insider*. Available at: https://www.businessinsider.com/nike-betterforit-women-campaign-2015-4.

Ots, M. & Nyilasy, G. (2017). Just doing it: Theorising integrated marketing communications (IMC) practices, *European Journal of Marketing*, 51 (3), 490–510. https://doi-org.acg.idm.oclc.org/10.1108/EJM-08-2015-0595.

Ots, M., & Nyilasy, G. (2015). Integrated marketing communications (IMC): Why does it fail?: An analysis of practitioner mental models exposes barriers of IMC implementation. *Journal of Advertising Research*, 55(2), 132–145.

Patti, C.H., Hartley, S.W., van Dessel, M.M. & Baack D.W. (2017). Improving integrated marketing communications practices: A comparison of objectives and results, *Journal of Marketing Communications*, 23 (4), 351–370, doi:10.1080/13527266.2015.1027251.

Payne, L.M., Peltier, J.W., & Barger, V.A. (2017). Omni-channel marketing, integrated marketing communications and consumer engagement: A research agenda, *Journal of Research in Interactive Marketing* 11(2):185–197. doi:10.1108/JRIM-08-2016-0091.

Picheta, A. (2020, July 11). Instagram and Facebook ban all content promoting conversion therapy, *CNN Business*, available at: https://edition.cnn.com/2020/07/10/tech/instagram-conversion-therapy-ban-scli-intl-gbr/index.html.

Pickton, D.W. & Broderick, A.J. (2004), *Integrated Marketing Communications*, 2nd edition. Financial Times Prentice Hall

Pickton, D.W. & Hartley, B. (1998) Measuring integration: An assessment of the quality of IMC. *International Journal of Advertising*, 17 (4), 447–465.

Rossiter, J.R., & Danaher, P.J. (2014). Advanced media planning. *Springer Science Business Media*. https://doi.org/10.1177/13548565211047342.

Schultz, D.E. & Schultz, H.F. (1998) Transitioning marketing communication into the twenty-first century, *Journal of Marketing Communications*, 4 (1), 9–26, doi:10.1080/135272698345852.

Sellers, P. (2012, 17 October). Coke's Facebook expert on how to build a "social" brand, *Fortune*. Available at: http://fortune.com/2012/10/17/cokes-facebook-expert-on-how-to-build-a-social-brand/.

Serdarevic, M. (2011, October 17) The public image: Contrex's exercise bike campaign: The agency opted for laughs while retaining the essential link between water and thirst. *FT*. Available at: https://www.ft.com/content/10fe18d4-f8c9-11e0-ad8f-00144feab49a.

Smith, P.R. & Zook, Z. (2019). *Marketing communications: Integrating online and offline, customer engagement and digital technologies*. New York: Kogan Page.

Strong, C. (2015). *Humanizing Big Data: Marketing at the meeting of data, social science and consumer insight*. London: Kogan Page.

Vizard, S. (2019, October 17). Adidas: We over-invested in digital advertising. *Marketing Week*. Available at: https://www.marketingweek.com/adidas-marketing-effectiveness/.

Walker, K.L., & Moran, N. (2019). Consumer information for data-driven decision making: Teaching socially responsible use of data. *Journal of Marketing Education*, 41 (2), 109–126. https://doi-org.acg.idm.oclc.org/10.1177/0273475318813176.

WARC Media (2023, April). *Global ad trends: Search 3.0*. Available at: https://content.ascential.com/search-3-0-thankyou.html?aliId=eyJpIjoiYW82aTFFZFJqOURMVmpZO-CIsInQiOiJCdzYxNFBXN205OWduUm9EY2R5T3B3PT0ifQ%253D%253D.

Weisbrich, S., & Owens, C. (2016). The creative challenge. In: Busch, O. (eds) *Programmatic advertising. management for professionals*. Springer, Cham. https://doi.org/10.1007/978-3-319-25023-6_10.

Wind, J., Sthanunathan, S., & Malcolm, R. (2013), Great advertising is both local and global, *HBR*. Available at: https://hbr.org/2013/03/great-advertising-is-both-loca.

Zandpour, F., Campos, V., Catalano, J. & Chang, C., (1994). Global reach and local touch: Achieving cultural fitness in TV advertising. *Journal of Advertising Research*, 34 (5), 35–63.

Zmuda, N. (2013, September 23). Media maven Ivan Pollard makes connections pay for Coca-Cola: Exec plots ways for brand to resonate with consumers globally, *Adage*. Available at: http://adage.com/article/special-report-media-mavens-2013/ivan-pollard-vp-global-connections-coca-cola/244129/.

8 Content Marketing: New media, familiar patterns

1 Branded content and content marketing

Branded content is all content produced and disseminated by a brand, to help achieve strategic goals (for a more extensive discussion on different definitions: Content Marketing Institute, N.D.; Hardy, 2018; Asmussen et al., 2016). Such content may appear on a brand's owned media, might be sent via email or appear in an app. Branded content could be posted for free, or get promoted as part of an online campaign. For example, a brand creates a "how-to" video, posts it on the website and on an Instagram account and then runs a campaign to boost this post to reach potential customers. Thus, content might help promote a brand's offering or might constitute an offering in itself, even if free.

Branded content might appear on another publisher's website. If this occurs for free, then it's earned media. For example, a big brand creates a new campaign and Adweek or Adage write a news story about it. However, a brand might pay for branded content to appear on a publisher's website as part of that website's content, having the publisher's tone of voice, style, and look & feel. This is the case of native advertising (Dens & Poels, 2023). Such distinctions are important to a website visitor. We should know who paid for the content we consume, because such transparency ensures we can assess such content more accurately. This is why trustworthy websites often label native articles using terms like "sponsored content". From a creative professional's perspective, however, such distinctions may be less relevant. Creatives produce branded content that can be either paid or organic or both.

Content marketing is a strategic marketing approach focused on creating and distributing valuable, relevant, content to attract and retain a clearly defined audience – and, ultimately, to drive profitable customer action (Content Marketing Institute, N.D. See also: Rowley, 2008; Beard, et al., 2021). Content marketing also covers targeting, dissemination, and outcomes, as part of broader digital marketing activities, running independently to maintain consumer interaction, or as part of integrated advertising and PR campaigns (Keller, 2001). However, as different organisational functions and different agencies might be involved in this process, achieving alignment is not always easy.

DOI: 10.4324/9781003330721-8

2 Engaging through content: three approaches

Brands may create content around product functions or around brand innovation or values, etc. The way content around brands or products and brand offerings in general is developed can take different directions and explore different possibilities, to achieve different strategic aims. In many cases, brands explore content territories that are not strictly speaking relevant to the product and yet can help create unique bonds with consumers. This section discusses three ways of strategic content planning.

First comes the **brand-as-publisher** approach. A publisher brand traces one or more territories of content that help establish a bond with significant target groups and then starts publishing content around these territories, not necessarily about the brand and its products. Thus, the brand offers content that users could normally find in news media or content websites. Publisher brands are often found in the business-to-business sector through corporate blogging like, for example, the Microsoft story labs, but are also encountered in other categories, even in the FMCG sector where an example would be Red Bull, the energy drink that engages with extreme sports not only as an organiser and sponsor but also as a publisher of news and feature stories in various formats (Burg, 2014). Publisher brands build content by demonstrating dedication, allocating resources, seeking expert help, organising entire newsrooms, and preparing longer term content plans which go beyond the narrow scope of a promotional campaign (Holliman & Rowley, 2014; Basney, 2014; Deloitte, 2016; see also: Johnson, 2023). To be a publisher brand is often considered laborious and not cost efficient. Successful brand publishing approaches rely on expert writing and top quality producing of multimodal and multimedia content.

Second, practitioners and academics have approached branded content by approaching the **brand as a storyteller**, arguing that the online environment helps brands convey narratives thus engaging not only with consumers but also with stakeholders and employees. Brand narratives promote innovation, values, visions, and not just products. Indicative examples include videos of brand activations like: "CIF Cleans Romania" or "Apple's Employee Recruiting Video". Brand narratives go beyond advertising and promotion to include stories which add to the meaning-jar of the brand and enrich its semiotic palette (Hackley & Hackley, 2019). Such stories may have to do with the product but may also focus on user experience, employees, heritage, and more. Great storytelling shared on social media allows brands to offer their side of the story, prevent or overcome crises, capitalise on their past, convey values, and build a positive image or an attractive, resonant personality. Big brands like Dove or Nike and smaller brands like Warby Parker or Ben & Jerry's have leveraged the power of storytelling, even without relying heavily on mass media advertising. Brand storytelling might boost brand image and sales, not instantly but in the longer run. This is a significant difference between display or programmatic advertising and content marketing (Dens & Poels, 2023; Crespo et al., 2022; Kemp et al., 2023; Kemp et al., 2021; Lou et al., 2019).

The making of strategic stories has been discussed extensively in Chapter 6. Content marketing can benefit from the tools presented there, to ensure not only creative originality but also strategic appropriateness. The key steps must first ensure the conflict of the story reflects strategic communication objectives literally or figuratively, then allocate narrative roles to include the brand and the message recipient and then work on the plot, starting from the climax.

Third, the **brand-as-community** approach has instigated considerable discussion and research since the 1990s. The term "brand community" describes a specific consumer–brand relationship characterised by shared consciousness of belonging; ritualistic elements and behaviours in interaction; and moral responsibility toward the preservation of the community (Muñiz and O'Guinn 2001; Miliopoulou, 2021). In brand communities, the brand should be a mere facilitator, not a controlling entity, enabling connections between members through events and other activities, while sharing special content, soliciting reviews, listening, and enabling, thus turning community members to willing ambassadors. Content and discussions mostly come from the users.

Brand communities could be very powerful in connecting global brands with local markets by tailoring content to local context and rewarding core users. Social media helped both build and kill brand communities. At first, social media enabled people with similar interests and feelings around a brand to gather online and form such communities. Later, communities were impacted by platforms' efforts to monetize user activity. Facebook now defines community as the number of a user's friends who like the same brand page. Thus, sense of belonging and moral responsibility toward the community are no longer a priority. The idea is that users interact with the brand individually.

***

There are signs of decline for content marketing and organic reach (Sehl, 2021; Sample, 2019) while content strategy becomes part of omnichannel marketing campaigns, as branded content requires significant resources and its benefits are sometimes doubted or take too long to become evident (Lou et al., 2019). Evidence indicates the results of content marketing are contextual, platform dependent and resource dependent (Bowden & Mirzaei, 2021).

3 Content marketing & product category

Best practices in content marketing vary per product category, not only in traditional advertising, as discussed in Chapter 2. Products characterised by high versus low involvement seem to differ slightly in the way they generate positive user experience, evaluation, and loyalty (Lou & Xie, 2021). Combining product involvement with investment, we can study best practices that emerge for different product categories in the areas of content marketing. Imagine that products can be classified on a horizontal axis from cheap on the left, to expensive on the right. Imagine also that products can be classified on a vertical axis, from utilitarian and functional, at the bottom, to emotionally engaging ones at the top. This would create four quadrants that help us understand how to plan for effective web and social media content (Miliopoulou, 2019; Morton & Devine, 1985).

Top right are products that are both expensive and emotionally appealing. Our mobile phone, our car, expensive outfits belong in this category. We spend a lot on our choice; therefore we need to know quite a lot before making an informed decision. Since these are products we care about, we are also more likely to connect on social media, to share, even create content for them. Thus, organic reach and content marketing is not such a huge challenge for these brands. Both informative and emotional or entertaining content, especially creative storytelling, is likely to resonate. User generated content like unboxing videos or product reviews is easier to achieve. Communities are likely to flourish. Brands who do well in this quadrant are Apple and Samsung, but also Volvo and Mini.

Top left are cheaper products we like or love. As we repurchase frequently, we are less likely to demonstrate extreme loyalty. We cheat on them occasionally. Our favourite chocolate or beer or bodywash might easily be replaced if something triggers our attention, like a competitor's offer or new flavour. These products need to stay "top-of-mind" and remind of their presence quite often. Thus, such products usually invest in a couple of strong bursts a year, using connection planning across all possible touchpoints, prioritising creativity to generate publicity that will last and leave a strong impact even after the campaign has ended. The Greek chocolate Lacta by Mondelez[1] and the Oreo Daily Twist[2] are such examples.

Bottom right are expensive products we need mainly for functional purposes. Banking and insurance services, home appliances… the wrong investment will have significant consequences, so we need to make informed choices. Content marketing is of essence here: long-form content, web apps for comparisons of alternatives, white papers, customer reviews and testimonies, infographics… all the tools brought by the new media can help products in this category establish content leadership and then brand leadership, thus gaining trust and preference, all other things being equal. Search Engine Optimisation and Marketing are also quite important here, as consumers will engage in active search once they define their need and start seeking the best way to satisfy this need. Slow-brewing long-form content, even when tiring, will become very important during the stage of consumers' research for more information. General Electric and the National Australia Bank are good examples in this quadrant.

Bottom left are FMCGs and all the functional, inexpensive goods our daily life relies on. We buy out of habit or demonstrating price consciousness and we consume their ads accordingly (Seiler & Yao, 2017). These are the products which invested heavily in mass media during previous decades and have a hard time standing out in the social media environment as users abstain from "liking" or "following" breadsticks, and detergents, even when in reality they do purchase such goods regularly. Content-wise, product information is less likely to instigate interest. Best practices in this quadrant come from products like Always or Persil or Dove that build on a social insight and on a motivating hashtag, rather than promoting the product and a tagline. "#likeagirl", "#freethekids", and "#realbeauty" create engagement in social media as these brands discover and present a salient "social self".

4 Content strategy and planning in steps

Content marketing is often ongoing, even when other campaign activities are paused; and yet it should be closely aligned with all these activities. To define the appropriate content strategy, one should follow the steps outlined in Chapter 1 and then covered throughout this book: assess the current situation and define objectives; specify target groups; select the appropriate message(s) and the online touchpoints that will be used; measure and optimise. All the above should derive from and be closely linked to the brand's overall communication strategy, as content may appear both offline and online, as in the case of video advertising (Lim et al., 2015). Once decisions have been made, the next step is planning.

Planning for branded content requires systematic, ongoing, iterative effort and constant monitoring. Autopilot does not help. This would be the process from scratch:

1 **Brand communication audit, benchmarking & (re)source-tracking**: the content team must become familiar with the brand's strategic priorities and study distinguished content practices not only from competing brands but from a wide range of products in different markets, paying close attention to backlashes. The team must also estimate available resources. Good content is costly.

2 **Organising & allocating**: the content team decides on pillars and formats discussed below in section 5, ensuring that content pillars will connect to strategy while content formats will leverage creativity and appropriateness. This is an iterative process. Every few weeks the team must assess results, project needs, and plan forward based on measurements and feedback.

3 **Creating & disseminating**: choosing which platform to use for which pillars and formats or for which target groups is laborious. There is a plethora of expert tips but only through trial and error can each brand create its own best practices. No universal rules apply, trends change, while platform content and interfaces gradually become homogenised.

    Some experts advocate that one can diversify content based on the users each platform attracts, thus matching audiences with content through the selection of each social media platform. For example, there is this notion that younger people visit Instagram and TikTok. Such notions change as platforms grow and expand. The average TikTok user in 2022 will not be the same in 2024.

    Others allocate content per platform, building on platform characteristics. Thus, some argue that more "visual" content is appropriate for Instagram, while long-form text is more appropriate in Facebook or LinkedIn. However, one may frequently see longer texts on Instagram posts – a frequent pattern for news publishers. So, trial and error it must be. Step 3 ends with the content calendar described in section 6 below.

4 **Measuring & optimising**: ideally speaking, each organisation should assess needs, create needs-based objectives, and then select the measurements that will prove these objectives have been achieved. Not-so-ideally speaking, organisations tend to start from free and accessible platform metrics, and then try

to connect these metrics with their objectives. They do not measure what they need; they need, eventually, what they can measure. Organisations should tailor composite metrics to make measurements relevant to their broader aims.

5 Branded content – pillars & formats

Content pillars are thematic areas, broad topics that content will be covering on a midterm basis. Such topics may emerge from brainstorming or benchmarking or through market research which brings to light a need to educate or inform or engage. Depending on budget, posting frequency, and long or short-term planning, a brand could rely on two or three pillars but more than that, for less than six months would probably mean the brand is spreading itself too thin. Because too much online content is redundant, outdated, or trivial (ROT), coming up with original and relevant pillars is challenging. Here are some examples that show relevance but not originality:

- A car brand could choose to develop content for a three-month period on the following pillars: a) eco-driving; b) electro-mobility; and c) passive safety, depending on the car features, the market and its trends.
- A cosmetics' brand could develop content for a yearly plan on the following pillars: a) seasonal trends; b) celebrity make-up; c) ingredient stories.
- A bank could develop content for a six-month period, on the following pillars: a) investment opportunities in certain domains; b) ethical, sustainable banking; and c) web & mobile banking tips and possibilities.

These pillars may help convey one key message each, like, for example: "drive green" or "fall for colour" or "we grow opportunities". Unless the content marketing plan revolves around a specific omnichannel campaign, having one tagline cover all pillars is not always best practice.

Pillars help an organisation set priorities on "what to talk about" with consumers or stakeholders. Pillars should be neither too vague (like, for example, good driving) nor too narrow (like, for example, how to make mobile transactions). Pillars should allow for a multitude of content that will be covered sufficiently by the end of the defined time period. Some brands focus on one pillar at a time, others alternate between a couple of pillars throughout the year.

Content format (or type) is the way a message will be materialised. The term is loosely defined among industry experts but usually refers to visual, audiovisual, textual, or multimedia executions. For example, we may create a series of tips on eco-driving. These can appear as visual posts with a quote and a link; each on its own or all in a carousel; or as long form content in the form of explanatory feature stories; or as short videos; or as a compiling infographic. Memes and gifs are also content formats.

A brand might start with plain textual formats and then provide more elaborate illustrations or animations, because content costs. This is called upscaling and depends on strategic priorities or pillar popularity. If, for example, a brand hosts an event and then chooses to post a digital release, they could write a plain text and, perhaps, add a photo. Later, the brand could release a carousel; or a white paper with the talks; one or more videos of what happened – usually ranging from the full long version to many cut versions covering different instances or speakers. With all the content cluttering surrounding users, good content needs high production values and standards. Creating or processing visual and audiovisual material requires expert help and software. Long form content takes time and expertise. These are often outsourced.

After defining content pillars & formats, the content team should consider resources and timing, and decide which content formats will be used to bring each pillar to life. These should be laid out on a spreadsheet which allows content managers to plan, assign, create, and get approvals before posting. The creative team might execute such content.

6 Content calendars

Every content marketing plan boils down to a content calendar, usually finalised and updated monthly, containing each post's working title, format, and the platform(s) it will appear in, per day or time of day if needed, as per the rough example on Table 8.1.

The web offers a lot of content calendar templates which facilitate alignment between content creators, managers, and the rest of the marketing team (indicatively:

Table 8.1 A monthly content calendar

Date	Headline	Format	Platform
October 1	Test your breast	Digital release	Facebook, LinkedIn
October 5	Know thy breast	Long form content	Posted on website, shared on Facebook & X
October 8	We care	Digital release	LinkedIn
October 12	The pink ribbon	Meme / Gif with link	Instagram post
October 15	The pink ribbon	Meme / Gif + link	X, Facebook
October 19	Expert interview	Podcast on Spotify and website + link	LinkedIn, Instagram story
October 22	Test yourself	Video	YouTube, Facebook, website
October 26	The pink ribbon (re-post and add 3 more)	Series of memes	Instagram story, Facebook carousel
October 29	The fight before (information on preventive testing)	Infographic	Instagram post, Instagram story, Facebook, website, LinkedIn
October 31	Our efforts to fight breast cancer	Long form content on website + link	Posted on website, shared on LinkedIn, Facebook, X

Kenan, 2023; Bernazzani, 2023; Newberry & Cohen, 2022). The calendar can receive pre-approval and then, once content is ready, it can be sent again containing every content unit to be approved. The first type of approval helps alignment with broader communication activities occurring during the same time, which is especially useful for omnichannel communication and for complicated integrated campaigns that also deploy traditional media. The second approval ensures content appropriateness and originality so that posting can be automated.

After content is published, community managers should anticipate reactions and responses. When a pillar has sensitive aspects involved, before it is published, content managers and community managers should plan on whether and how to address negative reactions preparing (and having approved) draft responses where applicable. Users react any time of the day or night, so the team should be proactive and stay alert to anticipate social media storms.

7 Metrics & KPIs

Though objectives should lead to metrics and not vice versa, many companies and agencies plan using available platform metrics which are sometimes escorted by third party measurements for a more complete picture. A list of essential, available metrics is presented in Table 8.2, per type of online site or activity, though composite and tailored measurements should always be sought.

The above metrics are basic, mostly associated with content marketing. There are more and more complex metrics (indicatively: Butow et al., 2020; Silva et al., 2020), and a lot of websites publish content on recent trends around measurements for the web and social media (indicatively: Chen, 2021; Digital Marketing Institute, 2021; Newberry, 2022; Carmicheal, 2023; Keyhole blog, 2023).

When a brand first engages in content marketing, generic KPIs are used, which then require fine tuning with patience. After the first results are in, the team should select which metrics to improve and how. When a campaign is running, real time monitoring gives the team good overview of what works or not, allowing for improvement. As measurements are fine-tuned, they may indicate not only which touchpoints and which content works better, but also how synergies may develop (Fulgoni et al., 2017). Though at first this seems laborious, tacit knowledge gradually enables fast moves and agility. Real-time optimisation helps content managers stop promoting inefficient content, address negative reactions early, boost content that performs better, and give feedback on all the above to content creators, for their forthcoming work.

However, one should always keep in mind that some content formats are "slow brewing" and do not yield results immediately (Lou et al., 2019). If the team chooses, for example, to invest in long-form reports, they should know that initial reports might go unnoticed even when promoted. If the effort persists, however, viewership might occur retrospectively, so the brand earns credit for having invested in this pillar. Some users start noticing the reports and then trace previous ones, which means that return on investment comes at a later stage, not immediately, as one would expect from a gif.

Table 8.2 Basic metrics per website type and platform or activity

Content website	Business website	E-shop	Native advertising	Social media	Email
Total traffic			Page traffic	Impressions	Subscribers
Unique visitors / First time visitors				Reach / views	Opt out rate
	Returning visitors			Page likes / followers	Open rate
Time on site				Post reactions	Conversion rate
Time on page			Time on page (compared to the website average)	Comments	
	Bounce rate			Shares	
Exit rate				Conversion rate	
	Page views (total or per visit)			Return on investment or engagement	
	Sources of traffic				
Device					
		Value per visit			
		Time to complete the buying process			
		Number of full carts (incomplete orders)			

Rich, informative, educational, entertaining, funny, clever, and engaging content is what brands can offer on social media.

8 A few words on virality

Thankfully, we are past the stage where clients asked for a viral video, though aiming at virality is a frequent IMC objective. Virality was impressive, spectacular, and exciting during the formative years of the web and social media but has now turned to a huge challenge. The vast amount of content and the way social media and their users devour such content makes it difficult for any piece of content to become viral. Then, there is also content going viral because of public outcry rather than because of a great idea. Furthermore, there is no guarantee that virality will increase sales or market share. Viral content leads to sales when such content includes informative not just emotional appeals (Akpinar & Berger, 2017; for a different view, Tellis et al., 2019). The combination of reason with emotion is a central mandate discussed in various parts of this book.

Few brands can anticipate negative backlashes and have the stamina to wait for the storm to pass. One such case was the Nike Colin Kaepernick campaign that was initially greeted with anger as consumers started to burn their NIKE apparel and sharing these videos on X. Nike responded with a simple grey post advising people on how to burn Nike products safely and gave useful tips. The irony was evident, the storm was short and then came a period of record sales and stock prices which lasted a while before the curve returned to normal standards (White, 2018).

An analysis of campaigns that went viral, indicates that three factors can help toward this direction. First is seeding (Nelson-Field, 2013). Content that is intended to become viral should launch in many different online touchpoints and become available to many different segments of the desired market. This is costly but helps give content a strong initial boost. Second is emotional intensity. Viral videos have one thing in common: they elicit strong emotions (Nelson-Field, 2013). Third comes positive emotional intensity. Videos that create positive feelings are more likely to become viral (Nelson-Field, 2013; Berger & Milkman, 2012; see also: Tellis et al., 2019).

As virality becomes harder to achieve, researchers try more complex ways to interpret virality, considering more factors such as arousal, defined as the degree of activation a viral video could elicit (Berger & Milkman, 2012); the context within which content appears on the user's interface; and the individual reasons why users may choose to interact with specific content (Reichstein & Brusch, 2019).

Case study: Volvo trucks

Imagine you are a copywriter invited in a brief to work for trucks. Volvo trucks. This is not the type of project that sounds exciting or intriguing. But a team in a Swedish agency thought otherwise. So in 2013, a YouTube video featuring Jean Claude van Damme making a perfect split while standing on the side mirrors of two huge trucks on the move, got millions on views within just a few days. This is one of the most awarded and celebrated viral videos of all time. Yet, it's just the tip of the iceberg.

Volvo trucks produced and released a series of videos on their official channel, some of which featured unbelievable stunts: a mouse trapped in a round cage on the steering wheel, drove a Volvo truck as the driver gently circled a carrot that the mouse followed. A man, said to be the company CEO, stood on a truck hanging vertically on a crane. Carefully and very creatively designed to promote product features, these videos were exciting to conceive and spectacular to produce but not so likely to go viral. The epic split, however, drove viewers to the official YouTube Channel where all the stunts awaited and the sum of all these views skyrocketed.

Soon after, epic split spoofs appeared that also became viral. Chuck Norris preformed a split standing on the wings of two adjacent flying aircrafts, while soldiers standing on his shoulder lit up Christmas candles. A Greek YouTuber performed the epic split drinking ice coffee and whisky while smoking. And Volvo trucks welcomed the effort.

The idea of epic stunts could have been considered frivolous had it not relied on a very good use of data and insights. Trucks are bought by drivers and by corporate executives. Both need rational arguments, but this does not mean they need dry, boring product information. Truck drivers, especially, spend long hours practically living in their trucks, watching videos late at night, participating in communities who share information about trucks, rest areas, and more. They know their trucks like no one else and they know what they need and what to expect. Finally, somebody offered them content that appeared relevant and fun, and this brought engagement, leads, and of course, conversions. Production costs were significant, but media costs were close to zero. When Volvo trucks submitted their application for award in the Cannes Lions Festival, spoofs were a welcomed part of the material they included and dealt with as an indication of success, not as tampering with the brand and its content.

Find out more, here:

- https://www.digitalstrategyconsulting.com/online-advertising/online-advertising-research-tips-and-news-for-marketers/cannes-winner-case-study-how-volvo-epic-split-got-73m-youtube-views/11486/
- https://www.fastcompany.com/3031654/how-volvo-trucks-pulled-off-an-epic-split-and-a-game-changing-campaign
- https://business-review.eu/br-exclusive/the-marketing-strategy-behind-that-epic-split-van-damme-did-between-two-moving-volvo-trucks-186348
- https://www.forsman.com/work/volvo-trucks-live-test-series
- https://contently.com/2016/03/08/volvo-trucks-turned-b2b-video-viral-artform/

9 Is the King dead?

In 1996, Bill Gates said that "Content is King". For over two decades following this statement, brands invested in content, experimented with formats, instigated discussions, strived for emotional engagement (Buffard & Papasava, 2020; Ashley & Tuten, 2014), and hoped that if their content proved worthy of attention, they would achieve the desired results.

To get around, these days, the King needs a lot of support. Social media algorithms do not prioritize branded content on the grounds that users want to be in touch with other users, not brands[3]. Branded content is hard to reach unless a user makes very specific queries. Users become selective. Mediators are needed to bring content closer to interested users. Such mediators may be influencers (further reading: Lou & Yuan, 2019; Hudders et al., 2021; Leung et al. 2022) celebrities promoting branded goods, social media ads and boosted posts, search engines, and more.

Content has become harder to find and expensive not only to create but also to disseminate. As discussed in the previous chapter, more and more resources go to content promotion and brands face a dilemma: create great content that will not reach consumers or create good content and ensure its reach? This becomes an either / or question because resources are limited, thus quality content divestment appears to be a reality for many brands.

With the advent of sophisticated AI tools to be used not only to generate text but also to undertake designing and editing in various formats, branded content is expected to change even more (Ammerman, 2019). Whether such changes will lead toward trivialisation or newly explored creative paths or both, remains to be seen.

* * *

10 "OK, Boomer"

Try to imagine a world where people stay in touch using the phone or fax, or even write letters; a world where if you wanted to meet new people, you would either have to travel or pay for "pen pals" or "matching" services. This was the beginning of the new millennium.

When the first social media platforms started going global, a new land of opportunity appeared, first for people, then for brands. When we first started sharing our thoughts, our photos, our favourite songs, and family moments, it was quite clear how these start-up platforms created value for us, but quite unclear how they could create revenue for themselves. The world wide web was already there, but mostly offered one way access to information, which was revolutionary already. Emails were there but, again, could link us all to those we knew already or spam us with sketchy offers.

Interactivity, and user generated content are, by definition, the two main contributions of social media. User content makes platforms what they are, for better or worse. Hopes were that users would make the world a better place by sharing what they know, developing their creativity and innovative powers, engaging with citizen journalism, exchanging informed opinions and experiences in a way that puts technology at the service of humanism and humanity. Plausible dreams. Shattered dreams.

Brands came on board, a bit more clumsily at first, to be "where consumers are". The argument was that, finally, brands would be able to engage with consumers, foster dialogue, co-create desirable products and solutions, improve based on consumer feedback, and build closer relationships that would lead to brand communities and ambassadorship. Especially for start-ups, new, smaller, local, or unknown brands, this promise was intriguing.

Once social media started offering advertising services to brands, things rapidly took a different turn, metrics were invented and re-invented, and today, if we stop scrolling over a branded post for a couple of seconds, this is an impression, counts as reach and is paid for. From a brand's perspective, return on investment becomes complex to calculate.

Once, the "Like" button was powerful. Liking a brand page meant a lot, and brands were trying to attract and reward likes, on the grounds that a "Like" signified brand salience. Today, isolated posts carry all the weight and some of these posts may never appear on the brand page. These are the so-called dark posts that leave ample room for fake news or inappropriate advertising messages.

The first three decades of social media would make a very interesting story. Understanding this story, composing a narrative is very important for users and brands alike, to assess where things may be going and understand forthcoming changes. Telling this story to cover the evolution of social media marketing, the story of big data and user attention as corporate assets goes beyond the scope of this book.

Some digital immigrants, people of older ages who taught themselves and followed the developmental stages of online platforms, often generate "OK, Boomer" reactions but at least remember how things used to be. Digital natives may find social media use more intuitive but are not necessarily savvy enough to assess content and publishing practices as users or as managers. Better communicators are the ones delving in the past as much as in the present.

Time to practise!

- Try to locate at least three brands in your home country, which:

  - excel as content publishers
  - engage in storytelling through various formats, not just videos but also podcasts or long form articles
  - built and maintain brand communities on forums or websites or on social media.

- Study these brands and try to consider:

  - Would you propose new pillars? New formats? Write a brief rationale for each pillar you came up with and create two indicative content formats.
  - How do these brands preform in comparison to their competitors?
  - Check one of these brands thoroughly on social media, going back one month and try to re-create the content calendar of that month based on the above template.

- Consider developing your own content marketing plan. Choose one brand. Follow steps 1–4 in section 5.3. Then, answer the following questions:

  - which of the stages proved to be more challenging and why?
  - are you satisfied with the KPIs you selected?
  - would your content ideas require expert help or outsourcing?
  - how frequently would you post and why? How frequently would you repost the same content?

- Create at least 10 different content units of different formats for a brand and a pillar of your choice. Consider multimodal and multimedia content.

- Create one full content marketing proposal for a low investment/ low involvement brand of your choice. Follow steps 1–4, then work on pillars and formats, then on a monthly calendar. Select your KPIs carefully. Create a presentation in which you cover all these topics in detail. This can be a group assignment to share in class.
- Combine the metrics provided in Table 8.2 with Think-Feel-Do; discuss whether they fall under the modelling or the behavioural paradigm (Chapter 2).

Notes

1 A 2021 case study available here: https://wfanet.org/knowledge/diversity-and-inclu sion/item/2022/01/27/Insight–Strategy-Dont-Ever-Leave-Me
2 The Effie case study available here: https://www.effie.org/legacycases/case/NA_2013_ 7709
3 Indicatively: https://about.fb.com/news/2018/01/news-feed-fyi-bringing-people-clos er-together/

References

Akpinar, E., & Berger, J. (2017). Valuable virality. *Journal of Marketing Research*, 54 (2), 318–330.

Ammerman, W. (2019). *The invisible brand: Marketing in the age of automation, big data, and machine learning*. New York: McGraw Hill.

Ashley, C., & Tuten, T. (2014). Creative strategies in social media marketing: An exploratory study of branded social content and consumer engagement. *Psychology and Marketing*, 32 (1), 15–27. https://doi.org/10.1002/mar.20761.

Asmussen, B., Wider, S., Williams, R., Stevenson, N., Whitehead, E. & Canter, A. (2016). *Defining branded content for the digital age. The industry experts' views on branded content as a new marketing communications concept*. A collaborative research project commissioned by the BCMA and conducted by Oxford Brookes University and Ipsos MORI. Available at: https://brandedentertainment.de/wp-content/uploads/2017/ 02/BCMA-Research-Report_FINAL.pdf.

Basney, B. (2014). Brands as publishers: Using content and paid media to fuel a brand transformation. *Journal of Brand Strategy*, 3 (2), 101–110.

Beard, F., Petrotta, B., & Dischner, L. (2021). A history of content marketing. *Journal of Historical Research in Marketing*, 13 (2), 139–158. https://doi.org/10.1108/ JHRM-10-2020-0052.

Berger, J., & Milkman, K.L. (2012). What makes online content viral? *Journal of Marketing Research*, 49 (2), 192–205.

Bernazzani, S. (2023, June 15). How to create a social media calendar to plan your content. *Hubspot*. Available at: https://blog.hubspot.com/marketing/social-media-calendar-tools# social-media-cal-examples.

Beveridge, C. (2022, January 13). What is user-generated content? And why is it important? *Hootsuite*. Available at: https://blog.hootsuite.com/user-generated-content-ugc/.

Bowden, J., & Mirzaei, A. (2021). Consumer engagement within retail communication channels: an examination of online brand communities and digital content marketing initiatives. *European Journal of Marketing*, 55 (5), 1411–1439.

Buffard, J., & Papasava, A. (2020). A quantitative study on the impact of emotion on social media engagement and conversion. *Journal of Digital & Social Media Marketing*, 7 (4), 355–375.

Burg, N. (2014). Could Red Bull become the new ESPN? *Contently*. Available at: https://contently.com/2014/08/07/could-red-bull-become-the-new-espn/.

Butow, E., Herman, J., Liu, S., Robinson, A. & Allton, M. (2020). *Ultimate guide to social media marketing*. Entrepreneur Press.

Carmicheal, K. (2023, March 6). Which Social media metrics are marketers tracking? | New Research]. *Hubspot*. Available at: https://blog.hubspot.com/marketing/social-media-metrics-ceos-cares-about.

Chen, J. (2021, March 26). The most important social media metrics to track. *SproutSocial*. Available at: https://sproutsocial.com/insights/social-media-metrics/.

Content Marketing Institute, (2022) *Branded content: Getting it right*. Available at: https://contentmarketinginstitute.com/articles/branded-content-right/.

Content Marketing Institute, (N.D.) *What is content marketing*. Available at: https://contentmarketinginstitute.com/what-is-content-marketing/.

Crespo, C.F., Ferreira, A.G., & Cardoso, R.M. (2022). The influence of storytelling on the consumer–brand relationship experience. *Journal of Marketing Analytics*, 11 (1), 41–56. https://doi.org/10.1057/s41270-021-00149-0.

Deloitte (2016) Brands as publishers. WSJ. Available at: https://deloitte.wsj.com/articles/brands-as-publishers-1481518936.

Dens, N. & Poels, K. (2023) The rise, growth, and future of branded content in the digital media landscape, *International Journal of Advertising*, 42 (1), 141–150, doi:10.1080/02650487.2022.2157162.

Digital Marketing Institute (2022, December 13). *The best social media metrics to focus on in your campaigns*. Available at: https://digitalmarketinginstitute.com/blog/the-best-social-media-metrics-to-focus-on-now.

Dunn, K., & Harness, D. (2019). Whose voice is heard? the influence of user-generated versus company-generated content on consumer scepticism towards csr. *Journal of Marketing Management*, 35(9–10),886–915. https://doi.org/10.1080/0267257X.2019.1605401.

Fulgoni, G.M., Pettit, R. & Lipsman, A. (2017). Measuring the effectiveness of branded content across television and digital platforms: How to align with traditional marketing metrics while capturing what makes branded content unique. *Journal of Advertising Research*, 57 (4), 362–367. doi:10.2501/JAR-2017-046.

Gavilanes, J.M., Flatten, T.C. & Brettel, M. (2018) Content strategies for digital consumer engagement in social networks: Why advertising is an antecedent of engagement, *Journal of Advertising*, 47 (1), 4–23, doi:10.1080/00913367.2017.1405751.

Gensler, S., Völcknerb, F., Liu-Thompkins, Y., & Wiertz, C. (2013). Managing brands in the social media environment. *Journal of Interactive Marketing*, 27 (4): 242–256. https://doi.org/10.1016/j.intmar.2013.09.004.

Hackley, C., & Hackley, A.R. (2019). Advertising at the threshold: Paratextual promotion in the era of media convergence. *Marketing Theory*, 19 (2), 195–215. https://doi.org/10.1177/1470593118787581.

Hardy, J. (2018). *Branded content: Media and marketing integration*. Routledge.

Holliman, G. & Rowley, J. (2014), Business to business digital content marketing: marketers" perceptions of best practice, *Journal of Research in Interactive Marketing*, Vol. 8 No. 4, pp. 269–293. https://doi.org/10.1108/JRIM-02-2014-0013.

Hudders, L., De Jans, S., & De Veirman, M. (2021). The commercialization of social media stars: A literature review and conceptual framework on the strategic use of social media influencers. *International Journal of Advertising*, 40(3), 327–375.

Jin, S.V., & Youn, S. (2022). "They bought it, therefore i will buy it": The effects of peer users" conversion as sales performance and entrepreneurial sellers" number of followers as relationship performance in mobile social commerce. *Computers in Human Behavior*. https://doi.org/10.1016/j.chb.2022.107212.

Johnson, M.J. (2023). Navigating the cultural landscape through publishing brands: A theoretical, gendered perspective. *Pub Res Q*. https://doi.org/10.1007/s12109-023-09953-1.

Keller, K.L. (2001) Mastering the marketing communications mix: Micro and macro perspectives on integrated marketing communication programs, *Journal of Marketing Management*, 17(7–8),819–847, doi:10.1362/026725701323366836.

Kemp, A., Gravois, R., Syrdal, H., & McDougal, E. (2023). Storytelling is not just for marketing: cultivating a storytelling culture throughout the organization. *Business Horizons*, 66 (3), 313–324. https://doi.org/10.1016/j.bushor.2023.01.008.

Kemp, E., Porter, M., Anaza, N.A. & Min, D.-J. (2021), The impact of storytelling in creating firm and customer connections in online environments, *Journal of Research in Interactive Marketing*, 15 (1), 104–124. https://doi.org/10.1108/JRIM-06-2020-0136.

Kenan, J. (2023, February 20). A complete guide to creating a social media calendar. *SproutSocial*. Available at: https://sproutsocial.com/insights/social-media-calendar/.

Keyhole Blog (2023, April 26). 9 essential social media metrics to track in 2023 [+ 6 Best Tools]. Available at: https://keyhole.co/blog/social-media-metrics/.

Kim, J. (2012). The institutionalization of YouTube: From user-generated content to professionally generated content. *Media, Culture, and Society*, 34 (1), https://doi.org/10.1177/0163443711427199.

Kitirattarkarn, G.P., Araujo, T., & Neijens, P. (2019). Challenging traditional culture? How personal and national collectivism-individualism moderates the effects of content characteristics and social relationships on consumer engagement with brand-related user-generated content. *Journal of Advertising*, 48 (2), 197–214.

Krishnamurthy, S. & Dou, W. (2008) Note from special issue editors, *Journal of Interactive Advertising*, 8 (2), 1–4, doi:10.1080/15252019.2008.10722137.

Kwark, Y., Chen, J., & Raghunathan, S. (2018). User-generated content and competing firms" product design. *Management Science*, 64 (10), 4608–4628. https://doi.org/10.1287/mnsc.2017.2839.

Leung, F.F., Gu, F.F., Li, Y., Zhang, J.Z., & Palmatier, R.W. (2022). Influencer marketing effectiveness. *Journal of Marketing*, 86(6), 93–115.

Lim, J.S., Ri, S.Y., Egan, B.D., Biocca, F.A. (2015). The cross-platform synergies of digital video advertising: Implications for cross-media campaigns in television, Internet and mobile TV. *Computers in Human Behavior*, 48, 463–472. https://doi.org/10.1016/j.chb.2015.02.001.

Lou, C., & Xie, Q. (2021). Something social, something entertaining? How digital content marketing augments consumer experience and brand loyalty. *International Journal of Advertising*, 40 (3), 376–402.

Lou, C., & Yuan, S. (2019). Influencer marketing: How message value and credibility affect consumer trust of branded content on social media. *Journal of Interactive Advertising*, 19(1), 58–73.

Lou, C., Xie, Q., Feng, Y. & Kim, W. (2019), Does non-hard-sell content really work? Leveraging the value of branded content marketing in brand building, *Journal of*

Product & Brand Management, 28 (7), 773–786. https://doi.org/10.1108/JPBM-07-2018-1948.

Miliopoulou, G.-Z. (2021). Brand communities, fans or publics? How social media interests and brand management practices define the rules of engagement, *European Journal of Marketing*, 55 (12), 3129–3161. https://doi.org/10.1108/EJM-09-2019-0692.

Miliopoulou, G.-Z. (2019). Revisiting product classification to examine content marketing practices. *Journal of Research in Interactive Marketing*, 13 (4), 492–508. https://doi.org/10.1108/JRIM-07-2018-0084.

Morton, J., & Devine, H.J. Jr. (1985), How to diagnose what buyers really want, *Business Marketing*, 70 (10), 70–83.

Nelson-Field, K. (2013) *Viral marketing: The science of sharing*. Oxford University Press.

Newberry, C. (2022, June 23). 16 Key social media metrics to track in 2023 [BENCHMARKS]. *Hootsuite*. Available at: https://blog.hootsuite.com/social-media-metrics/.

Newberry, C. & Cohen, B. (2022, September 27). How to create a social media calendar [2023 Guide]. *Hootsuite*. Available at: https://blog.hootsuite.com/how-to-create-a-social-media-content-calendar/.

Reichstein, T., & Brusch, I. (2019). The decision-making process in viral marketing – A review and suggestions for further research. *Psychology & Marketing*, 36 (11), 1062–1081.

Rowley, J. (2008). Understanding digital content marketing. *Journal of Marketing Management*, 24(5–6),517–540. https://doi.org/10.1362/026725708X325977.

Sahl, K. (2021, August 24). Organic reach is in decline – Here's what you can do about it. *Hootsuite*. Available at: https://blog.hootsuite.com/organic-reach-declining/.

Sample, J. (2019, August 6). Is organic reach dead? *Forbes Agency Council*. Available at: https://www.forbes.com/sites/forbesagencycouncil/2019/08/06/is-organic-reach-dead/.

Seiler, S., & Yao, S. (2017). The impact of advertising along the conversion funnel. *Quantitative Marketing and Economics: Qme*, 15 (3), 241–278. https://doi.org/10.1007/s11129-017-9184-y.

Shahbaznezhad, H., Dolan, R., & Rashidirad, M. (2021). The role of social media content format and platform in users' engagement behavior. *Journal of Interactive Marketing*, 53 (1), 47–65. https://doi.org/10.1016/j.intmar.2020.05.001.

Silva, S. C. e, Duarte, P. A. O., & Almeida, S. R. (2020). How companies evaluate the roi of social media marketing programmes: Insights from b2b and b2c. *Journal of Business & Industrial Marketing*, 35 (12), 2097–2110. https://doi.org/10.1108/JBIM-06-2019-0291.

Simatzkin-Ohana, L., & Frosh, P. (2022). From user-generated content to a user-generated aesthetic: Instagram, corporate vernacularization, and the intimate life of brands. *Media, Culture & Society*, 44 (7), 1235–1254. https://doi.org/10.1177/01634437221084107.

Tellis, G.J., MacInnis, D.J., Tirunillai, S., & Zhang, Y. (2019). What drives virality (sharing) of online digital content? The critical role of information, emotion, and brand prominence. *Journal of Marketing*, 83(4), 1–20. https://doi.org/10.1177/0022242919841034.

Tsiakali. (2018). User-generated-content versus marketing-generated-content: Personality and content influence on travelers' behavior. *Journal of Hospitality Marketing & Management*, 27 (8), 946–972. https://doi.org/10.1080/19368623.2018.1477643.

White, M.C. (2018, September 10). What boycott? Nike sales are up 31 percent since the Kaepernick campaign. *NBC*. Available at: https://www.nbcnews.com/business/business-news/what-boycott-nike-sales-are-31-percent-kaepernick-campaign-n908251.

9 Ethics & regulations in advertising

1 Introduction

For over a century, advertising has received intellectual criticism on several fronts. From a political perspective, advertising has been considered a powerful proponent of capitalism. From a sociological perspective, advertising has been associated with the implications of consumerism and cultural decadence. From a psychological perspective, advertising has been accused of creating false needs and narcissistic tendencies by tapping on human insecurities.

Prominent representatives from the Frankfurt School passed the torch of criticism. Horkheimer & Adorno (1998 [1947]) argued that advertising dominates the field of cultural production to create subservience to the system of consumer capitalism. Marcuse (2002 [1964]) has argued that advertising is an instrument of control and domination. Advertising has been criticized for instilling false needs (Berger, 2000) and its ideological functions have been put under scrutiny (Williamson, 1978). Even if advertising is often a scapegoat or usual suspect for broader social issues and challenges (Rotfeld & Taylor, 2009), the discourse around the impact of advertising is necessary and stimulating.

Advertising carries a long history of deceptive, misleading, and harmful messages. In the past, advertising has promoted addictive medication; unhealthy snacks to pre-teens; excessive alcohol consumption. Advertising has also made false claims about products; has concealed their disadvantages; has distorted or overstated their advantages; and the list goes on. To these, one should add gross stereotyping which has been offensive to women, LGBTQ+, the elderly, ethnic and racial minorities… making fun of otherness to sell (for an amazing collection of the worst ads of all time: Saatchi, 2015; see also: N.A., 2015).

Tobacco products can no longer advertise after it was revealed that for decades ads had been misleading consumers into thinking that some cigarettes help women stay fit or do not make throats soar (Stine, 2014; Maheshwari, 2017). Agencies and manufacturers had been concealing the harmful effects of smoking, while releasing ads that promised less coughing, more vividness, and a great style… After the first whistle blew, storming revelations led to the gradual banning of tobacco advertising. In the EU, not only is such advertising not allowed, but

DOI: 10.4324/9781003330721-9

the packaging must also promote health warnings. In the USA, the industry has been forced to finance anti-smoking campaigns (Maheshwari, 2017).

Repetitively, baby formula companies have promoted their product as superior to breast feeding, also making false claims that formula can prevent allergies (Nelsen, 2018; FTC, 2014; Solomon, 1981). False claims are often settled with fines or litigations but then, a few years later, find their way on air, again. For any curious student, scholar, or professional, deeper search into these matters will prove painfully enlightening.

Today, advertising is regulated in most parts of the world, and such regulation combines a legal framework with industry self-regulatory bodies and the respective procedures to prevent false, misleading, offensive, and harmful ads. The advertising industry frequently but not always treats regulatory initiatives as part of the sector's social responsibility, as do advertised brands. There will always be cases of ads who breech, bend, or ignore the rules, but, hopefully, some of these attempts will no longer go un-noticed. Active consumers, governmental and non-governmental organisations, tighter legal frameworks, and self-regulation processes try to mitigate the negative influences of inappropriate advertisements though the results of these efforts are often contested (indicatively: Kelly et al., 2019; Hastings et al., 2010; Jones, 2007). Everyday work in the agency is full of ethical tensions and dilemmas at the individual level, the agency level, and the industry level, despite effort to create best practices.

Advertising ethics is a discrete, outlined area of studies. However, ethical issues in advertising touch upon many different aspects. Advertising ethics can be approached from a marketing perspective. As part of the marketing mix, advertising can appear like a drop in a sea of ethical concerns which include: fair pricing, fair distribution, appropriate information disclosures, fair market practice, and much more (for a review: Nill and Schibrowsky, 2007). Advertising is also approached from a media perspective. Through this lens, advertising is already distinguished from other types of media content. Aiming first and foremost to persuade, advertising is bound to appear somewhat unethical when compared to informative or entertaining content (Patterson & Wilkins, 2008; Baker & Martinson, 2001).

Then, there is the distinction between the harm one isolated ad can do and the harm advertising in general can do. Gurrieri et al. (2022) acknowledge the multi-layered interplay between advertising and society, aiming to create a more thorough framework for future advertising research. They incorporate contributions from different research areas and suggest directions for scholars and practitioners toward social change. Finally, there is a difference between positivist and normative approaches (Nill & Schibrowsky, 2007) as will be discussed in section 9.8.

This chapter addresses some of the aspects that seem more relevant to creative professionals. We cannot cover all the ethical issues in advertising. We do not address topics relating to operations, financial or human resource management falling under the broader spectrum of business ethics. Issues of diversity and inclusion are covered in Chapters 2 and 4 because these improve strategic and creative output, not just ethical mandates. We barely outline the significant problems that have emerged around privacy, use of personal data, microtargeting, and influencer marketing which relate largely to dissemination and not (just) content.

We focus on what is more relevant to creative advertising, to help stream creativity toward ethically considerate directions; to instil ethical alertness; and to provide some basic guidance on a practical level, hoping to inspire toward a more sustainable and ethical approach which prioritises respect toward consumers (Kennedy & Laczniak, 2016).

This chapter follows a bottom-up approach. First, we examine self-regulation. Then we discuss ethical challenges on the level of one ad, along with some practical advice around claims. Then the scope broadens to discuss ethical issues on the macro-level and then we discuss advertising professionals' ethics from a normative philosophical perspective. By opening the lens gradually, this chapter aims to provide both practical support and theoretic understanding; the "how" and the "why", because the road to ethical advertising practice is long and bumpy.

2 Self-regulation in a nutshell

Imagine you are going to school, and you love to play hide and sick during the break. The headmaster has assigned a couple of supervisors to watch over the students. You and your friends are about to play, and you set the rules: do we count to ten or twenty? Can we hide in the classrooms or just in the courtyard? Too many rules, and you end up losing the entire break to agree without playing at all. Too few rules, and you end up disputing over right or wrong to the point where the headmaster interferes. So, you and your schoolmates set a basic set of rules and start to play. These rules may apply throughout the schoolyear or may be revised when something does not work. And while you are playing if someone breaks the rules, the game must stop, and the dispute must be resolved quickly and efficiently. This is self-regulation in a nutshell (an old, classic approach: La Barbera, 1980).

The headmaster is the law. Without the possibility of legal implications and sanctions, there is less incentive for agencies and businesses to endure systematically imposed self-regulation. Laws in each country often restrict both the content and the airing of ads, to ensure fair competition and protection of vulnerable consumer segments. The law applies to all but cannot always include provisions for every isolated case.

The supervisors are associations: advertisers' associations, media associations, and other involved stakeholders, depending on each country or market. Some countries also encourage consumer representation in the process of establishing rules and examining cases (Feenstra & González Esteban, 2019). The supervisors rely on pre-established rules and create procedures to ensure compliance. These rules constitute the code of ethics (or code of conduct), should be publicly available and frequently revised in alignment with the law, technology, as well as sociocultural changes. They must be stricter than the law so that issues can be addressed without the need for legal interference.

The players are clients and agencies, as well as consumers and other stake-holders in the advertising ecosystem, varying per country. They should know the rules and have incentives to promote fair play, protecting public interest and industry reputation.

The basic principles for every code of conduct, as indicated by European directives can be summarised as follows: **advertising must not lie or mislead; must not insult or offend; must not harm or promote dangerous behaviours.** These principles are developed into concrete, detailed rules addressing competitors' fair play, the protection of vulnerable segments, and the tackling of different topics like green advertising or food and alcohol advertising, to name a few. There are many approaches to self-regulation and their comparison becomes too technical and context specific (Miracle & Nevett, 1988). This overview focuses on the essentials adopting a European perspective, but without delving in member-state differences.

Following EU Directives, member states had to align their pre-existing legislation and self-regulation systems or create these from scratch. Each member state may follow a stricter or more lenient approach, depending on previous experience and overall mentality.

Once a code is in place, any individual or organisation can appeal, when they believe there are violations. What happens then? A team of certified experts, excluding members with potential conflict of interest, review the case following the code and decide whether to have an ad banned or amended or left as is. Usually, this is a corrective rather than punitive process. The emphasis is less on penalisation and more on restitution. Rulings must be publicly available for the sake of transparency, accountability, and further learning for all parties involved.

Self-regulation is quick and efficient, as opposed to long legal battles, and it is trusted in the hands of experts. Accumulated expertise may also offer valuable contribution to improve the legal framework within which self-regulation takes place. Furthermore, regulatory organisations in many countries don't offer only reactive but also proactive services. In Spain for example, an agency can ask for consultation and copy testing before publishing an ad (Feenstra & González Esteban, 2019). In France, ads must be cleared before airing. In most countries, these organisations also offer training on the code of ethics.

Self-regulation is not a panacea though. Funding is required to establish and maintain regulatory bodies and their services. This creates conflict (Harker, 2003, p. 99–100). Both laws and codes require frequent updates (Kerr & Moran, 2002), especially with the new media. Self-regulation requires a lot of effort and alertness; involvement of multiple institutions and stakeholders; constantly trained professionals. For complaints and appeals to arrive, aware, trained, ad-savvy citizens are also needed. Without active consumer engagement and the participation of interest groups or consumer movements, self-regulation is reduced to a battle among competitors blocking or stalling each other rather than caring about public interest (Jones, 2007).

Furthermore, self-regulation should consider the individuals' ability to process an advertising message. If we believe that consumers may take the "Red Bull gives you wings" tagline literally, as a court ruled (Culzac, 2014), and start jumping off roofs, then we need to reevaluate what can be taken as false or misleading. Advertising regulations and advertising literacy should walk in tandem (De Jans et al., 2017; Nelson, 2018). Ads need to be regulated while consumers need to be empowered to assess these ads, understanding the principles of self-regulation. The case study in this chapter is a good example of misalignment between consumers and watchdogs – and this is not about taking sides on who is right or wrong. Finally, a devil's advocate would argue that having advertisers assess their own work for the sake of society is like trusting the wolves to guard the sheep (Kerr & Moran, 2002). Transparency and accountability help mitigate such criticism but as mentioned, the effectiveness of self-regulation is often contested.

From a creative professional's perspective, understanding self-regulation and its basic principles leads to more appropriate executions and supports an ethical attitude toward the profession.

3 Some key ethical issues

This section briefly outlines some of the key issues facing advertising today but focuses on aspects that are more relevant to creative content and creative work. Beyond this outline, there are more issues calling for further examination and research.

3.1 Product category related regulations

No product evades the risk of misleading or harming if not marketed ethically. Thus, as discussed, the EU has issued directives for quite a few product categories (and for political advertising), which span the entire spectrum of their marketing and communication activities, not just advertising. Each member state then embodies the regulations by legislating, and although in each country the content of these directives might be more or less lenient and explicit, the basic principles should apply.

Here are some indicative examples:

- **Tobacco** products cannot be promoted anywhere but in the point of sales; should not encourage anyone to start smoking; should explicitly state on any promotional material and on their packaging the health risks associated with smoking, etc.[1]
- **Alcohol** should not be promoted to non-adults. Advertising should not show anyone who is or seems younger than 25; not associate alcohol with machine handling; not imply or claim that alcohol makes people more confident, relaxed, carefree etc.[2] In many countries, each ad ends with the message "Enjoy responsibly" promoting moderate consumption.
- **Prescription medicines** cannot advertise or be marketed directly to patients, and should be promoted to health professionals with caution. Certain paramedical products including food supplements also face limitations[3].

- **Cars** must display their CO emissions on all their promotional materials[4].
- **Investment products** must include in-ad warnings to protect investors from misleading claims or hidden conflicts of interest[5].
- **Food marketing** is also subject to regulation. Overstating the benefits of certain ingredients or concealing the harm or existence of others might prove to mislead or even harm. In the EU[6] and in Australia, food marketing should not target children. The rise of eating disorders has intensified this need.

If you are about to work on a brand for the first time, then make sure you check whether there are regulations and limitations you should consider.

3.2 Advertising regulations across categories

This section presents some of the regulatory initiatives which are not connected to a specific product category but may apply to advertising activities across different branded offerings.

- **Digital advertising**: The digital environment has generated new challenges for ethical advertising (Segijn & Strycharz, 2023). Personalised marketing relies on big data whose usage may prove to be manipulative, intrusive, discriminatory, or annoying. Microtargeting and customising advertising messages might mean that not all consumers have equal access to the same offer; that carefully isolated micro-clusters of consumers may receive disinforming or misinforming or even threatening messages; that minors can receive inappropriate messages. The effort to monitor such activity is extensive and resource consuming while citizens are not always aware of the risks, their rights, and the tools at their disposal. Attempts to regulate online advertising and content are obstructed by the global nature of the web and social media (López Jiménez et al., 2021; Dickinson-Delaporte et al., 2020), as well as by platform obscurity. Native advertising and influencer marketing, as well as their disclosure (or not) and potentially misleading claims are also under scrutiny (indicatively: Harms et al., 2022; Sweeney et al., 2022). These issues are not usually of direct concern to creatives whose task here is to ensure accuracy and appropriateness of their messages regardless of placement.
- **Advertising to children**: Moore (2004) provides a detailed overview of the risks of advertising to children. Each country or market should have special provisions to protect minors. Children are less likely to process an advertising message critically, to understand a metaphor or hyperbole. They may be susceptible to peer pressure and emotional appeals for social acceptance or popularity; less savvy about nutrition; more gullible to ads which suggest they persist until their parents buy them what they want or that they buy something against parental consent. That any such approach or insight is highly unethical feels obvious. It's not.
- **Green advertising & greenwashing**: advertising should promote brand initiatives which tackle environmental issues but often misleads consumers as

to the extent and impact of such initiatives. This is called greenwashing and appeals particularly to the environmentally conscious consumers who wish to adopt an eco-friendly lifestyle, hence green literacy is needed, along with precise regulation (indicatively: Schmuck et al., 2018; Fernandes et al., 2020). Limitations in advertising are suggested or imposed, especially for sectors with a significant footprint (indicatively: Teona et al., 2020). One more view to this subject is that green initiatives should penetrate the entire organisation and not focus too much on marketing and promotion.

- **Gender portrayals**: Advertising carries a long history of stereotyping and discriminating. As will be discussed below, each isolated ad can be called out or amended, but all the ads together shape the broader sociocultural context in ways that cannot always be traced and tackled. Some countries like the UK[7] take initiatives to prevent stereotyping by imposing limitations on the content of each ad but, still, what goes under the radar has a pervasive impact. Especially after the #metoo movement, many ads jumped on the female empowerment bandwagon. This is called femvertising and is also treated ambivalently. On the one hand, promoting female empowerment is important and often appreciated. On the other hand, female empowerment should not only appear in advertising but permeate organisational practice; and it should constitute a mid- or long-term goal, not a fad that will be forgotten when the next trending topic appears. The "Don't do as I do, just do as I say" attitude could be patronising and inauthentic. Consumers already show an understanding of this tension (Lima & Casais, 2021; see also: Kelso, 2019) accusing companies of piggybacking and woke-washing, wrongfully appropriating social issues for marketing purposes (Sobande, 2019).

4 Improving one ad at a time: the message and the claim.

Ethical advertising must not lie or mislead. A misleading ad is an ad that overstates product benefits and uses; or conceals product disadvantages and ingredients; or promotes overconsumption; or provides insufficient substantiation for the claims it makes. Also, ethical advertising must not offend, insult, or promote harmful behaviours especially to vulnerable segments. Advertising claims and imagery need to comply with these basic principles.

Creative professionals' task is to take a proposition stated in the brief and convert it to a compelling message through figurative language, use of images, and storytelling. The creative department, the entire agency for that matter, might not have the knowhow to evaluate truthfulness, accuracy, or quality of substantiation for each product. A designer cannot assess how much essential oil is in a bath foam or if a car's emissions are accurately measured. The client must ensure truthfulness and the agency must ensure accuracy and ethical compliance.

Figurative language is the copywriter's virtue and vice. It could be truth well told, as McCann famously claims, or partial truth, or too far from the truth. This has to do with facts and with the way these facts are stated and documented.

What creatives can do is disentangle creativity from deception by avoiding misleading statements. And there are two ways to do this: first, ensure that all claims are properly justified by fact and information; second, ensure that phrasing and visualisation of these claims, no matter how playful, is not deceptive. There is a fine line between playfulness and deception, which lies on the eye of the beholder and depends on their literacy.

An advertising claim is a statement about product attributes or benefits or comparative advantages. A claim is often stated in a brief's single-minded proposition and then appears as a headline or tagline. Advertising claims can be vague or even confusing in their excessive phrasings. Schrank (1974) provides a list and a critique of advertising claims, very interesting to read precisely because it refers to old messages that appear somewhat blunt, naïve, yet surprisingly still relevant.

When phrasing or editing claims, you should consider the following suggestions[8], both for the sake of ethics and for the sake of avoiding old-school advertising clichés:

- **Factual claims** should be verifiable even if upon request. For example, an insurance company that claims to pay within three days, should be able if asked to provide proof.
- **Comparative and superlative claims** should also be proven if requested, especially if competitors can be identified. It's best if proof of claim is evident on the ad. Unidentified superlative claims like "The best razor" or "The cooler refreshment" are less likely to be considered unethical, well, less likely to win a creativity award, as well. However, when it comes to food or environmental claims, stricter rules apply. "The greener cleaner" or "the healthier snack" would definitely have to provide justification to not be considered misleading.
- **Puffery and non-factual claims** usually evade ethical appeals, though we rely on the consumers' ability to correctly decode the message. "Stay on top of fashion" or "Your best chance at happiness' would not aggravate or mislead consumers, provided figurative language is plausibly decoded.
- **Parity claims** are usually not considered misleading either, though consumers are likely not to decode them properly. "No other cheese contains less fat than cheese X" is a parity claim. What it says, in fact, is that cheese x could contain the same amount of (low) fat as the competitors. If the cheese indeed contained less fat, there would be no ambiguity in the phrasing. This is truism or otherwise called vacuous truth in the sense that though the statement is true, it contains no argumentative value.

Advertising messages also make use of rhetorical fallacies. A fallacy is the use of inaccurate, faulty, or false reasoning used to construct a persuasive argument. Some fallacies use eloquent statements to compensate for the absence or the inadequacy of fact. Not all fallacies are misleading, but some may be, especially when addressing a non-savvy audience.

Table 9.1. presents an indicative, non-exhaustive compiled list of fallacies (Ruszkiewicz et al., 2014; Gula, 2018; Herrick, 2014; Dowden, n.d.) often

Table 9.1 Frequent fallacies in advertising

Fallacy	Advertising example	What is the problem?
The bandwagon argument (also formally defined as argumentum ad populum)	Six out of ten consumers trust X, so it's the best money can buy.	Trust of the many is not sufficient justification of superiority. The many have often been wrong.
Appeal to authority (also: ad Verecundiam)	• Doctors prefer to smoke X • The best beer according to [Celebrity].	Not all celebrities are experts around the products they advertise. Straightforward endorsements should be authentic.
Faulty / False / Hasty generalisations	• With six airbags, it must be the best car • Bigger company, better goods • The housewife's best ally.	Jumps to a general conclusion from only partial facts or arguments. Ignores all other information. When referring to consumers, generalisations are also closely associated with stereotyping
Slanting	The cooler, healthier, slimmer snack	Suppressing evidence that disprove a claim, like calories, preservatives, etc.
Faulty / False equivalency (or analogy; or association)	Orange juice X. As fresh as real orange.	Arguing that two things are similar does not mean that all their attributes are similar. Comparisons in general should be analogous. Especially food ingredient comparisons should be factual and justified. Packaged goods cannot claim to substitute fresh food.
Faulty causality Post hoc (after this); Ergo propter hoc (because of this)	• Toothpaste X. This is why they all flirt with you. • We would not be first, if we were not the best. • Fewer sore throats, better candy	Presenting the product as an antecedent though there may be no substantiated causal connection. The lack of proof for arguments or conclusions is formally defined as ignoratio elenchi.
Slippery slope	X insurance. Don't let a lifetime of effort be undervalued.	The consequences of an argument or proposition are overstated.
False dilemma / Either-or fallacy	It's the brand X's way or no way.	There are more than these two options.
Begging the question / Circular reasoning (Petitio principii)	The best soap because it's perfect for washing your hands.	The claim becomes part of the proof instead of relying on proof.
Red herring	They promise cleaner clothes. We give you a better life.	Turns attention from a competitor's claim by presenting a new argument, changing the topic, or distracting attention.

Fallacy	Advertising example	What is the problem?
Appeal to motive	• We are the best because we care. • Top quality. Would we ever lie?	Appealing to motive and good intentions does not render a claim true. Caring is only part of a brand's benefits or does not suffice to guarantee these benefits
Appeal to fear or force (Argumentum ad baculum)	Food supplement X or Your health is in great danger.	Scare tactics or shockvertising are considered unethical unless they are used for a broader social cause and not for commercial purposes, especially about health issues.
Appeal to tradition	Mascara X. Made the old way. Insurance X. We are better because we are old-school.	Not all goods and services were better in the past. Some were.
Appeal to ignorance (Ad ignorantiam)	The better investment bank. Have you heard otherwise?	Not knowing something is true does not make it false and vice versa. Not knowing something is false does not make it true. Conspiracy theories rely on appeals to ignorance.
Snob appeal	Appreciated by those who matter.	Promises that those who side with the product belong in a special, superior category of people.
Anthropomorphism	The fabric softener that loves you.	Projects uniquely human qualities onto something that isn't human, also described as the Disney fallacy (Dowden, N.D.)

encountered in advertising. Though we focus on the message, fallacies can also be traced on images and in storytelling, in the product's role, or in the plot, or in the message conveyed or elicited during denouement.

If the agency team or the client are about to adopt a claim that could be false or potentially misleading, offensive, or harmful, then anyone in the team should calmly voice their concerns. Everyone should maintain such alertness. Even if the outcome does not change, it is important to routinely apply an ethical filter on all ideas and keep the conversation running in the day-to-day agency life.

Time to practise!

• Watch this ad for McDonalds, aired in1996 https://www.youtube.com/watch?v=4MGI-EJQtgo. Do you consider it to be unethical? Why? Should certain products avoid using children or babies under a certain age in their advertising? Does the ad target babies? Should this make a difference? How would you put the ad's claim into words?

- Try a role-playing game in class. Form three teams. The first team appeals against an ad; the second team defends the ad; the third team must issue a decision on whether to allow, ban, or amend, based on the teams' arguments and the code of conduct in your country. Consider repeating this so all members experience all positions. Try to find overtly horrible ads but also look for ads with marginal violations. How does it feel to defend an ad which you consider unethical?
- Try to trace the type of claim or fallacy of the taglines below. Explore whether you can re-write these by replacing fallacy with an appropriate yet original creative scheme or trope. Where possible, stay close to the original meaning.

  ○ There are some things money can't buy. For everything else, there is MasterCard.
  ○ L'Oreal because you're worth it.
  ○ Toyota: Let's Go Places.
  ○ Papa Johns: Better Ingredients, Better Pizza.
  ○ Live in your world. Play in ours.
  ○ BMW. The Ultimate Driving Machine
  ○ No One OutPizzas The Hut.

- Could you interpret the ads below in a way that could bring to light a rhetorical fallacy? Would you consider such rhetorical fallacies to be unethical? In which cases? Justify your answer.

  ○ VW Passat – Darth Vader
  ○ Snickers – You're not you when you are hungry.
  ○ IKEA – lamp
  ○ The Grim Ripper (Australia AIDS advert).

5 Considering ads as a whole – Some key issues

Ensuring each ad is not unethical will not ensure that all ads together do not have an unethical impact. A lot of the criticism advertising faces is not about the impact of isolated ads as much as about the impact of all ads together. It's not one ad but advertising in general accused of stereotyping of objectifying women (Wolin, 2003) – and not just women; of using sex to sell (Latour & Henthorne, 1994); of perpetuating negative stereotypes and discrimination based on age, gender, sex (Landreth Grau et al., 2016), race, and more; of misrepresenting social groups (Borgerson & Schroeder, 2002); let alone promoting overconsumption (Nill & Schibrowsky, 2007). By projecting idealised images of idealised people and goods in idealised settings, advertising is accused of distorting views of reality and self-image (Gurrieri et al., 2022 who also provide a review of relevant literature). These have been described as unintended consequences of advertising (Pollay, 1986) and have also been approached from the perspective of media ethics (indicatively: Baker & Martinson, 2001).

Indeed, advertising often idealises or turns individuals to caricatures to represent targeted segments, seeking not authenticity but some grounds for identification. When profiling target groups or creating personas, what we do is assign individual traits to groups and group traits to individuals, which is by default what stereotyping does. And then, this is reflected in the creative executions. One-page images or thirty second stories do not suffice to build authentic characters, nor is this their purpose after all. Silly blonds, submissive housewives, aggressive alpha males, idealised bodies, naïve foreigners, roaring teenagers, rude bosses, cheesy experts, funny grandpas, and confident celebrities parade consecutively on our screens. We know they are not real, but do we? The impact of all ads together is harder to discern and assess.

Every generation re-negotiates the limits of tolerance of advertising and advertising must stay aware and respectful of what may (not) be considered funny or cute or creative. Take this series of posters that aired in France in 1981[9]. On the first poster, a young, slim woman in a swimsuit announces that two days later she will remove the top. Two days later, on the second poster, she appears topless announcing that in another two days she will remove the bottom. And she did. The third poster showed her back and revealed the name of the advertised brand, a poster company in France whose message was: "The poster company that keeps their promises". Indeed, replacing posters in just two days around an entire city or country is a great example of what a good poster company can achieve. The message back then was received positively, bringing publicity and awards. Could one argue that this ad objectifies the female body, misrepresents women, and promotes voyeurism? Would this ad be greeted so favourably today?

The connection between advertising, culture, and identities goes a long way back. Though there is research indicating that image advertising is not harmful per se and does not limit consumers' autonomy of choice, it is acknowledged that advertising can indeed "undermine consumers' self-esteem by collectively omitting images... and by combining impossible images with implied gaze" (Bishop, 2000, p. 371). This may be misleading. Or infuriating. Or both.

Advertising explores ways to tap on social issues and to make products constitute part of the social fabric individuals use to construct or convey aspects of their identity (Elliott & Wattanasuwan, 1998). Consumers are more likely to select brands which claim to share the same values or purpose (Hornsby, 2019). Femvertising and green advertising – or femwashing and greenwashing – become a trend, and not just in advertising, thus impacting attitudes and perceptions. Consumers often deplore ads which, they feel, do not represent reality accurately, even though up to some extent puffery is expected.

But then, as advertising takes a stance when it comes to politics, racism, sexism, gender rights, or body shaming, more and more people expect, or rather demand to be represented in advertising, even more so fairly and accurately. Identity politics walks in, but representation is means not ends for advertising whose objectives are shaped in a commercial context, as choice of utility, not principle. People symbolise idealised target groups or serve as props around the brand. Even when this can be regulated one ad at a time, it is very hard to assume that one can regulate the outcome of all ads together. If an ad for slimming products promotes unrealistic slim bodies, consumers can reject and react. But how about the myriads of ads who use tall, slim models to promote, let's say, toothpaste or credit cards? And the myriads of ads who neglect to portray non-mainstream consumer segments, as defined in each context, unless these segments are targeted? Would it help to set an annual percentage that would be considered socially responsible and representative?

Advertising influences our worldviews in more ways than we usually imagine, by artfully including and artfully omitting, by symbolising and by interacting with its contexts (Pollay, 1986; Kadirov & Varey, 2011; McDonald et al., 2020). Ethical issues then, might emerge even when we examine non-unethical ads.

Case study: Are you cancel culture ready?

In April 2015 an outdoor ad appeared on the London Tube portraying a slim young woman in a yellow bikini, asking: "Are you Beach Body Ready?" signed by a brand selling proteins. In no time, a wildfire of ire erupted with people cursing the ad on social media; vandalising the posters; erasing the "B" so as it read: "Each Body Ready"; creating parodies; taking selfies with gestures expressing their disapproval. Influencers called the ad out on all social media. In just a few days, about 40.000–50.000 signed a petition to have the ad removed and in a couple of weeks a march and protest was organised in Hyde Park. A well-known brand spoofed releasing a poster with three plus sized women on a yellow background and the headline: "Yes, we are beach body ready". The UK watchdog ruled that the ad did not violate any rules relating to harm and offense. The company refused to remove the ad arguing that the model was within acceptable weight standards and that the concept of preparing for the summer vacation is not a new one. Yet after protests continued, both the Advertising Standards Alliance and the advertised brand deliberated and agreed to not re-run the outdoor ads whose placement agreement lasted for three weeks. Compare this ad with the French example discussed above which aired in 1981 and contemplate on the limits and levels of tolerance demonstrated in different decades and different sociocultural contexts. This example is not here to provide a concrete answer on whether the Beach Body Ready ad should have been banned – this is up to you to decide. The example demonstrates that views change and that consumers might also have the power to shake things and make loud statements – today at least. So, food for thought, at the end of the day is it better to openly debate a problematic ad or to ban and not discuss it at all on the grounds of protecting consumers?

Sources:

- Clarke-Billings, L. (2015, April 27). "Are you beach body ready?" Protein World backlash grows as thousands sign petition calling for removal of "body shaming" ads. *The Independent.* Available at: https://www.indep

endent.co.uk/life-style/health-and-families/are-you-beach-body-ready-p rotein-world-backlash-grows-as-thousands-sign-petition-calling-for-removal-of-body-shaming-ads-10204601.html.

- Bajekal, N. (2015, April 28). "Beach body ready" advertisements spark widespread backlash. *Time*. Available at: https://time.com/3837979/bea ch-body-ready-protest-advertisements/.
- Sweeney, M. (2015, April 29). "Beach body ready" ad banned from returning to tube, watchdog rules. *The Guardian*. Available at: https:// www.theguardian.com/media/2015/apr/29/beach-body-ready-ad-faces-formal-inquiry-as-campaign-sparks-outrage
- Morgan, M. & Willgress, L. (2015, April 30). "Yes. We are beach body ready": New poster featuring curvy, bikini-clad women spoofs controversial Protein World ad. *Mail Online*. Available at: https://www.da ilymail.co.uk/femail/article-3062882/Yes-beach-body-ready-New-p oster-featuring-curvy-bikini-clad-women-spoofs-controversial-Pro tein-World-ad.html
- Hackman, R. (2015, June 27). Are you beach body ready? Controversial weight loss ad sparks varied reactions. *The Guardian*. Available at: http s://www.theguardian.com/us-news/2015/jun/27/beach-body-ready-am erica-weight-loss-ad-instagram
- Sweeney, M. (2015, July 1). Protein World's "beach body ready" ads do not objectify women, says watchdog. *The Guardian*. Available at: http s://www.theguardian.com/media/2015/jul/01/protein-world-beach-bo dy-ready-ads-asa
- Feller, G. (2016, June 13). The Disturbing Truth About Trying To Ban The Beach Body Ready Ads. Forbes. Available at: https://www.forbes. com/sites/grantfeller/2016/06/13/the-disturbing-truth-about-trying-to-ba n-the-beach-body-ready-ads/

6 Power relations between brands and consumers

How powerful is advertising? This is a question involving not just ethics but also ideologies. Post-World War Two, mass media, mass production, massive opening of new households and the massive need for a better life led to overconsumption and overpromotion of goods (an indicative non-academic review: The MIT Press Reader, N.D.). Judith Williamson (1978) opened her book with the lyrics of the Rolling Stones' song "Satisfaction" making a powerful statement about the pervasiveness of consumerism and advertising back in the seventies. A lot has changed since then. Product saturation, recessions, anti-consumerist movements, media literacy, tighter legislation and regulation, as well as new media among other factors, weigh in on the influences of advertising. Consumers' voices are heard louder. Advertising is a formative influence (Pollay, 1986) but does not shape its socio-cultural context all by itself. Advertising influences and is influenced by its context (McDonald et al., 2020; see also: Goddard, 1998). This is because advertising needs to persuade rather than alienate, so advertising does adjust, perhaps in a not so agile manner (McDonald et al., 2020). However, advertising may influence consumers directly while consumers may influence advertising statistically. The difference is huge. Within this discourse between brands and consumers both sides have different sources of power to leverage.

Advertising agencies and their clients are legal entities benefiting to some extent from the right to freedom of speech (Harker, 2003; Kulick, 2020). This right comes with considerable financial resources to publish persuasive content.

Brands and advertisers also hold significant symbolic power, which means they possess know-how, abilities, and resources to produce and exchange cultural meaning; to construct, establish and perpetuate our notions and views about reality (Bourdieu, 1991; see also: Cerne, 2021) and to contribute to the way we shape and negotiate our identities (Cannon et al., 2000). Thus, advertised brands not only impact media content but they also impact our broader understanding of the socio-cultural context we live in (Arnould & Thompson, 2005). They interact with consumers using symbols and they seek some degree of control over the symbolic landscape by creating resonant work. Creating and disseminating such symbols (Kadirov & Varey, 2011) brands become powerful players in the realm of the symbolic. To realise how pervasive advertising may be, old print ads are, again, useful. Today their messages may seem too overt or blunt or even outrageous, but this is not how they were perceived in the context in which they aired; on the contrary, they might have been well received or at least they might have appeared plausible and relevant. Advertising weaves part of the fabric of meaning we exchange and consume in our everyday lives, even though advertising is neither alone nor dominant in this process and should be examined in combination with other fields of symbolic power.

So, is the consumer powerless in this process? Conceptualisations of the consumer frame our approach to ethical challenges. If we perceive of the consumer as an autonomous, sovereign, media literate individual who can acquire information, solicit opinions, contemplate on the potential harms of advertising, and make well-informed decisions, then this consumer can use their analytical and critical skills to process any advertising message, thus no regulation or other mediation would be required on ethical grounds (for an old discussion: Lee, 1987). This would be a convenient solution for marketers who may shift the burden of tracing misleading advertising to the consumer (Kennedy & Laczniak, 2016). If, on the other extreme, we assume that the consumer is powerless and gullible when facing huge brands and their advertising budgets, then all advertising is unethical to some extent and paternalistic interference is needed (for a thorough discussion from a marketing perspective: Kennedy & Laczniak, 2016). Neither extreme is accurate and neither extreme can provide sufficient solutions to ethical challenges.

While unregulated advertising might be harmful, too much regulation may lead to censorship or to the infantilization and lack of literacy for consumers who do not learn to assess the stimuli they are exposed to and, worse, who have someone doing it for them. This is why every code of conduct should be carefully adjusted within local contexts and why there is no unified recipe for ethical decisions advertising professionals should make, beyond staying alert and fostering trust and respect.

7 Considering ads as a whole: Your moral compass

Casting a tall, slim, beautiful model to introduce, let's say, a dishwashing liquid is not unethical per se. Trying to convince clients and colleagues in a meeting room that casting a less perfect body will benefit society at large would be cringe, to say the least. How can creatives avoid stereotyping, objectification, and misrepresentation?

It all starts with ideation and then moves forward. This is not about casting and production. Here is one possible way to incorporate ethical concerns into creative thinking:

- **First step**: use automatic writing and divergent thinking openly, avoiding self-censorship, and writing down every possible idea that comes to mind; even the nastiest ones. Go broad, go bad, and go wrong.
- **Second step**: filter. Look for appropriateness and originality but prioritise ideas which are less likely to fall in the usual traps of stereotyping and misrepresentation.
- **Third step**: develop consciously. Develop your ideas (not just the ones you prioritised) using focused convergent thinking. At this stage you should also explore alternatives to avoid consumer clichés, discriminatory stereotypes, and mundane slice of life for all your ideas. Do so:

  a   by considering metaphors.
  b   by exploring aniconic illustrations.
  c   by engaging in better character building.
  d   by avoiding using people as props.
  e   by considering celebrity usage in unconventional ways beyond vain role-modelling and inauthentic claims.
  f   by considering if there is room for the under-represented, under a positive light.

  Such ideas always exist but require more effort to grow and gain approval. And, of course, alternative ideas should not be your only ideas but your preferred ones.
- **Fourth step:** talk about it. When presenting your ideas, make sure you mention this aspect in your rationale, even if it seems less of a priority to colleagues or clients. They might not fall for it but there is a double win: first, you learn to twist your creative thinking toward different directions; by not taking the well-worn path you grow professionally. Second, you keep the ethical discussion alive, fostering agency consciousness. If you engage in this process, you also mature ethically. And, frantically, you will only engage if you want to – it's all about intrinsic motivation.

Perhaps we cannot change the whole world one idea at a time but this approach might work because, sometimes, managers and organizations might change their ethical behaviours for better or for worse (Klein et al., 2006, also cited in Laczniak & Murphy, 2019). However, if we are not part of the solution, we are part of the problem. Each professional should pursue ethical advertising, challenge the ethi-cality of each proposal calmly, play the devil's advocate starting from their own ideas, avoid the corporate bubble and the use of clients as alibis for unethical choices, aiming at consumers' trust and respect. Ethical alerts seem to influence peers and managers within small teams in advertising agencies (Keith et al., 2003). Furthermore, when ethical issues are more openly addressed and more frequently discussed, individual misconceptions and stereotypes within each professional (Tuncay Zayer & Coleman, 2015) might be more openly addressed.

And this can only start from youth entering the agency world.

Time to practise!

- Read this article: https://www.theguardian.com/media/gallery/2015/nov/18/racist-sexist-rude-crude-worst-20th-century-advertising-in-pictures.

  ○ Discuss the implications of advertising pharmaceuticals and pre-scription medicine.
  ○ In which ads do you trace stereotyping?
  ○ Which of those ads might have been banned today? And which might have been criticised by consumers? Discuss differences between decades.
  ○ Take at least one ad as a case study and write an essay on ethics and regulation.

- Study this Arpege ad from 1967: https://www.periodpaper.com/products/1967-ad-arpege-perfume-fragrance-lanvin-dusting-powder-60s-hairstyle -fashion-215658-ymma1-060. Carefully trace visual & verbal elements that might be associated with sexism. Is there evidence of the "male gaze" on the ads? who is addressed and who is targeted? Discuss alternative views. Would this ad be suitable for both men's and women's magazines?
- Trace cases of advertising that backlashed and try to discuss the reasons why this happened and the role of context. Consider:

  ○ Pepsi-Kendal Jenner (2017)
  ○ Dove – T-shirts (2018)
  ○ Balenciaga apparel print / social media campaign (November 2022)

---

8 Normative ethics and deontology

This chapter has followed a bottom-up approach moving from hands-on issues to broader ones, aiming to facilitate students and professionals in creative advertising. Clearly, many ethical concerns cannot find simple answers and practical solutions. Rather than merely acknowledging, we can go one step further and consider how one should think and how things should be.

Implicitly, this chapter has approached advertising through the lens of normative ethics, providing suggestions on what a professional ought to do; on what regulation and self-regulation try to do; on criteria of what is right or wrong. Normative ethics is an area of moral philosophy, examining questions on how to act and how to live; on the moral judgement underlying our fundamental decisions in life (Kagan, 2018), on what "the right thing" is.

A frequent distinction in the marketing ethics literature is one between positivist and normative approaches where the former focus on "what is', being descriptive, while the latter focus on "what ought to be", being prescriptive (Tsalikis and Fritzsche, 1989; Harker, 2003; Nill and Schibrowsky, 2007; Laczniak & Murphy, 2006). This chapter prioritises the latter.

If we focus too much on "what is', we might end up taking too much for granted, adopting a passive rather than active stance toward ethical challenges. However "what is" provides a more accurate understanding of any current situation, its causes, and antecedents (Hunt & Vitell, 1986; 2006).

The industry seems to focus on "what is", on the grounds that marketing is objective and value neutral while ethical judgements can be subjective and arbitrary. Established micro-doctrines are often over-emphasised (Laczniak & Murphy, 2019). Micro-doctrines are the little things we take for granted, the ethical shortcuts "everyone else" takes, what we rationalise by evoking the mandate to please the clients. Research finds that a lot of practitioners adopt a utilitarian moral stance avoiding ethical concerns (Pratt & James, 1994); they demonstrate lack of interest on ethical research (Hyman et al., 1994) and adopt simplistic views of ethical issues (Nwachukwu et al., 2017). The term "moral myopia" describes professionals' distorted, blurry views of ethical challenges. The term "moral muteness" describes their reluctance to address such challenges (Drumwright & Murphy, 2004).

Of course, professionals do face ethical challenges (Schauster, 2019), but on the job, they tend to go with the flow. Advertising professionals' indifference (Drumwright & Murphy, 2004; 2009; Richardson-Greenfield & La Ferle, 2021) is often attributed to lack of training. The construct of bounded rationality (Simon, 1999) may provide a plausible explanation. According to Simon, within an organisation, individuals are bounded by what is available for them to know or what is advisable they do, and on what they get used to do, depending on their role. Their perspective is not all-encompassing. They learn and unlearn through the part they play. Individuals may develop tunnel vision and organisational culture may bound collective knowhow. After years in the industry, prior knowledge might fade away. Bounded rationality might explain the seeming indifference or ignorance researchers often find and justifies the importance of a routinely applied ethical filter on all ideas. A creative professional should have this in mind in the long run, maintaining ethical alertness and resilience. And agencies should ensure training, which is lifelong, not a once-off, tick-the-box attempt.

There are different streams of thought within the area of normative ethics, on the key questions of what constitutes a moral act. Deontological approaches examine if an act is inherently right (or wrong) according to non-debatable moral principles, rules, and standards (Timmons, 2012, p. 296; a different perspective in: Kagan, 2018, p. 99). Teleological approaches consider an act to be right if the outcome is the best among plausible alternatives, thus it is the consequences, the ends which justify moral acts, not a-priori abstract principles.

Self-regulation appears to follow a deontological approach, trying to establish accepted principles and then ensure that all actions are based on those principles. From a deontological perspective, decisions should occur after a careful balance of rights and duties, of tensions between an individual and a whole, like society, a company, or an agency. Regulation defines and then defends a common set of rules, and then enforces these rules, assuming that if we think right, then we will do the right thing.

From a teleological perspective, however, more effort is needed and more evidence that, indeed, the results of self-regulation prevent harm and have a positive impact on consumers and society. This type of evidence seems scarce (Jones, 2007). Regulatory bodies publish reports of handled appeals and complaints[10]. Such reports not only serve transparency and accountability but are also a way to document the efficiency of self-regulation. Critics argue, however, that effectiveness is still to be proven and that industry responses to appeals seem to resolve industry conflicts rather than community concerns, at least in some countries (Jones, 2007). A recent research report indicated that: "During peak viewing times, food and beverage advertisements that should not be permitted were higher in countries with industry self-regulatory programmes… compared with countries with no policies"(Kelly et al., 2019). We still have a long way to go to ensure that public interest is well served.

As advertising remains pervasive and audiences become more vocal and demanding, practitioners will have to adhere to higher standards of ethical conduct (Beltramini, 2003). Proactivity, alertness, and a moral compass are in need (Drumwright & Murphy, 2009) while agencies should have an ethical agenda. This shift remains challenging, fascinating, and indispensable for the long-term sustainability of the industry.

Notes

1 https://eur-lex.europa.eu/legal-content/EN/TXT/PDF/?uri=CELEX:32003L0033
2 https://ec.europa.eu/health/ph_projects/2004/action3/docs/2004_3_16_frep_a2_en.pdf
3 https://eur-lex.europa.eu/legal-content/EN/TXT/?uri=LEGISSUM%3Al21143
4 https://climate.ec.europa.eu/eu-action/transport-emissions/road-transport-reducing-co2-emissions-vehicles/car-labelling_en
5 https://ec.europa.eu/commission/presscorner/detail/en/ip_23_2868
6 https://iccwbo.org/wp-content/uploads/sites/3/2019/08/icc-framework-for-responsible-food-and-beverage-marketing-communications-2019.pdf
7 https://www.asa.org.uk/advice-online/harm-and-offence-gender-stereotypes.html
8 asa.org.uk
9 http://vintage.regioncentre.info/2020/04/23/jenleve-le-haut-pub-culte-de-laffi cheur-avenir-en-1981/

10 Here is the 2022 report by the European Advertising Standards Alliance: https://www.
easa-alliance.org/wp-content/uploads/2022/12/2022-EUROPEAN-
TRENDS-IN-ADVERTISING-COMPLAINTS-COPY-ADVICE-AND-PRE-CLEAR
ANCE.pdf

References

Arnould, E.J., & Thompson, C.J. (2005). Consumer culture theory (CCT): Twenty years
of research. *Journal of Consumer Research*, 31 (4), 868–882. https://doi org.acg.idm.
oclc.org/10.1086/426626.

Baker, S., & Martinson, D.L. (2001). The TARES test: Five principles for ethical persuasion. *Journal of Mass Media Ethics*, 16(2/3), 148–175. https://doi-org.acg.idm.oclc.
org/10.1080/08900523.2001.9679610.

Beltramini, R.F. (2003). Advertising ethics: The ultimate oxymoron? *Journal of Business Ethics*,
48(3), 215–216. https://doi-org.acg.idm.oclc.org/10.1023/B:BUSI.0000005847.
39154.69.

Berger, A.A. (2000). *Ads, fads, and consumer culture: advertising's impact on American
character and society*. Rowman & Littlefield.

Bishop, J.D. (2000). Is self-identity image advertising ethical? *Business Ethics Quarterly*, 10(2),
371.

Borgerson, J.L. and Schroeder, J.E. (2002), "Ethical issues of global marketing: Avoiding
bad faith in visual representation", *European Journal of Marketing*, 36(5/6), 570–594.
https://doi.org/10.1108/03090560210422399.

Bourdieu, P. (1991) *Language & symbolic Power*. Polity Press.

Cannon, J., Baubeta, P.A.O. de, & Warner, I.R. (2000). *Advertising and identity in
Europe: the i of the beholder*. Intellect.

Cerne, A. (2021). Speaking of business ethics: Bourdieu and market morality as a discursive
practice. *Environmental Economics and Policy Studies*. https://doi.org/10.1007/
s10018-021-00333-7.

Culzac, N. (2014, October 13). Red Bull awards $13m to its customers for not giving them
wings. *Independent*. Available at: https://www.independent.co.uk/news/world/america
s/red-bull-awards-13million-to-its-customers-for-not-giving-them-wings-9787627.html.

De Jans, S., Hudders, L., & Cauberghe, V. (2017). Advertising literacy training. *European Journal of Marketing*, 51(11–12),2156–2174. https://doi.org/10.1108/EJM-08-2016-0472.

Dickinson-Delaporte, S., Mortimer, K., Kerr, G., Waller, D.S., & Kendrick, A. (2020).
Power and responsibility: Advertising self-regulation and consumer protection in a digital
world, *Journal of Consumer Affairs* 54 (2), 675–700. doi:10.1111/joca.12295.

Dowden, B. (N.D.) *Fallacies*. The Internet Encyclopedia of Philosophy, ISSN 2161–0002.
Available at: https://iep.utm.edu/fallacy/#AdHocRescue.

Drumwright, M.E., & Murphy, P.E. (2009). The current state of advertising ethics:
Industry and academic perspectives. *Journal of Advertising*, 38 (1), 83–107.

Elliott, R. & Wattanasuwan, K. (1998). Consumption and the symbolic project of the self,
In: *European Advances in Consumer Research* Volume 3, eds. Basil G. Englis and Anna
Olofsson, Provo, UT: Association for Consumer Research, Pages: 17–20.

Feenstra, R.A., and González Esteban, E. (2019). Autocontrol: A Critical study of
achievements and challenges in the pursuit of ethical advertising through an advertising
self-regulation system. *Journal of Business Ethics*, 154, 341–354. https://doi.org/10.
1007/s10551-016-3423-0.

Fernandes, J., Segev, S., & Leopold, J.K. (2020). When consumers learn to spot deception in advertising: testing a literacy intervention to combat greenwashing. *International Journal of Advertising*, 39(7), 1115–1149. https://doi.org/10.1080/02650487.2020.1765656.

FTC (2014, October 30). *FTC charges Gerber with falsely advertising its good start gentle formula protects infants from developing allergies.* Available at: https://www.ftc.gov/news-events/news/press-releases/2014/10/ftc-charges-gerber-falsely-adverti sing-its-good-start-gentle-formula-protects-infants-developing.

Goddard, A. (1998). *The language of advertising: Written texts* (Ser. Intertext). Routledge.

Gula, R.J. (2018). *Nonsense: Red herrings, straw men and sacred cows: How we abuse logic in our everyday language.* Axios.

Gurrieri, L., Tuncay Zayer, L., & Coleman, C.A. (2022). Transformative advertising research: Reimagining the future of advertising. *Journal of Advertising*, 51 (5), 539–556. https://doi.org/10.1080/00913367.2022.2098545.

Hainneville, V., Guèvremont, A., & Robinot, É. (2022). Femvertising or femwashing? Women's perceptions of authenticity. *Journal of Consumer Behaviour, 1– 9.* https://doi.org/10.1002/cb.2020.

Harker, D. (2003) Towards effective advertising self-regulation in Australia: The seven components, *Journal of Marketing Communications*, 9 (2), 93–111, doi:10.1080/1352726032000050680.

Harms, B., Hoekstra, J.C., & Bijmolt, T.H.A. (2022). Sponsored influencer vlogs and young viewers: When sponsorship disclosure does not enhance advertising literacy, and parental mediation backfires. *Journal of Interactive Marketing*, 57 (1), 35–53. https://doi.org/10.1177/10949968221075834.

Hastings, G., Brooks, O., Stead, M., Angus, K, Anker, T., Farrell, T. et al. (2010). Failure of self-regulation of UK alcohol advertising *British Medical Journal*, 340(b), 5650 doi:10.1136/bmj.b5650.

Herrick, P. (2014). *Think with Socrates: An introduction to critical thinking*1st Edition. Oxford University Press. Available at: https://global.oup.com/us/companion.web sites/9780199331864/stu/supplement/

Horkheimer, M., & Adorno, T.W. (1998 [1947]). *Dialectic of Enlightenment.* Continuum.

Hornsby, S. (2019) The new brand-consumer contract: Tectonic shifts and new tenets. In: Montgomery, N. (Ed.). (2019). *Perspectives on purpose: leading voices on building brands and businesses for the twenty-first century.* Routledge, Taylor and Francis Group.

Hunt S.D. & Vitell S. (1986). A general theory of marketing ethics. *Journal of Macromarketing*, 6 (1), 5–16. doi:10.1177/027614678600600103.

Hunt, S.D., & Vitell, S.J. (2006). The general theory of marketing ethics: A revision and three questions. *Journal of Macromarketing*, 26(2), 143–153. https://doi.org/10.1177/0276146706290923.

Hyman, M.R., Tansey, R. & Clark, J.W. (1994) Research on advertising ethics: Past, present, and future, *Journal of Advertising*, 23 (3), 5–15, DOI: doi:10.1080/00913367.1994.10673446.

Jones, S.C. (2007), Fast cars, fast food, and fast fixes: Industry responses to current ethical dilemmas for Australian advertisers. *Journal of Public Affairs*, 7, 148–163. https://doi.org/10.1002/pa.256.

Kadirov D. & Varey R.J. (2011), Symbolism in marketing systems, *Journal of Macromarketing*, 31 (2), 160–171.

Kagan, S. (2018). *Normative ethics* (Ser. Dimensions of philosophy series). Routledge. https://doi.org/10.4324/9780429498657.

Keith, N.K., Pettijohn, C.E. & Burnett, M.S. (2003). An empirical evaluation of the effect of peer and managerial ethical behaviours and the ethical predispositions of prospective advertising employees. *Journal of Business Ethics*, 48, 251–265. https://doi.org/10.1023/B:BUSI.0000005786.09105.5c.

Kelly, B., Vandevijvere, S., Ng, S., et al. (2019). Global benchmarking of children's exposure to television advertising of unhealthy foods and beverages across 22 countries. *Obesity Reviews*, 20(S2), 116–128. https://doi.org/10.1111/obr.12840.

Kelso, T. (2019). *The social impact of advertising: Confessions of an (ex-)advertising man.* Rowman & Littlefield.

Kennedy, A.-M. & Laczniak, G.R. (2016), Conceptualisations of the consumer in marketing thought, *European Journal of Marketing*, 50(1/2), 166–188. https://doi-org.acg.idm.oclc.org/10.1108/EJM-10-2014-0608.

Kerr, G. & Moran, C. (2002). Any complaints? A review of the framework of self-regulation in the Australian advertising industry, *Journal of Marketing Communications*, 8 (3), 189–202, doi:10.1080/13527260210147333.

Klein, T.A., Laczniak, G.R. & Murphy, P.E. (2006). Ethical marketing: A look on the bright side, *Marketing Management Journal*, 16 (1), 228–243.

Kulick, A., (October 8, 2020). Corporate Human Rights? *European Journal of International Law*, Forthcoming, http://dx.doi.org/10.2139/ssrn.3707452.

Labarbera, P.A. (1980) Analyzing and advancing the state of the art of advertising self-regulation, *Journal of Advertising*, 9 (4), 27–38, doi:10.1080/00913367.1980.10673335.

Laczniak, G.R., & Murphy, P.E. (2006). Normative perspectives for ethical and socially responsible marketing. *Journal of Macromarketing*, 26(2), 154–177. https://doi.org/10.1177/0276146706290924.

Laczniak, G.R. & Murphy, P.E. (2019). The role of normative marketing ethics, *Journal of Business Research*, (95), 401–407, https://doi.org/10.1016/j.jbusres.2018.07.036.

Landreth Grau, S. & Zotos, Y.C. (2016) Gender stereotypes in advertising: A review of current research, *International Journal of Advertising*, 35 (5), 761–770, DOI: doi:10.1080/02650487.2016.1203556.

Latour, M.S. & Henthorne, T.L. (1994) Ethical judgments of sexual appeals in print advertising, *Journal of Advertising*, 23 (3), 81–90, DOI: doi:10.1080/00913367.1994.10673453.

Lee, K.-H. (1987). The informative and persuasive functions of advertising: A moral appraisal – A further comment. *Journal of Business Ethics*, 6 (1), 55–57. https://doi-org.acg.idm.oclc.org/10.1007/BF00382948.

Lima, A.M. & Casais, B. (2021), Consumer reactions towards femvertising: A netnographic study, *Corporate Communications: An International Journal*, 26 (3), 605–621. https://doi.org/10.1108/CCIJ-02-2021-0018.

López Jiménez, D., Dittmar, E.C. & Vargas Portillo, J. P. (2021). Self-regulation of sexist digital advertising: From ethics to law. *Journal of Business Ethics*, 171, 709–771. https://doi.org/10.1007/s10551-020-04471-y.

Maheshwari, S. (2017, November 24). Why tobacco companies are paying to tell you smoking kills. *New York Times*. Available at: https://www.nytimes.com/2017/11/24/business/media/tobacco-companies-ads.html.

Marcuse, H. (2002). *One-dimensional man: Studies in the ideology of advanced industrial society (Second,* Ser. Routledge classics). Routledge.

McDonald, R.E., Laverie, D.A., & Manis, K.T. (2021). The interplay between advertising and society: an historical analysis. *Journal of Macromarketing*, 41(4), 585–609. https://doi.org/10.1177/0276146720964324.

Miracle, G.E. & Nevett, T. (1988). A comparative history of advertising self-regulation in the UK & the USA, *European Journal of Marketing*, 22(4), 7–23. https://doi.org/10.1108/EUM0000000005278.

Moore, E.S. (2004). Children and the changing world of advertising. *Journal of Business Ethics* 52, 161–167https://doi.org/10.1023/B:BUSI.0000035907.66617.f5.

N.A. (2015, November 18). Racist, exist, rude and crude: The worst of 20th century advertising – in pictures. *The Guardian*. Available at: https://www.theguardian.com/media/gallery/2015/nov/18/racist-sexist-rude-crude-worst-20th-century-advertising-in-pictures.

Nelsen, A. (2018, February 1st). Nestlé under fire for marketing claims on baby milk formulas. *The Guardian*. Available at: https://www.theguardian.com/business/2018/feb/01/nestle-under-fire-for-marketing-claims-on-baby-milk-formulas.

Nelson, M.R. (2018). Research on children and advertising then and now: challenges and opportunities for future research. *Journal of Advertising*, 47 (4), 301–308. https://doi.org/10.1080/00913367.2018.1552218.

Nill A., & Schibrowsky J.A. (2007). Research on marketing ethics: A systematic review of the literature. *Journal of Macromarketing*, 27 (3), 256–273. doi:10.1177/0276146707304733.

Nwachukwu, S.L.S., Vitell, S.J.J., Gilbert, F.W., & Barnes, J.H. (1997). Ethics and social responsibility in marketing: An examination of the ethical evaluation of advertising strategies. *Journal of Business Research*, 39(2), 107.

Patterson, P., & Wilkins, L. (2008). *Media ethics: Issues and cases*. McGraw – Hill.

Pollay, R.W. (1986), The distorted mirror: Reflections on the unintended consequences of advertising, *Journal of Marketing*, 50 (2), 18–36.

Pratt, C.B., & James, E.L. (1994). Advertising ethics: A contextual response based on classical ethical theory. *Journal of Business Ethics*, 13(6), 455–468. https://doi-org.acg.idm.oclc.org/10.1007/BF00881455.

Richardson-Greenfield, P., & La Ferle, C. (2021). Insights about the ethical and moral state of advertising practitioners. *Journal of Current Issues & Research in Advertising*, 42(2), 197–213. https://doi.org/10.1080/10641734.2020.1780998.

Rotfeld, H.J. & Taylor, C.R. (2009) The advertising regulation and self-regulation Issues ripped from the headlines with (sometimes missed) opportunities for disciplined multidisciplinary research, *Journal of Advertising*, 38 (4), 5–14, doi:10.2753/JOA0091-3367380401.

Ruszkiewicz, J., Friend, C., Seward, D., & Hairston, M. (2013). *Scott Foresman handbook for writers*, The (9th ed.). Pearson.

Saatchi C.N. (2015). *Beyond belief: racist sexist rude crude and dishonest: The golden age of Madison Avenue*. Booth-Clibborn Editions.

Schauster, E. (2019). Ethics versus survival: The relationship between advertising ethics and new business challenges, *Journal of Current Issues & Research in Advertising*, 40 (1), 90–104.

Schmuck, D., Matthes, J., & Naderer, B. (2018). Misleading consumers with green advertising? An affect-reason-involvement account of greenwashing effects in environmental advertising. *Journal of Advertising*, 47(2), 127–145. https://doi.org/10.1080/00913367.2018.1452652.

Schrank, J. (1974). The language of advertising claims. *Media and Methods*, 10 (7), 44–51. Available at: https://eric.ed.gov/?id=EJ095925.

Segijn, C.M., & Strycharz, J. (2023). The ethical ramifications of surveillance for the industry, consumers, and regulators in contemporary advertising: Current issues and a future research agenda. *International Journal of Advertising*, 42 (1), 69–77. doi:10.1080/02650487.2022.2114700.

Simon, H.A. (1999). Bounded rationality and organizational learning. *Reflections*, 1 (2).

Sohande, F. (2019). Woke washing. "intersectional" femvertising and branding "woke" bravery, *European Journal of Marketing*, 54 (11), 2723–2745. https://doi.org/10.1108/EJM-02-2019-0134.

Solomon, S. (1981, December 6). The controversy over infant formula. *The New York Time Magazine*. Available at: https://www.nytimes.com/1981/12/06/magazine/the-controversy-over-infant-formula.html.

Stine, J.K. (2014, March 17). Smoke gets in your eyes: 20th century tobacco advertisements. *National Museum of American History*. Available at: https://americanhistory.si.edu/blog/2014/03/smoke-gets-in-your-eyes-20th-century-tobacco-advertisements.html.

Sweeney, E., Lawlor, M.-A., & Brady, M. (2022). Teenagers' moral advertising literacy in an influencer marketing context. *International Journal of Advertising*, 41 (1), 54–77. https://doi.org/10.1080/02650487.2021.1964227.

Teona, G., Ko, E., & Kim, S.J. (2020). Environmental claims in online video advertising: effects for fast-fashion and luxury brands. *International Journal of Advertising*, 39 (6), 858–887. https://doi-org.acg.idm.oclc.org/10.1080/02650487.2019.1644144.

The MIT Press Reader (N.D.) *A brief history of consumer culture*. Available at: https://thereader.mitpress.mit.edu/a-brief-history-of-consumer-culture/.

Timmons, M. (2012). *Oxford studies in normative ethics* (Vol. Vol. 2 /, Ser. Oxford studies in normative ethics, v. 2). Oxford University Press.

Tsalikis, J., & Fritzsche, D.J. (1989). Business ethics: A literature review with focus on marketing ethics. *Journal of Business Ethics* 8 (2), 695–743.

Tuncay Zayer, L. & Coleman, C.A. (2015) Advertising professionals' perceptions of the impact of gender portrayals on men and women: A question of ethics?, *Journal of Advertising*, 44 (3), 1–12, DOI: doi:10.1080/00913367.2014.975878.

Williamson, J. (1978). *Decoding advertisements: Ideology and meaning in advertising* (Ser. Ideas in progress). Boyars.

Wolin, L.D. (2003). Gender issues in advertising – An oversight synthesis of research: 1970–2002, *Journal of Advertising Research*, 43 (1), 111–129. DOI: https://doi.org/10.1017/S0021849903030125.

Online sources

DOI:www.easa-alliance.org.
https://www.easa-alliance.org/publication/guides-on-ad-self-regulation/.
https://www.easa-alliance.org/what-are-advertising-self-regulatory-organisations/.
www.eaca.eu
https://eaca.eu/advocacy/targeted-advertising/.
https://eaca.eu/wp-content/uploads/2023/03/C-level-report-FEB.pdf.
www.asa.org.uk.
https://www.asa.org.uk/advice-and-resources/resource-library.html.

https://www.arpp.org/.
https://www.werberat.de/.
https://www.autocontrol.es/autocontrol-eng/.
https://www.accc.gov.au/consumers/advertising-and-promotions.
https://adstandards.com.au/about.
https://www.acma.gov.au/complain-about-ads-tv-or-radio.
https://iccwbo.org/wp-content/uploads/sites/3/2018/09/icc-advertising-and-marke
    ting-communications-code-int.pdf.
https://iccwbo.org/wp-content/uploads/sites/3/2021/11/icc-environmental-framework-
    2021-final.pdf.
https://food.ec.europa.eu/system/files/2021-07/f2f_sfpd_coc_20210705_pledge_spirits-
    europe.pdf.
https://www.egba.eu/resources/eu-policy-documents/.
https://www.europarl.europa.eu/RegData/etudes/STUD/2022/703350/IPOL_STU
    (2022)703350_EN.pdf.
file:///C:/Users/user/Downloads/Global%20Guidance%20on%20Environmental%20Cla
    ims%202022.pdf.

Index